Sports and Society

Series Editors
Benjamin G. Rader
Randy Roberts

Books in the Series

A Sporting Time: New York City and
the Rise of Modern Athletics, 1820–70
MELVIN L. ADELMAN

Sandlot Seasons:
Sport in Black Pittsburgh
ROB RUCK

Reprint Editions

The Nazi Olympics
RICHARD D. MANDELL

The Nazi Olympics

The Nazi Olympics

Richard D. Mandell

UNIVERSITY OF ILLINOIS PRESS
Urbana and Chicago

Illini Books edition, 1987
© 1971, 1987 by Richard D. Mandell
Manufactured in the United States of America
P 5 4 3 2 1

This book is printed on acid-free paper.

Library of Congress Cataloging-in-Publication Data

Mandell, Richard D.
  The Nazi Olympics.

  (Sports and society)
  Reprint. Originally published: 1st ed. New York:
Macmillan, 1971. With new pref.
  Includes bibliographical references and index.
  1. Olympic Games (11th: 1936: Berlin, Germany)
2. Sports—Germany.   3. Sports and state.   4. Sports and
state—Germany.   I. Title.   II. Series.
GV722 1936.M3   1987   796.4′8   86-19347
ISBN 0-252-01325-5 (alk. paper)

TO
B. V. E. M. I.

Contents

Preface

This reprint edition permits me, in a new preface, to make corrections, provide for some additional shadings of meaning, and bring many of the book's characters up to date. Along the way, I will make some observations on the progress of sport-historical writing since 1971. And, at the risk of imposing upon my readers, I will use this welcome occasion to indulge in some autobiography.

A book on the Berlin Olympics of 1936 was not my idea. In 1968 the late Peter Ritner, an editor at the Macmillan Company, read my published doctoral dissertation[1] and invited me to New York for some expense account lunches. Ritner wanted me to write a book that would reach a general audience. After our third lunch, inspired by two double martinis and his suggestion (which included the title), I dashed to the catalog of the New York Public Library, where I found bibliographical riches. It was clear at once that I had the topic to myself and that it allowed, even demanded, lively writing. I was instantly embarked. I found pictorial and cinematographic riches at the Library of Congress. Later I collected a lot of material in archives in Berlin and Cologne.

The work was difficult, steady, and exhilarating. Macmillan promoted the book, which was published in the spring of 1971. My appearance on the "Today Show" roused congratulatory notes from friends unheard from for years. There were book club selections, kind reviews, and subsequently a paperback edition and translation into Japanese, German, and Hebrew. The success of the book altered my life in exciting ways.

Without anticipating it, I had become a sport historian. Then (and perhaps even now) sport history, particularly in America, was not an established endeavor. True, vast amounts of sport journalism appeared daily, as it still does. Some lyrically written, historical literature existed on baseball. And, in academia, some physical educators guarded the past of American sport with respectful, often hagiographic literature about the heroes of several sports. Upon reading *The Nazi Olympics,* many guardians of reputation and myth were annoyed. I had not only employed a conspicuously ironic style, but I had applied the critical eye of a conventionally trained historian to a subject not often examined: the Olympic Games. I showed that the Games of 1936 were far more than a series of athletic contests; rather, they were of major political and cultural significance.

The Nazi Olympics was an early, but minor, example of the intellectually iconoclastic output of its time. Sport could not stay apart from the turmoil. A lively, young neo-Marxist, Jack Scott, wrote and inspired some profound and, alas, rhetorically trendy literature on sport.[2] Sport-critical literature would continue to appear.[3] I subsequently learned that *The Nazi Olympics* encouraged two of the best later academic writers of sport.[4] Courses in the history, sociology, and literature of sport became ever more respectably established in so-designated academic departments; they even drew well.

So things are different now. Respectable journals with high editorial standards are devoted to sport history. The *American Historical Review* publishes articles on sport.[5] Some meetings of sport historians are international, both in participants and meeting sites. There are international journals of sport.[6]

Internationalism provides me with a transition. However much the book tarnishes the reputations of heroes such as Jesse Owens and Avery Brundage, it deals with a German festival that was only tangentially American. Coincidentally, when the book first appeared, the Federal Republic of Germany was preparing another enormous, expensive Olympic festival. The Munich Games of 1972, like the Games of 1936, would have portentous political and cultural ambitions. They were intended to *counter* the pretensions and some lingering impressions of the Berlin Games.

I had already collected a lot of source material for the book in Berlin and done a lot of interviewing elsewhere in Germany in 1969 and 1970. Munich was both topsy-turvy and euphoric with anticipation in the fall of 1971 when I visited the site of the planned Summer Games. Quite casually I called on the chief of the undertaking, the steel magnate Willi Daume, who was astonished to see me. He had just imposed my book, with its cautionary tales, as required reading for all his lieutenants. The postwar German Olympics were to be *anti*-Nazi Olympics. Patriotism was to be *de*-stressed. Red, the color of totalitarianism, was to be banned.

Over the next year I made a second talk show circuit, this time in Germany, as a celebrated sports critic and historian. Before television cameras I was addressed as "Herr Doktor Professor." I chatted with newscasters and cabinet ministers. Daume gave me V.I.P. status at the Games when they transpired. I was even provided with my own apartment and a chauffeur. The Leica people gave me a camera. Subsequently I enjoyed guest professorships at universities in Bonn and Cologne. All three of my books on sport have been translated and published in Germany.

While roaming the huge site of the sporting events in Munich in August 1972 I learned by accident that there would be a quiet reunion of former German Olympic heroes, including those of 1936. I appeared unannounced and uninvited at a large tent at a quiet part of the grounds. I was not unwelcome. Big, handsome Gotthardt Handrick (pp. 171–72, 210), whom I had already learned had been a fighter pilot in the war, boasted of his postwar success as a representative of Daimler-Benz in Hamburg. A lady who specialized in keeping track of German Olympic stars told me of many athletes of 1936 who had fallen in the war. Gisela Mauermayer had just died of cancer. Avery Brundage, whom I had met several times agreeably before (and after), was either unaware or impervious to the skeptical treatment I had given him in the book.

A major celebrity at this meeting, as indeed he was in 1936 and afterward, was Jesse Owens. This was the first time I had met him. Some awestruck reporters were about. We conversed in clichés. Owens was jovial and cynical. No remarks passed about my undermining of one of his treasured myths—that Hitler had refused to shake his hand.[7]

I giggled with pleasure when an interpreter presented me to wiry Kee Chung Sohn (as his name appears on the business card he quickly handed me and which I have kept). I had literally established him as a hero named Kitei Son, the 1936 victor in the marathon. Mr. Sohn, a track coach of the South Korean team, beamed with pleasure when I showed him his picture in my book. I promised to correct his name in the next edition.

By the late summer of 1972 the process of gathering evidence of errors in *The Nazi Olympics* was well underway. I learned that some statistics were wrong. There were typographical errors. I received notes from people eager to protect their reputations or to damage mine. Since the text is not being revised—the book is being reprinted by photo-offset and I cannot tamper with a single letter—I am taking advantage of the Press's offer of a new preface to add these corrections. Those I list are the ones that have been longest and most painfully on my mind.

1. In a letter postmarked Johannesburg, dated 1 August 1972, Rudi Ball (pp. 62, 76, 80, 100) told me he was half-Jewish and that he returned from Switzerland (not France) to play ice hockey as part of a deal to get his parents safely out of Germany . . . which he did.

2. A letter from William H. Allen, dated 4 February 1972, offers a pack of corrections:

a. Jesse Owens ran 10.2 in the second round of the 100-meter dash and 10.3 in his final.

b. I misspelled Ralph Metcalfe's surname.

c. The correct spelling is Martinus (not Marinus) Osendarp.

d. Owens's time for the 200-meter final was 20.7 seconds.

e. Reference to a "300-meter steeple chase" (p. 103) is a missed typographical error. It should read "3,000 meters."

f. Miquel White should be Miguel White.

Mr. Allen furnished a lot of speculation about the hasty and late decision to displace Sam Stoller and Marty Glickman on the American 400-meter relay team. He also suggested that my native language was not English.

3. The correct spelling is Dr. Arnold Fanck (not Franck).

4. The modern pentathlon includes a 1,500-meter run (p. 171).

5. I have concluded after a lot of discussion, particularly after arguments with sports scholars Arnd Krüger and John A. Lucas, that the outstanding performances of the German athletes could not be attributed to the extra inspiration of patriotic fervor but really were due to long and radically intense (for the time) training.

There are other minor matters I would have corrected if I had had the chance. With advancing years I have become a stricter stylist. There is an infinitive I would like to unsplit. I misused "presently." When I grade my students' work I caution them not to use the word "very," and I, in fact, used it several times.

Almost every one of the above errors are obvious and suggestions for setting them right were cautiously tendered. After all, *The Nazi Olympics* was sort of a first, so one might expect that it would be occasionally off the mark in its claims, details, and shadings. However, the admission of modest mistakes of judgment does not extend to two other aspects of the book—those dealing with Carl Diem and Leni Riefenstahl.

When discussing each of these figures I felt I had to be tentative in suggesting the extent to which they were opportunists or perhaps worse in the Nazi regime. I no longer feel that way. Each of these figures deserves separate attention here.

As I explained in the text, the organizer of the Berlin Games, Carl Diem, was rapidly rehabilitated into the respectable, democratic regime established in Germany after 1948. He was again a grand public figure at the time of his death in 1962. My claims that he had compromised himself with the Nazis affronted many elderly German sports officials—most particularly his wife, who was also an influential sports bureaucrat. Though established German periodicals and newspapers reviewed the book respectfully, several sports officials were, in fact, outraged. I had vandalized a monument. I responded by translating for an American sport-historical journal some of Diem's more hysterical patriotic rhetoric during the war.[8] This led some physical educationists in America and Germany to claim that I was not only antisport, but anti-German and anti-Olympic as well. Little damage was done to me or anyone else, but the dispute probably inspired more probing of Diem's past.

Several younger Germans have since published monographs providing evidence for the complicity of living and dead German sports officials in the Nazi regime. Recently, some careful German researchers have uncovered documents showing that Carl Diem's complicity with the Nazis went beyond his confessed use of them to promote sport. With his Nazi connections he settled brutally some old scores, and he stayed with the Nazis on ideological grounds long after their savagery was exposed and after coming defeat was apparent to all.[9]

A lot of people had been dependent upon Carl Diem and therefore were interested in protecting his reputation after the war. He could count on them to do some lying. Leni Riefenstahl was not so lucky; she had to lie for herself.

Riefenstahl, a great artist, is the heroine of the most praised and the most condemned chapter in this book. My discussion in chapter 9 of her masterpiece, *Olympia*, the film of the 1936 Olympics, intensified the already growing critical interest in her innovations as a cinematographer. There were no dissents from my praise. However, my skepticism regarding the purity of her artistic inspiration and the claims of her naiveté were not vividly enough expressed in 1971. I did not then have information that would allow me to document what I might have said.

It seems clear to me, as it has to other critics, that the beautification of mindless, masculine physical power is, in fact, highly supportive and perhaps a part of totalitarian ideology.[10] In addition, I believe that to portray the Berlin Olympics to the world in 1936 as a nonpolitical festival was not only deceptive but a political act as well as a lie. Besides, we now know that Riefenstahl was presenting political propaganda not only because she wanted to but because she was being financed by the Nazi regime with that object in mind.

Leni Riefenstahl has always been annoyed when accused of using her body as merchandise or as a bargaining chip in the turbulent years of the Weimar Republic and in the early years of the Nazi regime. This is not at issue here. What has been more reasonably debatable are her frequent claims that she was independent, always, from the ideology and politics of the Nazis. With the growing recognition of the grandeur of her work, she has been interviewed frequently on television; and when even tentatively asked if she was assisted by the Nazis or sympathetic to their cause, she has dependably become outraged and broken hearts with the lavishness of her tears. She was given an assignment as a journalist at the 1972 Olympics, yet while there she refused to see me. I heard that when my name was mentioned she burst into tears.

The archives of the Third Reich and a less-hurried attitude have permitted us to learn more about Leni Riefenstahl. It is plausible that, unlike Diem, who seems to have been an ideological convert, Riefenstahl was a knowing opportunist who would do almost anything to stay in café society and the movie business. She wrote admiring letters of support to Julius Streicher, the editor of *Der Sturmer,* an anti-Semite whose vulgarity occasionally offended Joseph Goebbels and even Hitler. We also know that she did not finance *Olympia* at all: the Nazi government did by means of slush funds managed by Goebbels, the minister of propaganda. While gathering footage for her film, Riefenstahl was troubled by sports officials but not by Nazi officials, who, in fact, she was able to call upon for protection from the sports officials. She claimed that the positions were exactly reversed. She later crossed the Nazis by taking so long to edit her sports film, which appeared late in 1938 and rather late in the establishment of the regime. The Nazis

dropped her when she proved herself unable to meet their dead-
lines for subsequent projects.

And so I am gratified for this chance, this reliving of a major event
in my life, to correct small errors. Major errors require time for
further reflection and, even more, the skills of other historians
working meticulously on some of the same problems.

We can now be more definite. As John Hoberman observed, sport
can serve as an "advertisement . . . for virtually any ideology."[11]
Modern, high-performance sport has been and will continue to
be an intricate part of modern ideology and modern high-stakes
politics.

Richard D. Mandell
April 1986

NOTES

1. Richard D. Mandell, *Paris 1900: The Great World's Fair*
(Toronto: University of Toronto Press, 1967).

2. See Jack Scott, *Athletics for Athletes* (Oakland, Calif.: Other
Ways Book Department, 1969) and *Athletic Revolution* (New York:
Free Press, 1971). See also, for example, David M. Meggysey, *Out
of Their League* (New York: Ramparts Press, 1971).

3. The best piece of American sports-critical literature remains
Robert Lipsyte's *SportsWorld* (New York: Quadrangle, 1971).

4. See Allen Guttmann, *From Ritual to Record* (New York: Columbia University Press, 1978); John M. Hoberman, *Sport and Political Ideology* (Austin: University of Texas Press, 1984).

5. See, for example, Donald Roden, "Baseball and the Quest for
National Dignity in Meiji Japan," *American Historical Review*, 85,
no. 3 (1980), 511–34; Elliot J. Gorn, "Gouge and Bite, Pull Hair and
Scratch," *American Historical Review*, 90, no. 1 (1985), 18–43.

6. *Stadion*, published in Cologne, is the best. The *Journal of
Sport History* steadily improves in quality and cosmopolitanism.
The *British Journal of Sport History* is broader in coverage than its
title suggests.

7. A thoroughgoing demything takes place in William Baker's *Jesse Owens: An American Life* (New York: Free Press, 1986).

8. Richard D. Mandell, "Carl Diem on Sport and War," *Canadian Journal of the History of Sport and Physical Education*, 5, no. 1 (1974), 10–13.

9. Despite the title the following article deals a lot with Diem: Hans Joachim Teichler, "Coubertin und das dritte Reich," *Sportwissenschaft*, 3 (1981), 361–78. Diem is the only major Nazi sports bureaucrat for whom there is no biography. Too many living people, some of whom control his papers, have a stake in maintaining his (still good) reputation. A critical biography would be an important contribution to sport history and to German history.

10. In the 1970s Riefenstahl published a splendid book of photographs on the Nuba, *The Last of the Nuba* (New York: Harper and Row, 1974).

11. Hoberman, *Sport and Political Ideology*, 1.

Preface to the First Edition

As the XIth Olympiad of the modern era opened, the masters of National Socialist Germany were tense. They had told the German people that their athletes were going to win the 1936 Olympics. Now everyone knew that German athletes as a group had never done well in international competition. Since the first modern Olympiad, in 1896, Americans had dominated the Games.

After the first day of the Berlin Olympics, American track and field athletes, many of the best of whom were Negroes, made a haul of medals. The Nazi leaders were fiercely embarrassed. They scrambled to devise some sort of scoring system that could hide the size of the American lead. One candidate would have disregarded all medals won by Negroes, whom the Nazis considered subhumans. Then, as the days went on, Germans, in events ranging from gymnastics to marksmanship and yachting won more gold, silver, and bronze medals than the athletes from any other nation, thus emerging victorious (though the ideologues of the Olympic movement forbade such rankings). German athletes, then, capped a festivity that at the time was a vessel without fissure, a seamless garment of happiness for the Nazis.

The Olympic Games of 1936 were an important episode in the establishment of an evil political regime. Giving some of the story away early, I shall claim that much of the success of the 1936 Olympics was due to the pursuit by the National Socialists of supremacy in mass pageantry. Hitler's success as a whole is inconceivable without the application of the contrived festivity that enveloped Nazism from beginning to end.

Festivity may be a societal need. We know, for example, that the success of early Christianity was in part due to its transformation of venerable pagan rites into the holidays of Christmas, Easter, and the innumerable saints' days. In a Mexican province I saw a large church whose great cross at the altar was entwined by a huge, gilded serpent, the persistent symbol of a pre-Columbian cult. Perhaps an aggravation of modern man's *ennui* and *Angst* has been the obliteration of any sort of mythological calendar that could reinforce communal solidarity and would guarantee, by its periodicity, the frequent expression, forced or otherwise, of joy. None of the bourgeois participants in the rites of the Masons or Elks believes in the efficacy of their silly ceremonies, yet the lodges live on—perhaps largely because it is fun to go through staged, unapologetically bogus festivals. To admit that modern man may welcome, indeed may need, this kind of synthetic recreation is to admit that he has bad taste as well as a gap in his rational facilities. The German festivals were, to be sure, purposefully contrived and could appear vulgar to cynical outside observers, but they were effective techniques for channeling the vigor of a skilled people. Comparisons of national susceptibilities to festivity are hazardous because modern competitors of the Nazis as festival makers just have not existed. The National Socialists were pragmatic and had a uniquely enthusiastic view of the didactic and civic uses of pageantry. Furthermore, it is much too simple to ascribe to the pageant masters of the Third Reich a desire for political power only. They actually sought to maximize the happiness of the German *Volk*. The millions of participants enjoyed themselves immensely.

As an example of Nazi festivity, the XIth Olympiad was exceptional because its intended beneficiaries were foreigners as well as Germans. The hundreds of foreign journalists, businessmen, and diplomats invited to the 1936 Games had their judgment skewed (a predictable consequence of festivity) by what they experienced there. Even as the thousands of athletes struggled before hundreds of thousands of onlookers and happy millions more reveled in the massed parades, flapping banners, and staged solemnities, there was ample evidence that the masters of Germany had charted that nation on a collision course. In August of 1936 Hitler was meddling purposefully in the Spanish revolution and becoming more ambitious in his plans for Austria and Czechoslovakia. The generous congratulations he and his lieutenants received for their Olympic successes were both emboldening to them and deceiving to their opponents. So, besides being a success, the 1936 Olympics were also a vast razzle-dazzle that blurred the outlines of a growing threat to Western civilization. I must state quickly, however, that it will be a point of this narrative to make clear that the results of the Nazi Olympics—immediately happy, though tragic in the end—were only partly due to such pageant masters as Hitler, Dr. Carl Diem, the chief of the organizing committee, Avery Brundage, and Leni Riefenstahl, the maker of the Olympic film. The artistic and falsifying aspects of festivity were in the modern Olympics from the beginning. Indeed, festivity was part of the seductive charm of the ancient Olympics as well.

The descriptions in Chapter 1 of sport in classical Greece are intended to introduce several themes. The Nazis viewed their sporting program as an integral part of their cultural renaissance and proclaimed themselves rivals of the classical Greeks as leaders of a golden age. I also wish to show (as almost no other writer on the subject has) that the connection between the ancient Games and modern ones is as tenuous as the temporal abyss might suggest. The individual most responsible for the foundation of the modern series of international sporting meets called the Olympic Games was Baron Pierre de Coubertin (1863–1937). Coubertin, in spite of the cant of peaceful idealism that now is his halo, originally hoped his international meets would reinvigorate French youth by shaming them and inspiring them with the spectacle of performances of superior athletes from other lands. Coubertin's skilled planning for periodic international meets included the use of decorative symbolism. And his festivals succeeded in seducing persons for whom the private joy (or indeed the supremacy) of agonistic effort was inconceivable. He also sought to convince ruling elites that sport for the masses (i.e., physical education) had paramilitary value. That the supreme levels of athletic excellence as manifested in the Olympics might have little relevance to democratic physical education (which in turn may have almost no relevance to the skills demanded for modern warfare) was not considered by Coubertin or by the Nazis or, in fact, by the military strategists of the 1970's. But these matters will remain largely outside the rubric of this book.

It is ironic that the anathema of Coubertin's youth, the nation that in the 1930's patriotically prepared its people to destroy peace, was the host for the Olympiad that reached an artistic and festive zenith. Ironically, too, the inspirational élan of superpatriotism appears (no other explanation is at hand) to have provided an extra boost for a few dozen German athletes who won all those medals.

My object in narrating the course of the actual athletic events of the 1936 Olympiad is merely to relate the facts. Therefore, I shall discuss most of the events as though they were parts of ordinary meets. A separate chapter will discuss the roles of three athletic heroes. But implicit in all the sports stories is my belief that all the athletes who competed at Garmisch-Partenkirchen and at Berlin were made to feel that they were the corporeal manifestations of intellectual and political forces let loose to compete in other spheres later in that troubled decade.

The world drew lessons from the Berlin Olympics. The effectiveness of the festive arrangements proved to many skeptics who had been incredulous in 1933 that the group of wild men in charge of Germany was administratively capable and would stay that way. The ranking of athletic victors by nationality was also instructive. Athletes from totalitarian nations performed strikingly well—and the most totalitarian performed best of all. The reinvigorated Germans were the winners and everyone knew it. The only democratic nation whose athletes ranked high was the United States, but we should note that the American team was larger than any previous one and that, in spite of this, the Germans put them in second place. Germany's enemies (and in 1936 the fateful lineup was already taking form), France and Great Britain (or rather their athletes—I use the rhetoric of 1936), did badly—thus indicating to many the wave of the future. Depending upon what side you were on, many immediate lessons of the 1936 Olympics, even at the time, were grim.

Other lessons might have been learned from the 1936 Olympics. The superior performances of American Negro athletes, particularly those of Jesse Owens, a hero even to the Germans, were a flat refutation of certain of the National Socialist race theories. Why did the Germans not learn from this? The athletes harmonized at the Olympic Village, as planned. The great numbers of polyglot spectators fraternized without friction. Why was this peaceful intermixing not continued? The Reich could arrest Jew-baiting for the Olympics, apparently without suffering therefrom. Why was this ghastly campaign not permanently reversed? The technicians of the new Germany had demonstrated that they could manage the German people extremely well. Why did they not rest there? As a whole, the sporting festivals of 1936 offered to a troubled era a political rest and colossal, sensuous theater. The 1936 Games, then, were an amalgam of the potentially good and the potentially bad. But the end result was tragic, because the new Germans were almost universally viewed as not only powerful and stable, but respectable as well.

The impression dominant among us as to what took place at the 1936 Games has been largely due to Leni Riefenstahl's film, *Olympia*, which was released in 1938 and which has gained status as a popular classic in the last decade or so. In her film, this great director almost invented the sport film as art. I have tried to cast Leni as a priestess of art at the 1936 Olympics.

Many individuals who played important roles at the Berlin Olympics are still alive. The reader will notice that I have avoided recent personal recollections of many of the actors there. Leni Riefenstahl is a case in point. She has granted many interviews since 1945. Her stories of the Nazi years are inconsistent and at odds with statements she made before the war. The repeated yarns that Jesse Owens pulls forth for historically oriented journalists become more sweetly nostalgic as time goes on. I have avoided Owens for I feel no need to embellish a tale that is splendid enough when based on sources from the time when he was a young Olympic victor. I must also confess my distaste for an aging gentleman who uses his glory as a youth to huckster beer as Jesse Owens did in the revolting commercials that interrupted the television viewing of the 1968 Olympics for the American public. I met and spoke with Avery Brundage, but we were both in transit and were unable to arrange a lengthy interview.

As I worked on this book, I tried to determine whether the 1936 Games as an episode and the modern Olympics as a movement have been forces for peace—as Coubertin's admirers loyally claim. I have already stated my belief that the festivities of 1936 disguised the extent to which the diabolical aspects of National Socialist ideology were being used against an unfortunate people. I claim that the Olympics were an obscuring layer of shimmering froth on a noxious wave of destiny.

It is absurd to think that an amalgam of competing patriotisms will result in peaceful idealism; yet the ideologues of

Olympism treasure this belief. Inevitably, journalists feed "incidents" to the yellow and not-so-yellow press whose readers are too torpid to experience kinesthetic empathy with sport's great individuals and who are impatient with the formal drama of contests between teams. The patriotic pressure for the prestige that winners bring has made victims of the physically endowed citizens of many nations. Patriotic sports czars have consciously deformed youths to make them the kept monsters of ambitious political regimes. One reads of Hungarian and Polish coaches feeding male hormones to female teenagers in order to give them the sinews for victory in the international arenas of sport. The girls' lives are, of course, ruined. Already in the modern Olympics the figure of the loser is often a focus of national disgrace rather than merely a poignant case of individual disappointment.

Ought the Olympics to go on? There is no question that— barring military calamity—they shall. The moguls of television reap harvests from sports broadcasting and the public appetite for it. The International Olympic Committee is now financially dependent upon the quadrennial sale of world-wide televising rights at the Games. Still I grasp this opportunity to urge international sportsmen to labor to remove some of the patriotic rites from the modern Olympics. We could start by eliminating the victory ceremonies with their inappropriate clanging of national anthems. Anthems, flags, point systems, ranked victory platforms, medals (and especially national totals of them) have played roles that are more dangerous than they are irrelevant. The world would be better off—certainly the world of sport would be better off—if the Olympics centered on the athletes and the sporting contests rather than on collectives that have only the weakest ties with sport's outstanding personages and teams.

This book is one person's effort. I alone am responsible for its claims and unintended errors. Nevertheless it could not have been accomplished without the help of generous institutions and friends. I worked on the manuscript during the year 1968–69 while in the private luxury of a Humanities Fellowship at Duke University and the University of North Carolina. This fellowship was financed jointly by the Ford Foundation and my home University of South Carolina. The Educational Foundation of the University of South Carolina helped by providing funds for some travel and other research expenses. The most useful store of sources was that monument (I shiver with awe when I enter its doors), the New York Public Library. I also obtained documentation at the headquarters of the International Olympic Committee in Lausanne, at the Carl-Diem Institut in Cologne, at New York's Olympic House on Park Avenue which is the office of the American Olympic Committee, at the Library of Congress, and to a lesser extent at other libraries and depositories of documents. The staff at the film archives at the Museum of Modern Art, New York, and the Library of Congress were especially helpful in furnishing films, leads to other films, and materials on Leni Riefenstahl. Bradley Bargar, Peter Becker, Brian O'Farrel, Singleton Carty, Elizabeth Kehr, and others helped by commenting on parts of earlier versions of the text.

1
The Olympics Revived

As the Germans prepared for the Berlin Olympics of 1936, National Socialist sports leaders and, indeed, much of the nation succumbed to an old German temptation. They sought—and found—parallels between German culture and that of the ancient Greeks. As athletics had been an integral part of classical Greek culture, the Nazis felt that athletics had to play a large role in the creative dynamism they were directing.

Athletics did figure in the life of Greek citizens to an extent that we can scarcely imagine today. Physical beauty and sporting excellence were paramount personal qualities. Every city-state had its gymnasia and *palestra* or health clubs, reeking of sweat and raucous with the grunts of agonistic effort, where youths and older men could gather for workouts, conversation, or homoerotic looking. The pagans' anthropomorphic gods, besides delighting in poetry, music, and love, also took joy in demonstrations of physical skill. The *Odyssey* and the *Iliad* contain sports stories and, as in Odysseus' entertainment by Alcinoüs of Phaeacia, rich descriptions of athletic meets.

In fact, we have known for some time a lot about Greek athletics.[1] Despite some similarities in the athletic spirit of modern meets and that of the ancients, there are many differences in detail. For example, the costumes of the athletes differed from our own in more than the absence of fabric. The athletes customarily rubbed themselves with olive oil and then were dusted with powders of various minerals and colors— each powder being attributed with qualities such as swiftness, endurance, and, for the wrestlers, enforced grippability. Records existed for such measurable events as the discus throw and the long jump (which was lengthened by carried and aptly swung iron dumbbells). The javelin was thrown through a ring for accuracy and not for distance. For the foot races the ancients had no chronographs and had no means of comparing performances of runners except in proximate combat. The usual sprint was a stade, or the distance equal to the interior length of a stadium, customarily about 200 meters. Distance men ran races of several stades and, like the swimmers of today, executed abrupt 180-degree turns (risking deliberate fouls and accidental sand-sprayed collisions) around marking posts or at raised marble banks.

Military, diplomatic, and business affairs all demanded that the Greeks cultivate long-distance joggers for urgent intercity communication, but there is no record that the Greeks had foot races of more than three miles. Perhaps the wretched appearance of the long-distance runner at the end of his race offended their so-often disobeyed maxim, "Nothing in excess," as well as their sensitivity for physical beauty. The spare, stringy athletes who are the successful distance men were not models for sculptors as were the Hercules-like sprinters and wrestlers. The Greek pentathlon consisted of the long jump, the discus, the javelin, a sprint of one stade, and wrestling. A large athletic meet would also have separate events for rugged specialists in wrestling and boxing. The rules of both of these sports allowed much rougher stuff, such as kicking and gouging, than modern rules, which guard against maiming. At the Nemean Games of about 400 B.C. Damoxenus of Syracuse surprised Creugas of Epidamnus with an open-handed jab into the stomach and ripped out his entrails. It was a filthy foul and Creugas, who died on the spot, was awarded a crown post-humously.

Most of the ancient peoples played some sorts of ball games. Egyptian wall paintings show precursors of hockey sticks, teams of players, and various kinds of balls that were hustled by cooperative effort from one goal to another. No doubt Greek children also had spontaneous team sports, but socially blended sporting efforts had no place in the Greek festivals which demanded supreme physical efforts by individuals alone. Nor did the ancient Greeks have relay races as part of their festivals. True, there were torch races in those days when fire was kindled with difficulty and was still surrounded by a pre-cious aura of magic; they were eerie and splendid adjuncts to many religious festivals. However, in these relays, the ob-ject of the passing of the fire was not only to cover a distance with the torch, but to arrive without extinguishing the flame. Passing the torch was enchanting to witness. Plato recalls in the *Republic* an experiment consisting of a torch race held on horseback.

The first Olympic victor of whom we have record is a certain Coroebus, a cook from Elis, who won the dash of one stade in 776 B.C. However, at the sacred site among quiet rivers, green forests, and low hills in a vale in the Peloponnesus, the tradi-tion of quadrennial athletic-religious celebrations is much older. There were probably regular sporting contests four or even six centuries before—myth attributes the founding of the Olympic Games to Hercules. In any case, by 600 B.C. the program at Olympia was nearly complete and remained remarkably stable for almost a thousand years. Later additions were a few events for boys and some competitions for trumpeters and heralds—the last being of practical importance, for the crowds were large and chatty. Strong lungs and tough larynxes were needed for announcements. The heralds won their prizes for the volume and not for the sweetness of their notes.

The Olympic festivals were held every fourth year about the

time of the summer solstice when a new moon announced the month of Hieromenia. As the date neared, heralds were sent from nearby Elis, host of the Games, to be welcomed and publicly entertained in all the cities of the Greek world—including the distant colonies in Spain, Sicily, and the Black Sea. All the Greek festivals initiated truces, but usually the rest from scheming politics and war was only local. For the Olympic Games, the sacred truce was more pervasive. The Elian hosts declared the whole territory of Elis to be sacrosanct. No soldier could enter Elis; all competitors or pilgrims going to or coming from Olympia were declared to be under the direct protection of the gods, and to molest travelers was sacrilege.

The social tone at the Olympic festival was hardly one of sanctimonious somberness. The panoply of anthropomorphic Greek gods presided over a raucous scene somewhat like a large fair. The wealthy arrived on horseback and were attended in their decorated tents. Others, like Socrates, walked to the Games and, at night, rolled in their blankets, listened to the rustling river Altis and looked up at the stars over one of the most beautiful spots in Greece. The Games were the occasion for the meetings of musicians, artists, playwrights, philosophers, and merchants. Between the contests hucksters sold souvenirs and bankers from distant cities used the occasion to conclude long-term business contracts. There were side shows of jugglers and acrobats.

Many more were present than the 40,000 that the stadium held. (Actually there were few seats as such. Most just lolled on the grass.) The atmosphere was gruff and masculine; the only woman allowed to be present was the priestess of Demeter, who was seated alone on a white marble throne opposite the judges.

The pressure to *win* at the Olympics was awful. Significantly, history has recorded almost no Greeks who took second place. The sporting representatives of various communities were told that they were the corporeal representatives of the home city in symbolic, but important, battles. A victor, particularly one who took several events or who triumphed in successive festivals, was feasted, sculpted, and celebrated in verse and would have his name inscribed in the temples of his home city. In later years a great athletic hero could approach semi-divine status. City-state athletic rivalry was intense. By means of costly prizes, luxurious Sybaris tried to establish an athletic festival that would rival the Olympics. Bribery tempted renowned athletes to leave their home city to compete as the citizens of another. One Olympic victor, Astylus of Croton (a town famous for its athletes) was induced to compete in his third Olympiad as a Syracusan, whereupon the outraged citizens of Croton destroyed his statue and turned his house into a prison. With so many sporting festivals and so many prizes to be won, Greece saw the rise of the pothunter who traveled quite purposefully as a professional. A Theogenes of Thasos is supposed to have harvested some 1,400 prizes.[2]

The Romans continued the ancient athletic meets, as they did so many Greek institutions. Games continued and even became more frequent and grander. But Roman sports were separated even more from the fabric of life by greater professionalism and by the Roman taste for decorative showmanship. The spectacles went on a downward slide that ended in the truly awful. The ancient Greek educationalists proposed (if they only sometimes produced) physically fit, intellectually vigorous all-rounders. The Roman trainers were practical impresarios who forced the narrow specialization of the mass entertainer. The contrast is revealed in Greek and Roman statues of athletes. The body of the Greek Olympic victor was idealized as an illustration of physical and spiritual harmonies. The sculpted Roman wrestlers and boxers depict for us pathetic, brutalized muscle-men. The Roman crowds liked best the wrestling, *pankrátion*, and boxing. To make the matches more visually stimulating (i.e., bloody) the fists of the boxers were wrapped with the murderous, weighted thongs of the *caestus*. Athletic festivals were commonly supplemented by gladiatorial shows and fights of wild animals. It is recorded that human blood was inadvertently sprinkled on the front rows of the Panathenian stadium at Athens—for the Greeks, under Roman domination, also cheered the gruesome festivals of the decadent Imperial world.

The Romans adored luxury. An advertisement for some athletic games to be staged at Pompeii held out as attractions the promise of awnings and sprays of perfumed water (*vela et sparsiones*) for the spectators.[3]

However, deep in the Greek Peloponnesus, the Olympic Games continued with rare interruptions and few changes. So prestigious were the Olympics that the Romans were unsuccessful in upsetting the ancient Mediterranean rule of establishing chronology in terms of Olympiads, or periods of time four years long dating from the first recorded Olympiad in 776 B.C.—when history was supposed to have begun. The early Greeks had confined their entries to Greek-born citizens. Under the tolerant, assimilating Romans, the Olympics became polyglot and the last Olympic victor of whom we have record was an Armenian prince, Varaztad, who won a boxing match in A.D. 385. After this, Rome's vigor declined sharply and the Olympics became scarcely noticed, sentimental side shows. The termination of the Olympic Games is as obscure as their beginning.[4] The last meeting occurred in the early fifth century and one of the Christianized Roman emperors stopped the series because they were pagan rites. In any case, Olympia and its museums and temples became victims of the Goths who dispersed their treasures. The brilliant stucco peeled from the massive stones of rough, gray, shell limestone. An earthquake in the sixth century toppled the temples and diverted the course of the Altis which subsequently hid the site with layer upon layer of mud.

As the Christian era of history progressed, memories of Olympic glories persisted. Certain Latin emperors attempted majestically to have their reigns reckoned in "Olympiads." His-

torians who continued to use classical authors as sources referred from time to time to the Olympic Games. Various words
derived from the site, the four-year period, and the Games
passed into European languages from the Latin *Olympias*.
William Shakespeare used the sentence, "Such rewards as victors weare at the Olympian Games," in Act Two of *Henry VI*
and referred to "Olympian wrestling" in Act Four of *Troilus and
Cressida*. John Milton recalled the "Olympian Games" in his
Paradise Lost in 1667. After the sixteenth century linguistic
forms and derivatives of *Olympias* were far more common in
English than in any other language.[5]

Indeed, the English seem to have been the modern leaders
in evolving among themselves a feeling for and a pursuit of
sport that could be compared with ancient Greek athletics. In
the early seventeenth century a wealthy Captain Robert Dover
established at his provincial estate in the heart of the Cotswolds
a yearly series of "Olympick Games" that took place on
Thursday and Friday of Whitsun week. Dover planned these
gaudy celebrations as a protest against the infectious puritanism
that was spreading throughout the country. In fact, the settings,
ceremony, and feasting accompanying the athletic events were
throwbacks to the medieval tradition of courtly pageantry. The
extremely popular Dover, as chief official, rode about the playing fields on a white horse, with a broad brimmed hat and a
flopping, fluted ruff. For a time the Cotswold "Olympicks"
were widely known and consisted of "wrestling, playing cud-
gels, fencing, leaping, pitching the bar, throwing the iron hammer or handling the pike [javelin?] while the young women
were dancing to the tune of a shepherd's pipe."[6]

We know about these baroque Olympics principally because
of the survival of a book of poems dedicated to Dover. The list
of poets included Ben Jonson, Michael Drayton, and Thomas
Haywood and is almost a *Who's Who* of English poetry in the
early seventeenth century. All the poems harken back to the
glories of ancient Greece. Dover was often eulogized as a sec-

ond Hercules. At the conclusion of his own poem which closes
the little volume, Dover observes:

> Whilst Greece frequented active Sports and Playes,
> From other men they bore away the prayse;
> Their Common-Wealths did flourish and their Men
> Unmatch'd were for worth and Honour then:
> But when they once those pastimes did forsake,
> And unto drinking did themselves betake,
> So base they grew, that at this present day
> They are not Men, but moving lumps of Clay . . .[7]

There can be no doubt that, despite her tiny population,
England in the eighteenth and nineteenth centuries demonstrated extraordinary economic, political, and even intellectual
energy. Continental social critics came to Great Britain to observe its society and institutions in hopes that they might de-
tect some exportable essence from Albion's experience. Explanations for the success of Englishmen were, of course, many-
sided, but a number of travelers wistfully admired the Englishman's exceptional passion for sport and drew conclusions from
this passion. Montesquieu, Voltaire, and other Anglophiles, in
turn, expressed disgust at the effete elegance of super-civilized,
continental intellectuals. Once, while happily participating in a
sporting festival on the banks of the Thames, Voltaire felt himself "transported to the Olympic Games."[8]

During the later nineteenth century there was another British series of yearly "Olympics" that enchanted a young French
social critic. For more than forty years a Dr. W. P. Brookes had
staged a series of races for men and horses and some tennis
and cricket matches on his "Olympian fields" at Wenlock in
Shropshire. As with the festivals of Rovert Dover, these pageants
were accompanied by band music and contrived rituals such
as the passing of silver bowls of champagne, the casting of
flower petals, and the gallant awarding of laurels by fair ladies
to kneeling victors. Brookes also hoisted banners with mottoes in

classical Greek and commissioned special odes which he had set to music. The reigning Greek sovereign was notified of the English "Olympics" and he sent from afar a special silver cup to be awarded at these modern Games. Brookes responded with the planting of a seedling oak dedicated to the distant monarch. Baron Pierre de Coubertin, a young Frenchman who observed the Shropshire games, befriended Brookes and commented later,

Since ancient Greece has passed away, the Anglo-Saxon race is the only one that fully appreciates the moral influence of physical culture and gives to this branch of educational science the attention it deserves.[9]

Philhellenism has been a strong intellectual current in Europe in the modern age. The English were not, of course, the only modern nation to claim the mantle of classical culture. Germany too was culturally vigorous in the eighteenth and nineteenth centuries. In terms that were at once mystical and lordly, intimate and arrogant, the Germans have long claimed a spiritual kinship to the artists and philosophers of the classical golden age.

A major figure who both exemplifies the German fascination with Greek antiquity and was himself an influence in the *Aufklärung*, or German Enlightenment, was Johann Joachim Winckelmann (1717–1768). A poor boy, early singled out for special attention because of his intellectual liveliness, Winckelmann was channeled into the German university system in order to prepare him as a theologian. He balked at this, yet did no better in his studies in medicine, for as a boy he had developed a tough curiosity about Greek art and literature. Various positions as a librarian for wealthy patrons in Italy eventually permitted Winckelmann to indulge his curiosity further than previous classical scholars had. Winckelmann absorbed the contents of the galleries of Greek art assembled by the Renaissance princes and popes. He himself was a pioneer in scientific archaeology. His many thoughtful essays and his monumental works published with large, careful line etchings of antique monuments in the 1750's and 1760's were imaginatively conceived and his prose was a model of German style. The writer and his works were admired everywhere, but nowhere more than in his homeland.

Winckelmann presented a picture of Greek life and culture that was at once dazzling and restful. He described a lofty, intellectual society of individuals distinguished by discipline and subordination to principles of rationality, balance, and restraint. Sculpture, the salient Greek art form, was characterized by "noble simplicity and calm greatness" and by athletic types which repressed details like tendons and veins to emphasize ideal, perfect proportions. Implicit in Winckelmann's essays is an explanation of why the Greeks were able to create such a corpus of literature, art, philosophy, and science—a contribution so stupendous as to fascinate without cessation the following millennia. Greek intellectuals self-consciously isolated themselves from the hurly-burly of ordinary life. Their thrills were interior and their working milieu was one of clean air, calm, and "Olympian" separation. At least this was the belief of the Germans of the Enlightenment.

As a later, more subtle admirer of classical antiquity, Friedrich Nietzsche, was to show, Winckelmann's lovely explanation ignores the sweat and stink of the palestra, the shrieking abandon of the Dionysiac orgies, and the illogical horrors of the Eleusinian mysteries; it also neglects to appraise the Greek taste for wild music and sensual dancing. But the durability and impact of the myths of classicism have been incalculable. Neoclassicism was an artistic current in the late Enlightenment of all Europe. Classical motifs determined the forms and surfaces of creations ranging from those of the English cabinet makers to the setting by Jacques Louis David for Napoleon's coronation; the popularity of these symbols of ancient excellence owed a great deal to Winckelmann's publications and to his inspiration.

The rich creativity of German artists and intellectuals continued into the nineteenth century. Growing numbers of Germans felt that so brilliant a people ought to have a strong state just as the other Western European peoples did. Consequently, Germany in the nineteenth century produced some persuasive theorists of nationalism and some vigorous panegyrics for the sovereign, national state. The philosopher Johann Gottlieb Fichte (1762–1814), laboring at the University of Berlin under Napoleonic occupation, gave and published lectures on German patriotism. In the eighteenth century, many German intellectuals had used French. The brothers Jacob (1785–1863) and Wilhelm (1786–1859) Grimm, in their studies of German folk culture, established the historical and popular basis for manifestoes of the antiquity and richness of the German language and a specifically German past. An ever growing and more determined German nationalism spread among the middle classes throughout the hundreds of states, principalities, free cities, bishoprics, and trading towns that had kept Germany fragmented for so long.

A jarring and vulgar note was also added to German nationalism during the period of Napoleonic domination. A leading ideologue of aggressive, muscular, German patriotism was Friedrich Ludwig "Vater" Jahn (1778–1852). In his pamphlet, *Deutsches Volkstum* (1810) Jahn appealed for an upsurge in German national spirit to be based upon a submission to the ideals of militaristic, hierarchical Prussianism. Prussian pride was arrogant, uncultured, and at odds with the tolerant cosmopolitanism of the German literary figures. To base one's hopes for a German regeneration on the toughness and loyalty of the German *Volk* was quite different from pride in the spiritual monuments of the *Aufklärung*.

Though an author of German intolerance and aggression, "Father" Jahn was probably more famous as a popularizer (the *inventor* was Johann Guts Muths, 1759–1839) of massed gymnastics in the *Turner* societies which became such a distinctive element in German education and German society in the nineteenth century. Jahn and his *Turnerschaft* preached *mens sana in corpore sano*, but his *Turners* had little in common with the Greek or the English ideas of sport. The German gymnasts met and performed in disciplined rows and did simple or extremely strenuous maneuvers in unison. The object was to synchronize one's slightest gesture with those of one's companions in the brotherhood. The organizers of German gymnastics sought to organize very large numbers of performers in grand, rigidly programmed tableaux that offered a powerful impression to the observer and produced in the participator fierce feelings both of internal joy and communal solidarity. In massed gymnastics, the individualism of the Greeks was absent. The ideals of the good loser, fair play, and rapid ingenuity in team cooperation, all English attitudes, were simply foreign to athletics in nineteenth-century Germany. The *völkisch* gymnasts, young and old, mere amateurs and the most dazzling laborers at the parallel bars or the flying rings, were in deadly earnest. They were organized into quasi-military hierarchies and formed paramilitary clubs and networks of clubs that were meant to prepare the German *Volk* for a test against its enemies who were preventing German political self-realization.

German nationalism gathered determination. Finally, beginning in the 1860's and culminating in the decisive six-weeks war with France in August and September of 1870, Germany was united in a rough approximation of a modern state. The task was accomplished by pitiless military logic and diplomatic duplicity—both masterfully wielded by Otto von Bismarck who, in order to consolidate the gains of *Realpolitik*, appealed to the crude discipline and the vulgar pride of the German masses.

Before the military surprises of the disruptive years 1866–70, Europe's outstanding success had been Great Britain. The British led the Industrial Revolution after its beginnings in the late eighteenth century. After Napoleon fell (largely because of the steady application of English gold to the enemies of

France), Britain became "the workshop of the world" and the arbiter of Europe's political and economic destinies. After 1870, when statistical data and new techniques for interpreting the data were demonstrating that it was so, Germany's triumphs were more striking. Germans became prosperous on the basis of new industries such as electrical equipment and heavy chemicals and competed vigorously in fields such as insurance, banking, shipbuilding, and foreign trade in which the British had been superior. Bismarck made Germany the makeweight in critical diplomatic decisions. By the end of the century, in the pretty land which most cultivated Europeans had earlier conceived of in terms of castles on the Rhine, love in the Schwarzwald, and merry elves with turned-up shoes—in short, the country where toys came from—people were breeding faster, forming new industrial cities, and evolving more potentially destructive military techniques faster than the people of any other nation in the world. And, because the Germans could afford it and since *Kultur* did not threaten the state, German artists, intellectuals, and scholars were allowed to be as vigorous and as richly creative as ever.[10]

Supported by local German governments, the well-subsidized universities were hives of scholars working on the large problems and the little mysteries posed by the evidence left by the *Volk* which had so long ago altered the world with *its* accomplishments. The written evidence the Greeks left behind was lamentably fragmentary. Germans devotedly compiled archaeological evidence that would add to the literary remains of the people for whom the nineteenth-century Teutons felt such ideological propinquity.

One of the potentially richest archaeological sites, Olympia, had been neglected for so long that its exact location had been unknown even before the Ottoman Turks overran Greece. An English antiquarian, Richard Chandler, correctly ascertained the location of the site in 1766. Two years later Winckelmann himself was working on a proposal to the Sublime Porte. The

German was planning to import a hundred foreign workmen to Olympia at the time of his death. Some travelers visited the site thereafter. The first excavations took place in 1829, shortly after the modern Greeks, at a terrible cost, shook off the Turkish yoke.

Ernst Curtius (1814–1896) was a lively and brilliant young man who, like other great Germans, loved to read Greek history and literature. He rose to early fame in German academia on the strength of his mastery of, and enthusiasm for, the sources of Greek civilization and in 1838, at the age of twenty-four, visited the buried temples of Olympia as an archaeological researcher. Later, as a professor in Berlin and as tutor to the Crown Prince of Prussia, Curtius single-mindedly pursued his schemes for major excavations at the lonely site in the Peloponnesus. In 1875, as Prussian-dominated Germany was booming with self-confidence, Curtius had the satisfaction of leading a generously subsidized expedition. The resulting excavations, because of the layers of mud often at depths of sixteen or more feet, were more arduous than expected and lasted six years. Curtius unearthed coins, vases, inscriptions, whole temples, and complexes of sporting architecture—all of which tended to verify the surviving descriptions of the Roman traveler, Pausanias. The German classicist brought back plunder in the form of sculpture and antique decorative art to enrich the museums of Berlin.[11] At one time or another, the most distinguished classical scholars in Germany played some part in this vast project, the success of which was sentimentally linked with the grandeur of the Prussian and Imperial royal house.

The Germans came to consider themselves exceptional in all respects, athletics included. "Vater" Jahn's disciplined, massed gymnastics was, however, almost exclusively German. (A kind of gymnastic training had become popular in the Scandinavian countries as well, though without the sinister *völkisch* overtones.) The *Turnvereine* (athletic clubs) multiplied and established journals and gymnasiums and special *Turnplätze* (exercise fields) for their large assemblies. The conventions or *Turn-tage* usually took place on patriotic holidays. The *Turnfeste*, when teams numbering thousands competed to music and were surrounded by ranks of local and national flags, drew vast numbers of participators and few spectators who did not at some time participate. The Germans were enthusiastic about sport—or at least their own variety of it.

It ought not to be astonishing that, in the light of German sympathy for classical antiquity, German inventiveness, German sport, and German organizing ability, there would be some proposals for a sentimental revival of the Olympic Games. One of the theoretical founders of the German system of gymnastics, Guts Muths, had proposed a revival of the Olympics. Ernst Curtius gave a public lecture in Berlin in January 1859 in which he discussed the Olympic Games and urged that they be re-instituted. But, it should be noted, these nostalgic proposals for a revival of an ancient festival came from the custodians of a sort of German culture that was isolated from the sectors that actually enjoyed German sport. The classicists represented the old, dreamy, cosmopolitan ideal and were hardly chauvinistic Teutons.

Besides various English "Olympics," which in their festive orientation were actually vestigial medieval celebrations, and the German intellectuals' yearning for a return to the sport of their cleaner, classical incarnations, there were also in the nineteenth century several athletic meetings in Greece itself which were called "Olympic Games." Evangelios Zappas, a nostalgic Greek living in what is now Rumania, left a large fraction of his considerable fortune for the purpose of reestablishing the Olympic Games in his only recently independent fatherland. The young government built a large hall and exhibition complex in Athens to be used, among other things, for athletic practice and meets. The Greeks also staged a series of "Panhellenic" or "Olympic" Games after 1859.

Clearly, in the last years of the nineteenth century, Olympism (or the term at least) was in the air, particularly in England, Germany, and Greece; and English ideals of sportsmanship were spreading all over the empire, including India, which had enthusiastically adopted cricket and field hockey. In the United States the rapid adoption of college athletics had led some editorial writers to decry the "sporting craze" that would very likely affect studies badly. Germans too were, in their own fashion, promoting athletics more assiduously and had even self-righteously proposed themselves as custodians of the classical ideals of sport. Athletic extravaganzas sometimes called "Olympic Games" had been staged in the capital of modern Greece. Ironically, however, the actual impelling force for modern international sport as we know it came from a nation where competitive athletics were almost unknown.

As was noted earlier, a pivotal event in recent modern history was the defeat of France by Germany in 1870. Few felt the gravity of this upset more deeply than young Pierre de Coubertin. Coubertin interpreted the results of the six-weeks war as conclusive evidence of the deterioration of the quality of the French people from some earlier zenith of moral and, most particularly, physical perfection. Born in 1863 into a great noble family that had served France for centuries, Coubertin as a youth assigned himself the task of reinvigorating French youth by means of a reform of the national educational system. *Revanchards*, those Frenchmen who favored vigorous military preparations against Germany, were far from rare in France after 1870, but Coubertin's plans were unusual, not only in his concrete proposals, but also in the results he actually produced.

In the 1880's and 1890's Frenchmen of all levels of talent forced themselves to devise new assessments of the essence and strength of their culture and of their nation. For the very bravest, those tough enough to look into the vortex and talk with the devil, it was obvious that Germany had much to teach France, most particularly in the philosophy and operation of public education. If power, glory, a surging national wealth, and ebullient cultural vigor were all objectives to be pursued after 1870, much of German technique in many areas deserved dispassionate examination and, conceivably, adoption. Young Pierre de Coubertin, in the process of becoming a social theorist and a zealous political reformer, was not one of the bravest Frenchmen. Indeed, for him to embrace any aspect of German culture in the 1880's would have also required him to affront well-dressed, banqueting, literary, French society—a prospect he could not then face.

Now Anglomania was not new to upper-class Frenchmen. Parisians of the *belle époque* had adopted English words ("week-end," "smoking," "jockey"), English tweeds, and English race horses. Though the British fell short of German expansiveness after the pivotal date of the century, 1870, they were still surging with economic and intellectual vitality. The British had evolved in the direction of democracy without the calamitous revolutions so familiar to the French. Pierre recalled the embarrassment of his youth when, in the multiple, disparate "effigies" on the jingling coins in his pocket, he saw in microcosm the "repeated disarray" in French politics and the "ridicule of our instability."[12] Like Montesquieu, Voltaire, and Hippolyte Taine before him, Coubertin traveled in England, stayed at aristocratic country houses, was dined in London's paneled and leather-tufted clubs. When he was shown about England's vastly spacious, turfed, and gray-stoned schools for boys, young Coubertin was convinced that he was breathing the distilled essence of power and success. If France was to be glorious in the future as she had been in the past, there had to be reform. Great Britain would be the model. As Germany's success was generally attributed to her educational system, he decided that England's success must be due to her schools. Furthermore, Coubertin felt that the crux of English education was the unique fostering of athletics along with formal intellectual training.

In 1886 began Pierre de Coubertin's copious stream of articles, published speeches, and books that, in the guise of praise of English education, were really hosannahs to the English rich and were intended somehow to revitalize France. After 1890 his writing dwelled increasingly on the methodology of pedagogical sport, gleaning most of his ideas from the growing quantity of theoretical literature on sport available in English. The young French aristocrat embarked on a campaign to gain administrative control of amateur athletics (such as they were) in France. Single-handedly he established himself as an expert on athletics and his impeccable social connections (for he did not repudiate salon society) led to his role as occasional consultant for high government bureaucrats. The results of a questionnaire he sent to scondary schools in the British Empire and the United States convinced him that almost all favored a balance of physical and intellectual activity.

The young baron went to the United States in 1893 to observe the World's Columbian Exposition in Chicago and journeyed as far as the University of California at Berkeley where he endowed a prize for public speaking. He himself gave several public speeches. At Princeton he began his friendship with the socially prominent historian, Professor William Milligan Sloane, also a sports enthusiast.

Back in France, Coubertin continued to organize amateur sport and to enlist the support of strong public figures. A catch was the celebrated orator and educator, the Dominican priest, Henri Martin Didon (1840–1900). The courageous Père Didon had become nettlesome as a leftwing critic of orthodox views on divorce and the Trinity, as a prophet of Germany's dangerous economic vigor, as a castigator of French decadence, and as an experimenter with new curricula (including physical education) at his lycée, Albert le Grand. Chiseled into the stone over the entrance to Didon's school was its motto, *Citius, Altius, Fortius*—Farther, Higher, Stronger.

In Paris Coubertin would hound newspaper editors to publicize his fencing matches in the great hall of the Grand Hotel and equestrian competitions and "cross-country" (the English term had to be used) races in the Bois de Boulogne. Once the spectacle of inexpert French boys somehow flopping their way through the Anglo-Saxon specialty of a hurdle race brought eruptions of ill-bred guffaws among the sparse French spectators. The jealous little societies of French yachtsmen, rowers, and gymnasts resisted the baron's attempts to form a union of all sports and especially resented his internationalism. Coubertin suffered keen embarrassment when the French gymnasts boycotted a laboriously arranged exhibition of Swedish gymnasts at the Nouveau Cirque.

Pierre de Coubertin used his own money and that of a few wealthy supporters to buy trophies, to advertise, and to stage the banquets, oratory, and accompanying music that lent his assemblies and meets a familiar, festive appeal that was apart from the equivocally viewed athletic contests themselves. By 1893 Coubertin dominated the Union des Sociétés Françaises des Sports Athlétiques (U.S.F.S.A.). To offer a beautiful picture of French athletics to the world, Coubertin called an international congress of sporting enthusiasts to meet at the Sorbonne in June 1894. The declared purpose of the meeting was to discuss the forever thorny problem of defining and enforcing the concept of "amateur" and to consider the possibility of promoting international sporting meets.

Though internationalism, which we can conveniently date from the Crystal Palace Exhibition in London in 1851, was an ever stronger and ever more varied theme of these decades, international sport was scarcely known at all. Even in England and in the United States intercollegiate sport was in its early infancy. Coubertin had earlier been daringly experimental when he arranged for some meets between French and English rowers at Henley and in Paris. There had been a few meets among the best gymnasts of Scandinavia. However, the first international track meet of any significance did not take place until September 21, 1895, when the London Athletic Club team met the men of the New York Athletic Club at Manhattan Field. Americans, incidentally, won all eleven events.

What Coubertin was plotting in 1894 was to stage an athletic meet to be a subsection of the next Universal International Exposition of Paris scheduled for 1900. The French hosts planned this world's fair to be the largest ever. The conservative projection of attendance was sixty million. Far more comprehensive than later examples of the genre, the nineteenth-century world's fairs included international competitions in art and industry and congresses for librarians, physicians, mathematicians, and biologists. Why not a congress for athletes?

In July 1892 the French Republic had published a decree establishing the date and purpose of the next international exhibition in Paris. Four months later at a large assembly of French sportsmen Coubertin had first proposed "on a basis conforming to the conditions of modern life, a great and beneficial project: the reestablishment of the Olympic Games."[13] As Pierre planted this bomb, he throbbed with excitement. But his missile had a long fuse. His audience in 1892 was unmoved. He might just as well have suggested a resurrection of the Eleusinian mysteries or of the Oracle at Delphi. It should be noted here, that Coubertin himself had almost no enthusiasm for the glories of antiquity. His ambitions at the time were directed at improving the quality of French education, specifically physical education, by the observed examples of superior athletes from other nations. The young Coubertin (he was twenty-nine in 1892) was bored by sentimental anachronisms. He said "Olympic Games" in 1892 because he had been impressed by Dr. Brookes' festival and because the term was more festive and potentially inspiring than any other at hand.

Two years later, at Coubertin's eight-day international meeting of sportsmen and physical educationalists in June 1894, his ideas had gathered more precision. He had prepared a tentative program for an athletic congress to codify rules of all the sports that were then internationally practiced, including track and field events, horsemanship, sailing, gymnastics, fencing, and wrestling. His advance program for the delegates included an announcement that projects for the revival of the Olympic Games would be discussed last. The little man was a bureaucratic wizard and a master of subtle persuasion. As the gentlemen in Paris discussed amateurism and the standardization of techniques and rules, they were also treated to lunches at the townhouses of titled millionaires, speeches, choral concerts (a high point was the special performance of an ancient "Hymn to Apollo" discovered, deciphered, and orchestrated shortly before[14]), and those indispensable social lubricants of the epoch, banquets. Once, after a banquet, the lawn of the Croix Catalan was surrounded by a thousand torches as the delegates were treated to horse races and mock battles on horseback. There were martial music and trumpet voluntaries and the evening ended with a display of fireworks. Coubertin seduced and enchanted the conferees. When he finally introduced the question of modern Olympism, they rapturously applauded it.

The baron himself seems to have been euphorically transported. Nineteen-hundred was six years off. Might he be risking the evaporation of all this enthusiastic harmony if they waited so long for the first, grand, international athletic festival? The Swedes, gymnastically sophisticated and in the vanguard of the century's internationalism, proposed Stockholm for preliminary meets in 1896. But what about a more cheering climate and the redolent air of Greece itself? Shortly before the final banquet, the Greek delegate, the poet and historian Demetrios Bikelas (1835–1908) had offered as much to Coubertin. The French impresario queried Bikelas with his eyes as the banquet drew to a close. A nod—murmurs everywhere— a motion carried the delegates unanimously.[15] Athens would be the site of the first revived Olympiad, just two years away. When George I, the king of Greece, was informed of the congress's action, he telegrammed thanks "for the establishment of the Olympic Games."

Another act of the Congress of the Sorbonne (to use the

designation established in Coubertin's later writings) was to form a *Comité International Olympique* of which Coubertin was duly chosen secretary. As was characteristic of his strategy, he then named a figurehead president. Some keen supporters such as Bikelas and Professor Sloane immediately joined the Committee. Others were accepted as members when they expressed uncritical warmth for Coubertin's projects; still others were informed of their membership (their presence at that or subsequent meetings not being a prerequisite for eligibility) by mail. In short, in the formative years of the Olympic movement, Baron Pierre de Coubertin and he alone was the effective International Olympic Committee, the new letterhead of which consequently became Coubertin's own.

Bikelas returned to Athens to be the liaison with the government there. To help the Greeks, Coubertin sought out and gathered information from the many constituent bodies of his U.S.F.S.A. Experts gave him the distances for various foot, cycle, and swimming races, schedules of point systems for fencing, wrestling, and gymnastics, and sets of rules for judges and coaches. He thus, incidentally, assured that the then feebly established rules prevalent in Paris would gain a foothold in cosmopolitan sport. He convinced the noted sculptor, Jules Champain, to design the silver and bronze first- and second-place medals. Gold—putrid, tainted with lucre—was banned from the Olympic Games of 1896. It was Coubertin who wrote the official invitations and sent them along with schedules of events and rules and the first copies of his new *Bulletin du comité international des jeux olympiques* to all the constituent bodies of his personal international organization.

When Bikelas wrote from Athens that the first Olympiad was about to abort (the government suddenly declared it could not even begin to finance the Games due to a crisis bordering on bankruptcy) Coubertin left Paris almost immediately. Shortly before Coubertin left France a prominent Hungarian friend had written him to offer Budapest as a site for the 1896

Games. While in Athens Coubertin often brought forth the Hungarian letter to be held in the palm of his left hand and slapped with the back of the right. Coubertin wrote an open letter to the newspaper *Asty* that contained the following observation: "We have a proverb which says that the word 'impossible' is not French. Someone told me this morning that the word is Greek, but I didn't believe him."[16] The royal family (which had no legal access to the treasury which, in any case, was empty) and public opinion were on the scrappy Frenchman's side. Eventually the Crown Prince and a few other personages outside the government called for a public subscription plus appeals, through the consulates, to wealthy Greeks abroad. Astonishingly, heavy donations poured in. An Alexandrian merchant, George Averoff, agreed to pay for the restoring of the once glistening marble of the Panathenian stadium of Herodes Atticus, at the time just a weedy ravine. The mass of smaller contributions permitted plans for a high standard of staging.

The nature of the teams tells us much of the state of sport at the time. Joyous at the prospect of hosting such a festival, the Greeks imported an English trainer and went into a whirlwind sporting Renaissance. Policemen cleared city streets so boys could practice the long jump and put the shot at impromptu competitions. Chuffing, lean peasants jogged the dusty 25-mile distance from the village of Marathon to the center of Athens. An old friend of Coubertin's, Michel Bréal, a classicist and a linguistics scholar, had promised a chased silver cup to the winner of the "revived" marathon race. This was the genesis of an event that Coubertin secretly felt was too ghastly to draw entries and which subsequently was to mar so many of his early festivals. Another Greek specialty was the discus throw. Certain sailors and soldiers were given special leaves to train for it.

The first large team to arrive was the Hungarians. Cocky, high-spirited, they marched about Athens five or six abreast, were assiduous depositors of commemorative wreaths and responded with alacrity to requests for snapshots. One memorable Magyar, though he posed in a jersey shirt and short, tight trousers, wore about his bunching calves high black socks that required garters with little buckles just below the knuckled knees.

From the start, the Athens Games were marred by the German muddle. Wilhelm II's Reich, making so great a mark in the world, was planning to send a large team. Then, a German newspaper alleged that Coubertin had boasted that the enemies of France had been barred from the Sorbonne Congress of 1894 and that he would exclude them from the international meet of 1896. There followed an explosion in the German press as a whole. Diplomatic maneuvering. Denials. Apologies. Bitterness. Finally the Germans sent a small but expert gymnastics team led by a burly, elderly man who was willing to enter almost any event. The Germans held themselves separate from the rest of the athletes and nettled the others by standing sternly at attention before launching into their routines.

From the rest of the continent there were just a few individuals: a Danish weight lifter with a remarkably thick neck and *cheveux en brosse*; a Swedish runner and a Swiss gymnast who were passing through. The sole Italian to appear had come the entire distance from Milan on foot in order to train, but could produce no amateur credentials upon his arrival and was not permitted to compete. Despite Coubertin's elevated position in the French sporting world, he could rouse only two very good cyclists, a few fencers, and a M. Lermusieux who was a runner of some verve (he drained bumpers of wine before his races and wore white gloves when he was to appear before the king) who planned to enter both the dashes and the marathon.

Had the publicity been better planned at the English universities, there might have been a representative British team. Only six Britons competed. One was, in fact, a South African hurdler. The favorite for the distance runs was Mr. Flack, an Australian member of the London Athletic Club. Mr. Boland, who took the tennis singles and was assisted by a Greek for the doubles, just happened to be in Athens when the Games began. The Athenian British community caused a hubbub when they almost succeeded in barring two young English cyclists from the races, because they were working men, servants at the Embassy, and therefore outside the embrace of the aristocratic, English amateur rules.

The American team was larger. Coubertin's friend, Professor Sloane, who was in fact the American Olympic Committee at the time, got his dean at Princeton to give four eager juniors part of the spring semester off. Two Boston athletic clubs sent a squad of Harvard students and alumni, thereby interjecting intercollegiate rivalry into the international meet. There were also two marksmen and a lone swimmer from Boston. All arrived at Athens on April 4, 1896, somewhat shaky from the long journey of several steamers and a variety of trains between New York and Piraeus. They had stopped to do their workouts on the fields of the British officers at Gibraltar.

Since the Games of 1896 were independent of the paralyzed Greek government, the royal family seized upon the festivities to promote their own prestige. King, queen, princes, princesses, their spouses and fiancées posed as patrons and inserted themselves into the judging and the award ceremonies—all to the delight of the spectators, almost all of whom were Greeks, for there were few foreigners who came to Athens specially for this strange anachronism, "the Olympic Games."[17] At one point the queen inaugurated a specially built shooting gallery using a pistol engarlanded with chains of little flowers. The king was host at a huge breakfast for all the athletes and officials in the colonnaded main ballroom of the royal palace. There were lunches and other parties. Madame Schliemann, widow of the rediscoverer of Troy and Mycenae, offered a picnic for the Americans at her villa in the vale of Daphne. The heavy cruiser *San Francisco* was anchored in the harbor. Its officers gave a reception and the band of American sailors offered concerts of *Waldteuffel* and (naturally) Sousa waltzes and marches. For a special *fête de nuit* intended to add fantasy to the Games, the *San Francisco* contributed a fireworks exhibition and speeded its whining dynamos for a dazzling display of hundreds of electric lights in the great ship's rigging. During the ten days of the festival, the Athenians had torchlight parades, band concerts in the parks, played selections from *Lohengrin* (for some reason), performed a new cantata, "The Young Sailor," and gave many offerings of an "Olympic Hymn" composed by a Greek for the occasion. There was also a newly staged version of Sophocles' *Antigone* for which a local composer devised special music that, in turn, gave rise to critical controversy in the Greek press. Coubertin had tried to have formal music competitions included as part of the Games of 1896, but at the last minute the Greek bands dropped out, pleading a lack of time to practice.

The results of the Athens Games can be summarized quickly.[18] Even according to the expectations of that time, the records were dismal. The only entries who knew that in order to do well one had to *prepare* for an event—not just enter it—and the only athletes who knew about and were willing to undergo training were the English and the Americans—and they arrived badly out of shape. Besides, the facilities were generally poor. The track surfaces were loose, the turns in the ancient stadium too sharp, the weather chilly and gusty, and the competition often pathetic.

The outstanding hero of the Games and a towering national hero thereafter was Spiridon Loues, a spare, dusky peasant from the village of Marousi. He won the first marathon. Loues lagged far behind at the beginning of the dusty, rocky 40-kilometer distance (about 25 miles) from the bridge at the village of Marathon to the restored stadium. However, Loues was just one of many lagging entries in the early part of the race. At the start, Lermusieux, the French showman, had rushed to the lead and convinced all the non-Greeks to follow him. Totally unaware of how one paced for this novel kind of torture, almost all came to grief shortly after the half-way mark. The Australian, Flack, was carried raving to a following hospital van. Loues took the lead very late in the race. Lermusieux actually finished and so did a Hungarian, but eight of the first nine were Greeks. Greeks also won in the flying rings, some minor fencing competitions, one contest in marksmanship, and a unique bicycle marathon of 80 kilometers, from the Athens velodrome to Marathon and back.

The two Frenchmen dominated the cycling. One special race was a twelve-hour-long spin around the ⅓-kilometer track. The winner went almost 900 revolutions and the man who was runner-up was just one lap behind him. Some French fencers also did well. The thick-necked Dane took the two-handed jerk in weight lifting. By doing intricate and risky maneuvers (with inevitable mistakes), the German gymnastics team beat the cautious, but more graceful Greeks, favorites of the crowd. The stern Germans thereby became the villains in Athens. Their position was not helped when a versatile, elderly German who was also ugly, downed a tall, fair, and excessively handsome Englishman and then two natives in the wrestling. The stocky German was the only athlete in the 1896 Games who was hissed. The sole Hungarian athlete who performed well at all was a Jew, Alfred Hoyos, who took both short and long distances in swimming. The races were held at the little bay of Zéa at Piraeus. The American swimmer, accustomed to the pools of home, had found the Mediterranean in April intolerably frigid.

The other Americans performed much better. They were, for example, the only runners to use the crouched start, invented by Charles Sherrill in 1888 at Yale. With the exception of the distances, they swept the track and field events, scoring upsets in the hurdles, the shot put, and the discus. The last two events were taken by Robert Garrett, captain of the

Princeton team. Tall, long-armed Garrett who had only begun to practice for the discus just after his arrival in Athens, won over two powerful Greek favorites. The American marksmen took first and second in every event they entered.

The Americans, in fact, had a marvelous time which was marred by the eruption of Harvard-Princeton rivalry. An embarrassment during the first few days was the very frequency with which the "stars and stripes" shot up to the top of the standard at one end of the stadium. This patriotically stimulating flag ceremony for victors was invented for the first revived Olympics. Garrett's victory over the Hellenes' candidate for hero in the discus was almost tragic for the Greeks and there was a strain, for a while, about the American presence in Athens. The fabulous marathon victory on the fifth day erased local resentment, though, and the Ivy League cleancutters, with their open good looks and their hair parted down the center then became really popular. Their college cheers, so novel to the continentals, made them an entertainment sensation; they cleverly modified the "tigers" and "locomotives" by grafting onto them a *"Zito Hellas!"* (Hooray Greece!).

The final day of the Games, several times delayed because of bad weather (which, incidentally, caused the cancellation of the scheduled yachting races), was designated for the conferring of the awards. The herald, a certain Captain Hadjipetros, summoned the individual winners to appear before the king. The prizes were the medals, certificates (which the Americans called "diplomas"), and branches of olive for the victors and branches of laurel for the runners-up. The athletes assembled by nationality and marched, all fifty or so of them, around the track of the restored stadium of Herodes Atticus. The crowd of about 100,000 which overflowed on the hills above the rows of seats, was especially joyous when some master of the revels turned loose several hundred pigeons trailing ribbons of the Greek national colors. Some spectators tossed flower petals into the air on schedule. Ranges of massed thousands exploded into volleys of cheers when, modest and upright, Spiridon Loues paraded waving a miniature Greek flag that an adoring countryman had thrust into his hand. After the tumult that accompanied their circuit, the cosmopolitan group assembled before the royal patron who announced, "I proclaim the ending of the first Olympiad."

Though they launched the series and were remarkably effective as festivity, the Athens Games also marked the beginning of some new and serious troubles for the International Olympic Committee—i.e., Pierre de Coubertin. So enchanted were the Greeks with the prospects of the Olympic Games that even before they had opened the Greeks excluded all foreigners, including Coubertin, from being officials, and when the French baron reappeared in Athens, he was cast as just another journalist. The Crown Prince Constantine and a circle of intimates immediately began a campaign to retain the Olympics forever in Athens. Thus the struggle to keep the Games ambulatory preoccupied Coubertin as he planned the second Olympiad as part of the colossal Universal Exposition of 1900 in Paris.

Coubertin early convinced the organizing committee of the great Exposition that athletics should be included. However, during the years 1897 and 1898 he was slowly squeezed out by a pack of third-string bureaucrats in the Ministry of Education, educators who were utterly without finesse or a taste for festivity and whose sole intention seemed to be to include as many sports as possible.[19] They had none of the wizard's faith in the value of galas; none of the aristocrat's skill in meticulously arranging entertainment. Consequently in 1900 the events dragged through most of the summer. Besides track and gymnastics which Coubertin felt should be the focus of the modern Olympic competitions, there were judges, prizes, and, incredibly, large fields of entries for ballooning, fire fighting, life saving, and even pelota, the Basque game. Earlier, Coubertin had desperately scrambled to stage some international competitions in Paris *apart* from the Exposition.[20] In the end all he accomplished was to gain the recognition that the Exposition's athletic festival was indeed the second modern Olympiad. In some cases not even the athletes knew of the "Olympic Games" until they read the inscriptions on their medals.

Still, even Coubertin had to admit that there were many more athletes from many more countries than had been in Athens four years earlier. Anglo-Saxon sport was a transferable taste.

The next Olympiad was yet more sadly conceived and carried out. Coubertin had tried to get New York, then Chicago as a site, but in the end he had to accept again the encompassing rubric of a world's fair, this time the Louisiana Purchase Exposition in the summer of 1904 in St. Louis. Of the five hundred athletes to show up in St. Louis, there were only a few Europeans, principally German and Hungarian swimmers.

The biggest controversy to arise in the course of the St. Louis Games was over the marathon. It developed that the first joyously greeted man over the finish line had come part of the way in an open touring car; it was later learned that the man *then* declared victor had been given periodic doses of strychnine by his trainers who drove beside him in a light runabout. The man who led most of the way, a tiny Cuban, was felled by stomach cramps not far from the finish. He had eaten too many stolen apples.

A combination of Coubertin's intransigence and their own ill-considered foreign military adventures prevented the Greeks from staging another "Olympiad" until their rump festival of 1906. This time the news of the Athens Games was circulated in the English universities and attracted many well-conditioned British athletes. France also sent a large team that did well in fencing, tennis, and marksmanship. The events of this second meeting in Greece and a general sympathy with the ideals of international amateur competition meant that the 1906 Games were well reported in the world press. All this surely strengthened Coubertin's International Olympic Committee which, about this time, became somewhat more of a group working in concert rather than the structure of one idealist. Greece, however, was never again able to stage a rump Olympiad.

Determined that the new quadrennial Olympiads, which he had personally endowed with a near sacred significance, somehow had to go on, Coubertin was forced to give his 1908 Games to London where, once again, they were subsumed under a larger festival, this time the Franco-British Exhibition. This big exhibition itself was one manifestation of an earlier major shift in British foreign policy which was, contrary to previous practice, intent upon having staunch allies in the face of the growing power and irresponsibility of Wilhelm II's German Reich. Great Britain was wooing France from a position of strength and there were lavish facilities for the display of artistic and manufactured goods and for the athletes as well. An international group of journalists was on hand as were huge patriotic crowds.

For the English were pursuing glory—even in athletics and even then in the face of the reputations of the American track teams. The rivalry reached back into the 1890's when in fact only Englishmen and Americans could produce a track team at all. Tensions were not eased by the fact that many of the American athletes were Irish or of recent Irish descent. British arrogance confronted aroused American braggadocio. Before a crowd of 65,000 at the opening ceremonies, the British neglected to display the American flag at the stadium. During the parade of athletes, the Yankees carried their banner and, unlike the other teams, refused to dip theirs as they passed King Edward and Queen Alexandra. An American afterward boasted, "This flag dips to no earthly king," and the incident established a tradition for American Olympic contingents. Newspaper editorials complained that the Americans wore clothing that was too tight. The British officials openly cheated in the 400-meter race to disqualify the American victor and probably did so other times. They cheered on their own champions with megaphones. One of many grim and scandalous moments occurred at the finish of the marathon when hosting officials assisted a collapsing Italian up to the tape in order to squeeze out a still-functioning Yankee who was coming up fast. The American, Johnny Hayes, was subsequently declared victor, but the intervening ruckus was ominous and I.O.C. thereafter removed the judging from the hosting nation and placed the responsibility in balanced, international juries.

In 1908 in London there were many offenses to patriotism. At the opening ceremonies the Swedish flag (like that of the United States) was missing and when the Swedes unsuccessfully protested a decision in a wrestling match, they quit and went home. Finland, then part of the Russian empire, obtained permission to compete as a separate team, but was denied the use of the Finnish flag. Deeply hurt, the Finns marched flagless. The Russian ambassador was enraged. National pride and the corrosive, single-minded pursuit of victory were now vital factors in the Olympics. Still, Coubertin and his followers began fashioning a modern Olympic mythology, part of which was that international athletics would promote, by the mixing of peoples, international harmony.

The I.O.C. gave the 1912 Olympics to Stockholm. At last Coubertin was able to see a proper athletic festival. Twenty-eight countries, including Japan, sent teams. National Olympic committees were functioning in many countries and had been able to arrange a series of early tryouts in order to assure the presentation of their best. A general determination to uphold the rigid standards of amateurism resulted in a bitter disappointment to the American team when the American Indian, Jim Thorpe, because he had earlier played professional baseball, was shorn of his victories in the pentathlon (at the time consisting solely of track and field events) and the decathlon.

The 1912 Games were richly financed by the proceeds of a Swedish national lottery. There was a great deal of new athletic architecture. The harmonious opening ceremonies (including the still flagless Finns and the non-dipping Americans) emphasized, for the first time, Coubertin's personally designed Olympic flag of five rings (representing all five continents) of the colors of *all* the national flags. At the opening of the Stockholm Games a chorus of over 4,000 sang "A Mighty Fortress is our God." The I.O.C. gained impeccable respectability when the king of the Belgians accepted the honorary presidency. Most of Europe's royalty permitted Coubertin to use their names on his various letterheads and proclamations. In 1912 the kings of Sweden, Italy, and Greece, the emperors of Germany, Austria, and Russia all personally presented or donated special trophies.

The revived Olympics approached their mature form. The Games for 1916 had been awarded to Berlin and Coubertin was entertaining a triumphant and festive meeting of the secure International Olympic Committee in Paris on July 28, 1914, when news came from Sarajevo of the assassination of the Austrian Archduke and heir to the Hapsburg throne.

2
The German Atmosphere

Olympism in 1914 was very different from what it had been in 1896. Great numbers of people—Europeans and Americans, journalists, athletes, international idealists—knew what the modern Olympics were and also felt some confidence in their continuation. Notions concerning the worth of team sports, individual competitiveness, and fair play—confined principally to the Anglo-Saxon upper crust before 1896—had continued their conquest of the world. Pierre de Coubertin had changed from a narrow French patriot to a sincere, altruistic internationalist and the International Olympic Committee became, in fact, what its name suggested it was. As the years of the young twentieth century progressed he grew to be less of a patriot and political philosopher and more of an intellectualizer of sport. Coubertin's musings about sport were antithetical to French ideas of "civilization" and, during his lifetime, he attracted more sympathy abroad than among his countrymen. In Paris he presented "anniversary" festivals or "jubilees," in the case of the five- or ten-year milestones of some holy date connected with the history of the International Olympic Committee. Distinguished and, whenever possible, titled guests from all over

Europe and from across the sea would flock to Coubertin's banquets, receptions, and exhibitions to offer him the respect absent in his everyday personal relationships. Royalty and the presidents of republics readily lent their names to his Olympic movement. International sport, which Coubertin originally conceived of as leading to the *"rebronzage"* (a neologism of his, meaning re-stiffening, re-gilding, and re-strengthening) of French youth, had been a favored part of a wider campaign to fortify France generally. After 1906 international sport received the attention of an ever greater proportion of Pierre de Coubertin's formidable intelligence and zeal. He conceived of the Olympics as great events leading to world peace. They had to go on and become ever grander. What is perhaps most significant for the modern Olympic movement is that he succeeded in implanting his views of sport and his dedication to quadrennial Games in many of his polyglot followers.

By the time of the Stockholm Games of 1912 there were representative, rigidly principled, national Olympic Committees which maintained Coubertin's high standards of amateurism. These committees were led by men who at home and as members of the International Olympic Committee were as sincere as Coubertin about the moral tone to be maintained at these festivals. After 1912 the former *revanchard* had few bitter feelings about Germany and worked harmoniously with Theodor Lewald, Chairman of the German Olympic Committee. Lewald, in turn, had to deal with the politically irresponsible, but patriotically ambitious Kaiser Wilhelm II to prepare the VIth Olympiad for Berlin.

The plans for these German Olympic Games were far grander than those made by the Swedes for 1912. Quite aware that they had not fully taken over the notions of the Anglo-Saxon sport that were overwhelmingly evidenced in the modern Olympic program, the Germans imported the well-known American track coach, Mr. Alvin Kraenzlein. Earlier called "the father of modern hurdling," Kraenzlein had been the first to use the straight-leg method and had been a star sprinter and long jumper as well.[1] His bitter rivalry with Meyer Prinstein, a Jew of Syracuse University, for records in the long jump and triple jump had been one of the exciting elements in the 1900, 1904, and 1906 Games and in American intercollegiate sport as well. Prince Karl, the Kaiser's son, became one of Kraenzlein's all-around athletes. The VIth Olympiad had already been the object of a great deal of German organizing talent, wealth, and affection when the directors were jolted by the outbreak of war in August 1914.

Each of the teams in the Great War was confident that it would be victorious and that their military victory would be rapid and relatively bloodless. Despite demands from the Entente powers that he do so, Coubertin resolutely refused to shift the site of the 1916 Games from Berlin and even moved the headquarters of the International Olympic Committee from Paris to Lausanne on the shores of neutral Switzerland's Lake Geneva. On April 10, 1915, Count von Francken-Sierstorpff of the German Olympic Committee announced that the next Olympiad would take place in Berlin when the war ended. Coubertin declared, "In olden times it happened that it was not possible to celebrate the games, but they did not for this reason cease to exist."[2] Then, on May 4, 1915, shortly after the German army first used chlorine gas at the trenches of the stalemated eastern front, Coubertin stated that rules (never specifically cited) made it impossible to shift the 1916 Games to France or America. None would be held.

Somehow, Coubertin convinced the Belgians to host the VIIth Olympiad which was held in 1920, on schedule, in Antwerp. Belgium had suffered more damage than any other participant in the Great War and she had only a year in which to prepare for her guests. Almost needless to say, Germans and Austrians were not invited. Nor were the Russians who for more than three decades afterward were assumed by the conservative members of the I.O.C. to be inhabiting territory poisoned for athletics as for other things by Bolshevism. In Antwerp in 1920 the standards of accommodation were meager as were the festive trappings and the enthusiasm of the small crowds. The hosts were concerned with but few parts of the large program and, understandably, had more serious things to worry about. A hero of these Games was Paavo Nurmi, the poker-faced Finnish youth, who made his international debut at the Antwerp Games as a victor in the 10,000-meter run and the 10,000-meter cross country. Though in the unofficial scoring systems invented by sports writers with eyes on the patriotic home markets (the I.O.C. recognizes no victorious nations) the Yankees were still winners, athletes from tiny, newly independent Finland also took the shot put, discus throw, javelin, pentathlon and the marathon. Rye bread became a health fad in the nineteen-twenties when journalists reported that this food bulked large in the Finnish diet.

A new standard of showmanship was set with the 1924 Olympics in Paris. However, the French were probably drawing more on their experience in hosting world's fairs than they were on an athletic tradition. In fact, the festive opening ceremonies with crowned heads, ambassadors, teams of hundreds, and accompanying officials, plus orchestras and speeches all occupied so much time that the sports, as such, had to wait until the second day. Again the Finns performed marvelously. Nurmi, now dubbed "a mechanical Frankenstein created to annihilate time," besides winning the 10,000-meter cross country one day, on another day of the Games took the 1,500 and 5,000 meters within a two-hour period. The 1924 Games were also remarkable because of the expanded program that included boxing, a great variety of rowing events, and a program of winter sports that took place earlier in the year at Chamonix in the French Alps. Europeans also saw the first appearances of superior American Negro athletes, one of whom, DeHart Hubbard, won a gold medal in the long jump (gold as a first prize had been used in 1900 and ever since).

In the Amsterdam Games of 1928 (the winter Games were at St. Moritz and were dominated by the Swiss hosts and the Norwegians) 43 nations entered a total of more than 4,000 competitors. As with the Games of 1920 and 1924, there were, inevitably, numerous disappointments and even personal tragedies due to stumbles, flubs, bad days, caught infractions, misperceived non-infractions, lapses in protocol, and offended national pride. However, in the Olympiads of the 1920's "good sportsmanship" overcame all; athletes, journalists, and whole teams seemed good-naturedly to have a shoulder-shrugging attitude toward bad luck—or at least they all accepted festivity and supposed international amity as a reward for forbearance.

Coubertin had long since ceased being a French chauvinist. The grand staging of vast numbers of participants in the Games in Holland seemed to corporealize his dreams (dreamed in the 1920's, but claimed to have been reveries before 1896) for international sport. Even the victors were becoming ever more international. Canadians and Scandinavians were rivaling the Americans for supremacy in track and field events. Germans (who were competing for the first time since 1912) made good showings in rowing and gymnastics. Mikio Oda, a Japanese, took the triple jump in 1928. El Ouafi, an Algerian, won the marathon; a Chilean was second. A grand sensation of the winter Games was the exquisite champion figure skater, Sonja Henie.

The same atmosphere of international geniality was pervasive at the 1932 Games in Los Angeles (the winter Games were in Lake Placid in New York State). Upon receiving news in 1928 that they would have the Xth Olympiad, the Californians characteristically gave themselves up to joyful anticipation—a mood that turned to embarrassment as the nation (and the world), after the stock market crash of October 1929, went deeper into the slough of depression. Money was short, but the treasurer of California found $1,000,000 to give the organizing committee. The Los Angelenos floated a special bond issue of $1,500,000. This money plus the nationwide appeal for contributions of dollars (in exchange for which the donors would get a button) furnished that without-which-nothing for a successful pageant, cash.

All was deluxe. The chief stadium held 104,000 and had the best track surfaces and apparatus obtainable. There was a new auditorium for wrestling and boxing, a large complex for swimming and diving, shooting ranges, and even stands for 17,000 spectators of the rowing races at Los Alamitos Bay. A long-standing gripe of American teams had been the rude living quarters they had endured at the sites of previous Olympiads. For their guests, the open-handed Angelenos constructed a special "Olympic Village" at an area then known as "Baldwin Hills" on the western outskirts of the city. Here, on a barren hilltop with views of the mountains and the sea, the best from all nations would mingle on 250 secluded acres living in Spartan but comfortable cottages. There were halls for socializing and Hollywood generously donated films for the athletes to view at night. Bonhomie was established early.

Since President Herbert Hoover was off campaigning for re-election, Vice President Charles Curtis opened the Games. No strangers to the spectacular and the fabulous (the lots of the studios were nearby) the hundred thousand revelers at the opening ceremonies were offered salvos from ten cannons, plenty of bands, and hundreds of flags flying in fresh, sunny weather—which stayed that way. The American hosts revived a touch used in Athens in 1896 when they released hundreds of white pigeons. Hollywood even added an appealing (if entirely original—for there were no historical antecedents) "Olympic flame," a torch that was to burn in a big brazier over the peristyle of the main stadium until the Games ended.

All contemporary observers noted the nobility and consistency of Olympic sportsmanship. The deep rivalry of two American sprinters, Ralph Metcalf—tall and elegant—and Eddie Tolan—a squat, cheery fellow who held his horn-rimmed spectacles on with adhesive tape, reached its climax in the 100-

meter dash. The winner of this race was popularly known as "the fastest man in the world." (Relative to the performances in this event, it is noteworthy that Percy Williams, winner of the 100 meters at Amsterdam in 1928 with a time of 10.8, was unable to qualify in his semi-final heat in Los Angeles with the same time.) Known to be a slow starter, Metcalf in the final heat of the 100 meters pulled up dramatically at the end of his race with Tolan. The roars of the vast stadium greeted the tall man as winner. After two hours of agonizing due to the firm dissenting views of some judges (later confirmed by the photoelectric timer which revealed that Tolan had won by two inches), Metcalf was told he was the second fastest man in the world, though both were clocked at 10.3. Later Metcalf lost the 200-meter dash to Tolan. Handsome Ralph's chagrin, however, was exceeded by the apparent sincerity with which he congratulated little Eddie. The runner-up became a kind of champion in his own right—a sort of gentleman hero of the crowds.

An unexpected observer of the Los Angeles Games was Paavo Nurmi who came to California eager to compete and triumph in his fourth Olympiad. Upon his arrival he was astonished to learn that he had been barred from amateur competition because of the lavish "expense account" he obtained for an exhibition tour shortly before. His teammates were seething. One, Lauri Lehtinen, twice fouled the American Ralph Hill as Hill tried to pass near the finish of the 5,000-meter run.[3] The last lap was run in 69.2 seconds. Both, incidentally, broke all previous (including Nurmi's) records. The crowd was outraged, vociferous, and almost inconsolable. Bill Henry, the stadium's announcer, finally succeeded in quieting the spectators by intoning, "Remember that these athletes are our guests." Once more there was an agonizing period before the decision. The judges, very likely over-eager to avoid an "incident" declared Lehtinen the victor. However, at the award ceremony, most of the fury of the audience was wiped out when the Finn tried to pull Hill up with him on the victor's pedestal and the general mood became joyous approval when Lehtinen pinned a little Finnish flag to Hill's sweater.

Another case: The British Lord Burghley and Morgan Taylor, an American, were known to be the world's best hurdlers. Taylor had been assigned the task of carrying the American flag in a parade—rather a tiring job. In order not to gain an unfair advantage, Burghley carried a British flag at the same time. Ironically, both lost (at third and fourth places) to an Irishman, Robert Tisdall, and an American, Glenn Hardin. All four broke the previous Olympic record—Burghley's.

Politest of all were the Japanese who showed up in Los Angeles with a team of 143, the second largest squad. The Japanese had been instructed to congratulate the winners of each event they, the Japanese, competed in. Japanese coaches and judges made a practice of shaking the hand of a judge who shared the nationality of the victorious athlete or team. Toward the end of this great meeting, the practice became contagious and in southern California where fears of the "yellow peril" were pervasive and occasionally vicious, the crowds became partisans of Nippon. The Japanese gave startling performances in the aquatic events where the American swimmer, Buster Crabbe, was one of the few to challenge their domination.

Finances, festivity, and sportsmanship were not the only ways in which the Los Angeles Games were outstanding. It happened that almost all the Olympic records were dramatically altered. This was so not only in the track and field events (only the records for the long jump and the hammer throw remained) which were, as in most Olympics, most closely watched. Records tumbled in the large rowing program, in the swimming, cycling, and gymnastics competitions. And records were smashed by women, too. The expected peak performances by great athletes were made more stringent. Some records of the 1932 Games stood until the 1950's. Actually, if the year marks a summit in the level of sportsmanlike good feeling, it also marks the beginning of a new era in athletic training. After 1932 an oppressive intensity entered athletic conditioning, which, in order to set new records, subsequently led to placing an almost monstrous value on a sporting championship.

Superior performances were not confined to Americans, Finns, and the Japanese. In the track events Luigi Beccali of Italy took the 1,500 meters; Polish Janusz Kusocinski sprinted the last of the 26 laps around the track to break a long monopoly of Finnish victories in the 10,000 meters. The first figure to enter the stadium through a dark tunnel and chug up, waving his white linen hat, to the finish line of the marathon was that of Juan Carlos Zabala, a tiny Argentine (he weighed just 114 pounds) with fine white teeth and black curly hair. All three were "upset" winners and all three destroyed the existing records for their events. In cycling there was a varied program of sprint and distance races for individuals and for tandem bikes. Italian wheelmen nosed out the French and the Dutch to take most of the victories. In almost every case the winning times were Olympic records. Italians also excelled in the men's and women's gymnastics competitions, sharing victories with Hungarians, Americans, and the Dutch. Frenchmen did very well in the fencing. At the winter Games at Lake Placid the performances of Scandinavians convinced many Americans that they should exploit their geographical and climatic resources for skiing, bobsledding, and ice skating. Once more the world's favorite at the winter Games was the bubbling figure skater, petite Sonja Henie.

What about the Germans? Despite the fact that the Weimar Republic was reeling from the depression (Germany's decline was rivaled only by that of the United States and came after a series of other social disruptions), she sent the third largest team. Since the war the Germans had become even more sports-minded and more conventionally sports-minded at that. In the summer of 1930 Daniel J. Ferris, secretary-treasurer of the American Amateur Athletic Union, while in Germany, observed that many public playing fields were better equipped than those of rich American universities. He claimed the Germans were more enthusiastic sportsmen than any other Europeans and predicted that German athletes would sweep the Los Angeles Games.[4] Despite the costly effort, the team from the Berlin Rowing Club won the only German gold medal in the coxed fours; the same quartet took second in the uncoxed fours. The German water polo team also carried a silver medal home. A German journalist grabbed a crumb when he boasted that Arthur Jonath, a German, was the fastest *white* man in the world.[5] In the 100 meters he had finished just behind Tolan and Metcalf who were Negroes.

The German world of sport was painfully depressed and perplexed. News of the record smashing by others came just as the Germans pondered a new and awesome responsibility. As was noted earlier, the plans for the Berlin Games of 1916 were aborted by the war. However, the intended stadium and some other facilities remained and German desires for another chance gathered strength throughout the Weimar period. In May of 1930 the International Olympic Committee had a large congress in Berlin. The elderly president of Germany, former Field Marshal Paul von Hindenburg, opened the meeting and proclaimed, "Physical culture must be a life habit." Ferdinand Schmidt, rector of the University of Berlin, warned in his speech, "If formerly too much effort was placed on intellectual as opposed to physical culture in Germany, the pendulum now threatens to swing in the other direction." Dr. Theodor Lewald, the president of the German Olympic Committee, in his speech recalled (as so many Germans seemed compelled to do) the role played in deepening our knowledge of classical Olympism by those great Germans, Johann Joachim Winckelmann and Ernst Curtius.[6] At the time the Germans were vying with Spain for the XIth Olympiad which would be in 1936. Just before the Los Angeles Games, so disappointing to the German teams, the I.O.C. announced the decision that the IVth winter Olympiad would take place in Garmisch-Partenkirchen in Bavaria and that the summer Games of 1936 would be in Berlin.

Therefore, two of the closest observers of the Los Angeles Olympics were Lewald and Dr. Carl Diem, a burly type of older athlete and the world's most distinguished historian of sport. Both men had been grief-stricken when their preparatory work in 1913 and 1914 had been wrecked by the war. As Lewald filled ceremonial functions in Los Angeles, Diem was behind the scenes, seeking masses of material: "sketches, models, addresses, flags, programmes, tickets, etc., that had been carefully collected for us. . . ."[7] Diem took notes as he chatted with the designers of the elevator and telephone systems. He photographed garages and workshops and stooped and stretched calibrated tapes to take metric measurements of the cottages in the Olympic Village. He recorded in his files the statements of the cooks as to the dietary preferences of the participating nationalities.

Germany was suffering from a worsening series of economic and political upheavals when Lewald and Diem had left with their teams in the early summer of 1932; the political situation was much worse when they returned in the fall. Germany, in fact, was beginning some of the most extraordinary convulsions endured by a modern state. Fearfully Lewald and Diem worked on—anguished that perhaps, once more, political violence might rob them of the chance to glorify Germany in their own peaceful fashion.

The Weimar Republic, established in July 1919 as part of the confusing aftermath of Germany's defeat in the Great War, was dying in 1932. The Republic was fundamentally feeble in the first place. Conceived in shame and economic wreckage, its government was entrusted to an electorate which Bismarck and then Emperor Wilhelm II had convinced was unsuited for self-government. The decline of Weimar was especially rapid after the market crash of 1929 which precipitated the Great Depression. By 1932 six million Germans, or more than 20 per cent of the work force, were unemployed; more were working only short hours. Exports, essential to the whole economy, fell steadily as international credit almost dried up. In the two years after 1929 the price index fell more than 25 per cent and the great agricultural landlords of Prussia and Pomerania, who had so long furnished the military and bureaucratic elites for the nation, were as a class desperate for survival. The ancient ruling caste was only one of several large groups which had been restlessly quiet or suppressed under the best of conditions during the rosiest years of Weimar. In 1931 and 1932, with the deepening of economic disorder and the resulting political disruption, the military caste, the Communists, and various supernationalist parties began actively to attempt to take advantage of social discontent. All hoped to manipulate chaos in order to reform society in the light of their various notions as to what society ought to be.

Since March of 1930, even before the International Olympic Committee met in Berlin in May, Germany had been nominally ruled by a coalition of centrist and rightist parties which effectively surrendered their debating and legislative powers to the cabinet of Chancellor Heinrich Brüning who, in turn, governed by emergency decrees. As the depression and the resulting social confusion became increasingly disheartening, the wealthy and middle classes became more and more frightened by the growing numbers and militancy of the tactless, bombastically revolutionary Communists. At first with distaste and then with some eager curiosity they flocked to the political leader whose followers most faithfully battered the Reds in their street fights and who surpassed the Reds in the crudity and effectiveness of their propaganda.

The story of the rise of Adolf Hitler and of the National Socialist Workers' (Nazi) Party deserves a summary here. Hitler came of undistinguished parentage and had no particular professional skills, yet his oratory of hatred against the Versailles settlement and against those upon whom he hung the guilt for it gained him a following after the war ended. Hitler favored the pageantry of banners, standards, and dramatic lighting to accompany his beer hall speeches. With some devoted and opportunistic followers he attempted a *Putsch* in Munich in 1923, the failure of which led to a short prison term. While in jail Hitler dictated to Rudolf Hess his memoirs and a political program, later published as *Mein Kampf* (my struggle). The Nazis, who had declined in numbers, then prospered dramatically with the coming of the depression. Hitler gathered to him a cadre of skilled and fanatically ardent deputies. In skill and fanaticism the party Chief of Propaganda, Joseph Goebbels, surpassed them all. Even before the depression began the Nazis had a working system of street armies (the Storm Troopers—*Sturmabteilung* or S.A.), a nucleus of a youth movement, and a bureaucratic structure. The "movement" or *Bewegung*, as it began to be called, acquired ceremonials and an appealing (because skillfully devised) mythology. Goebbels manufactured one of the Nazi martyrs when he constructed a splendid funeral after the death of a young, anti-Communist street brawler and sometime pimp named Horst Wessel who, before his murder (by a leftist rival in love for a whore), furnished the party with a poem, "*Die Fahne hoch!*" The verses happened to go well with one of the Communist marching songs. As the "Horst Wessel Lied" this song became a sort of Nazi anthem. The party rallied financial support and founded a series of newspapers each of which came under the protection of a ranking deputy. One of them, *Der Angriff* (the attack), belabored the enemies of the Nazis. Another, *Der Völkische Beobachter* (observer of the Folk), preached patriotism and played the role of preserver of traditional German culture. Julius Streicher's *Der Stürmer* specialized in anti-Semitism. By 1930 there were party headquarters in most of the cities in Germany and several huge, black, be-nickeled Mercedes-Benzes for Hitler and his staff to tour in.

In September of 1930 began that extraordinary series of elections that recorded the acceleration of Hitler's appeal. After that Reichstag election, the Nazis with 107 seats were second to the Social Democrats (non-revolutionary Socialists) who got 143 seats, and were ahead of the Communists who got 77 seats. In March 1932 Hitler felt strong enough to run for president against the living monument, von Hindenburg. Hitler was second; the Communist candidate was again third. Since no candidate got a majority, there was a runoff which Hindenburg won. As economic and social conditions became desperate, the Nazis (contrary to their usual practice) were able to combine with other parties and to trade favors which produced for the Nazis the nullification of legislation that had curbed their most vicious propaganda and their brawling. Membership in the party grew in numbers and in heated devotion. As the German Olympic team was traveling across the United States to Los Angeles, the Reichstag elections of July 31, 1932, returned 230 of Hitler's candidates, but the house had to be dissolved—the Nazis lacked a majority and would form a coalition with no others. After the election of November 1932, the National Socialists, though they lost some votes to the Communists, were still the largest party. Parliamentary procedure was impossible because neither the Nazis nor the Communists would cooperate with anyone. Hindenburg merely personified the desperation of the German people when, on the advice of Franz von Papen, he named Hitler chancellor on January 30, 1933. New elections were scheduled for March 5 and, though the Nazis failed again to get a majority, they formed coalitions with some other nationalist parties just long enough to enact a radical program which was, in effect, a seizure of power.

The National Socialists imposed their "new order" in less than a year. The old, inefficient federal system inherited from the unification was ended and Germany became a national state held together by the party bureaucracy. The Nazis infiltrated and purged the whole governmental administration. The judicial system was overhauled in functioning and in philosophy in order to introduce haste and to fasten the hegemony of the party's theoretical apparatus more securely upon the nation.

There were laws against the use of the word "Republic"; concentration camps were established for keeping opponents out of the political scene. On July 14, 1933, the National Socialist party was declared the only legal political party in Germany.

Had the other nations in the world been less distracted by their cares, they might have been more alarmed both by the atrocious methods and by the ease with which the imposition of the "new order" was accomplished. As it was, the most sensational news to come from the Nazi news networks (there were no others in Germany) was that they were vanquishing the depression. With the dissolution of all the workers' parties, which traditionally had strong ties with the unions, the interests of labor were then shepherded by the Nazi Labor Front, the purpose of which was to sidetrack and, if necessary, to crush potentially disruptive labor disputes. In any case, strikes and lockouts were forbidden by a law of May 17, 1933, and the employers' associations thereafter had wide discretionary powers within their industries. Wages, and this was an important factor in the success of Germany's economic schemes, were kept very low. Unemployment was almost eliminated (or at least cleverly hidden) partially with the help of labor camps for young men and women (like the Civilian Conservation Corps of the American New Deal) and by large-scale public works and rearmament. Much of the financing of the revival was traceable to unorthodox fiscal policies that juggled exchange rates, forced internal loans, and seized the profits of industry before they could be distributed. As life became cheap, synchronized in the *Gleichschaltung* (coordination, forceful bringing into line, or elimination of the opposition—a word much used in Germany after January 1933), busy and irrationally purposeful, life in Germany also became happy.

It is a mistake to see only coercion in the Nazi triumph. Any prepared Nazi occasion, whether it was a party meeting, a holiday (such as the ones set aside for their martyrs, for example), or the preparation of an election—all these occasions were accompanied by a panoply of neo-pagan, festive trappings. As early as October 13, 1931, Hitler was able to assemble marching columns of cheering, disciplined Storm Troopers to the number of 100,000. After the revolution, the numbers taking part in Nazi festivities were limited only by the then existing state of logistical techniques. Nights glowed with bonfires and torch-lit parades and resounded gloriously with marching or patriotic songs from the throats of enchanted masses delighted to submerge their private worries into the infinitely grander majesty of the *Volk*. All were led by loudspeakers which could also direct the tribal joy of the community into channeled energy which could be, and often was, constructive. Through the years following the revolution the numbing of the critical faculties led to a peculiar mood which, to be sure, did not envelop every last German, but led the whole nation nearly berserk. The prodigious, long-accumulated talents of an energetic people were diverted away from private cares and offered to the state which, in theory at least, assumed the functions of society. Community was molded by the incessant propaganda. Many who were idle before had their leisure time absorbed by the *Kraft durch Freude* (strength through joy) movement which, despite the howls of mirth that its name aroused among foreign and some German cynics, provided welcome mass entertainment and cheap vacations to millions. Incredulous outsiders from a world still toiling with an unresponsive, apparently malignant economic system recorded that the frantic Germans were terrifically keyed up and often literally on the verge of joyous tears.

The Nazi success would have been inconceivable without the application of the contrived festivity which enveloped Hitlerism from beginning to end. It is apropos of the subject of this book to consider the most striking examples of artificial festivity of the modern age.[8] These were the annual gatherings of the Nazi party held in Nuremberg beginning in 1933. The Nuremberg rallies had notable precursors in the 1920's. In Munich on January 27 and 28, 1923, the young N.S.D.A.P. had a formal gathering to hear speeches of Hitler and his intimates. A bogus (but effective), cultish note was the ceremony of consecrating the newly concocted Nazi banner of the *Hakenkreuz* (hooked cross) or swastika. A crowd of more than 15,000 watched 5,000 Storm Troopers dip their red, white, and black banners and vow never to forsake their sacred mission to produce a revived Germany. A second rally, called "German Day," was much larger and assembled more than 70,000 participants at Nuremberg on September 14, 1923. Eager responsiveness among Hitler's audiences was capable of highly elating him and may well have emboldened him to attempt the *Putsch* of November 8–11 that same year. The *Putsch* was put down, but the subdued party gained a day of martyrdom, November 9, thereafter set aside to honor those who shed their holy blood in Munich in 1923. Temporarily checked, the Nazis had to stage their next rally on July 3 and 4, 1926, in Weimar, since Thuringia was one of the few parts of Germany where the laws permitted Hitler to speak publicly. The meeting demonstrated the spread of the party out of southern Germany and featured harangue after harangue, but the number of parading men was small, partly because these were the same days when the Weimar Republic appeared durable.

In its confidence, the Republic eased the restrictions on the Nazis and Hitler's group grew rapidly just before the "Day of Awakening" on the weekend following Friday, August 19, 1927. Railroads cooperated in carrying some 160,000 celebrants to the ancient, beautiful city of Nuremberg. It took thirty men several weeks of full-time work to arrange sleeping accommodations.[9] The city was a railroad hub and nearby had vast grassy meadows that could be used for assemblies and the raising of camp cities. Nuremberg had cultural and artistic associations. It had many medieval monuments from a period especially venerated by the German *völkisch* historians. Albrecht Dürer was born and had worked there. Hitler later remarked:

As I wished as many towns as possible—big, medium, and little—to participate and to become centers of German cultural life, I chose

Nuremberg for our rallies, and our annual gathering there must, I think, give the city for ten days the atmosphere of the Olympic Festival of ancient days.[10]

At the four-day congress in August in 1929, attendance was slightly enlarged by greater national representation and by Nazi delegates from France, North and South America, the Sudetenland of Czechoslovakia, and South Africa. There were some innovations in technique. One was a fireworks display before a crowd of 150,000. At the finale a high, frail scaffolding burst into a blazing swastika surrounded by a circle of green leaves, the whole surmounted by the Nazis' distinctive, chunky eagle. Another novelty was an especially grand and somber ceremony before Nuremberg's memorial to the dead of the Great War. After the service, from which Christian symbolism was barred, brass voluntaries and cannon introduced for the first time a new "consecration" ritual where, among constricted throats, twenty-five new standards and eleven new S.A. flags were passed before Hitler who touched the tip of each to the "blood flag," a hallowed banner so stained in the 1923 street fighting in Munich.

No more party meetings were held at Nuremberg until the annual series began in 1933. Immediately after Hitler took control of the German nation, the open fields around the medieval city became the objects of public works projects intended to surpass those of the pharaohs and the Caesars. The rustic improvisations of earlier party meetings were to be replaced by vast, acoustically perfect congress halls, colossal stadiums, parade squares, granite towers and reviewing stands, and by comfortable quarters for the international press. Although with some exceptions all serious content was to leave the rallies, they were patriotic demonstrations of stunning power. Construction of new facilities continued, in fact, until 1944 when Allied troops forced the abandonment of the works for a towered, battlemented arena with stands for 400,000 and a travertine marble congress hall 1.3 times longer and 1.7 times wider than the Roman Colosseum.[11]

Of the annual party rallies beginning in 1933, the one of 1934 interests us most. It was during the planning and execution stages of the 1934 rally that the Nazi regime determined to give the Berlin Olympics the benefit of their festive organizing experience and almost limitless financing. In 1934 the rallies reached their mature form. Further evolution would be in refinement of technique toward amassing larger numbers of participants and toward permanence in the form of Albert Speer's monumental architecture. The celebrations which occupied the week following Tuesday, September 4, 1934, however, had their own special, nervous overtones.

Hitler recognized that his progress toward total control of the state was blocked by the fear and disgust which the Prussian generals of the Wehrmacht had felt for the hoodlums of the S.A.; consequently, he had formed and released the blood purges of the "Night of the Long Knives" of June 30, 1934. Thousands of potential dissidents, both within the party and outside it, were murdered or otherwise removed from their threatening positions. On August 1, 1934, the day after the long-imminent death of the old monument, von Hindenburg, Hitler proclaimed the amalgamation of the offices of president and chancellor, and as Supreme Commander of the Wehrmacht demanded and received the army's unconditional oath of obedience.

The 1934 Nuremberg rally was scheduled for September, a month later. Hitler had just forsaken old loyalties for the elites of the old Germany. It was far from certain that those present at the Nuremberg rally—180,000 political leaders, 88,000 remaining Storm Troopers, 12,000 S.S. men, 60,000 Hitler youths, 50,000 Labor Service troops, 120,000 party members, and 9,000 S.S. functionaries (the special police to handle traffic and the staff of organizers have not been counted)—would accept the degradation of so many of Hitler's *alte Kämpfer*, the old, loyal brawlers who had assisted in his rise. Though the 1934 meeting was dubbed "The Party Days of Loyalty," throughout the proceedings throbbed an insistent emphasis on *German* patriotism rather than the narrow *party* loyalty of the past. Taking a risk, Hitler included the Wehrmacht in the festivities. For the first time since the odious Treaty of Versailles, crack mobile units of the army—shined, pressed, and impeccable in jangling military hardware—executed flawless parade maneuvers in public. The approval of 300,000 ecstatic spectators on the special "Army Day" approached frenzy. Hitler himself was in a state of auto-intoxication. After the Führer's final speech, Hess, who was cast as the crowd's symbol to say goodbye to the leader, was unable to quiet the massed ranks of adulators who, like Hess and Hitler themselves, were nearly delirious with emotion. When Hess was able to present his rhetoric, it was as follows:

The party is Hitler; Hitler, however, is Germany just as Germany is Hitler. Heil Hitler! Heil Victory! Heil Victory! Heil Victory![12]

In addition to the employment of Panzer units, several traditions were established (this phraseology can be used here) with the 1934 rally. Hundreds of pampered journalists present awaited a major policy statement; there was none and thereafter these climaxes of the Nazi year were almost always cult orgies only. In the evening of the first day's full assembly, the eagerly awaited leader's appeal was not a harangue, but a prayer for sacrifice and obedience. This invocation coincided with the onset of darkness. Loyal functionaries struck bonfires all along the horizon. Vertical beams of a circle of searchlights surrounded the vast assembly. These infinitely long shafts of light also enclosed, in twentieth-century columns, thousands of torchbearers, twelve abreast, as they followed the pensive leader out to his enormous, glistening touring car. One later assembly featured crisp, stern-visaged masses of youths in the Labor Service Corps who manipulated ceremonial spades in a military fashion. In deep, passionately sincere choruses, they responded to the electrically amplified lead phrases of barked directions. Choir leaders and regiments shouted.

One Folk, one Führer, one Reich—Germany! Today, unified by work we labor in the quarries, on the dunes, and on the dikes of the North Sea. We plant trees. We grow forests. We build roads from village to village, from town to town. We clear new fields for the peasants. Forests, grain, and bread—for Germany![13]

The problems posed in planning these extravaganzas were solved by the genius of a people whose special talent was organization. Party hacks chose the participants (after 1933 only a fraction of the members could be present) months in advance for drilling. As the time for the assembly approached, rehearsals occupied all the evenings of the work week and then even the weekends.

Before the departure, every participant received several special slips with all the necessary information about the trip, the arrival, and the quarters. There was a green slip on which were printed the province, the participant's unit (e.g., Hitler Youth Choir), his town, and his number—every participant was given a number. There was a yellow slip on which were printed the participant's name, home town, the number of the truck on which he would travel, his place of departure, time of departure, and the number of his seat on the truck. There was a red slip on which were his name, number, section of the tent camp in Nuremberg, and number of the tent in which he would sleep. There were, furthermore, all kinds of coupons. . . .[14]

Marchers received printed descriptions of the proper posture. While passing before the Führer in the traditional review of the troops at the center of the old city, each row of twelve was to be separated by 114 centimeters.

The left hand of the marcher was to be placed on the belt buckle; the thumb was to be inside, behind the buckle, and the other fingers slightly bent, with the finger-ends at the right edge of the buckle.[15]

In a society that was being rapidly molded by the ubiquitousness of the patriotic, up-to-the-minute loudspeaker, the Third Reich's technicians devised for the rallies a new, mushroom-shaped loudspeaker that was at once delicate and powerful and which even at full volume would not buzz or produce echo effects.

The party rally of 1934 subsequently received so much attention not because it was the grandest (the rally of 1939, stopped by the outbreak of the Second World War, would have surpassed it by far in every way), but because it was transmuted into cinematic art by Leni Riefenstahl. Hitler yearned to have the maximum number take part in the cult gatherings. Himself a movie addict and alert to the propagandistic possibilities of the cinema, he desired a film that could communicate to millions the cohesive tribalism that could only, in fact, be felt by the hundreds of thousands on the spot. Since her career will be discussed in some detail later, I shall mention here only Riefenstahl's work on the resulting effort, *Triumph of the Will* (*Triumph des Willens*), which was released in 1935.[16] When she arrived in Nuremberg a week before the rally was to begin, the city's fire-fighting equipment and public utilities were put at her disposal. Her crew numbered 120, of whom 16 were cameramen, each with an assistant.[17] The filming, from airplanes, cranes, wheelchairs, roller skates, pits in the ground, and specially built tracks, was done according to a script. Indeed, many of the special massed assemblies of the 1934 rally were staged for the camera and were not repeated afterward. The resulting film, then, is a sort of twentieth-century *Gesamtkunstwerk*, or union of several arts. It celebrates a quintessentially twentieth-century political rite and preserves it on celluloid with accompanying artistic distortion and the dubbed music of (among others) Richard Wagner, whose quest for a synthesis of several arts this film certainly realizes.

In this film the viewer is pulled effortlessly through the days flowing into nights and then dawns of Nuremberg during the festival. The film participant moves amid vast numbers of persons, standards, and banners. It seems as though the viewer is given an all-perceptive, grandly manipulable, invisible spot that he can move at will forward or back in space and onward in time at the pace that will most intensify the glory of what is taking place about that miraculous, infinitely seeing bit of disembodied vision. All the participants in 1934 were commanded not to notice the many queer-looking cameras with their extended telephoto and squat wide-angle lenses. In the film itself only briefly do we glimpse the ribbed shadow of the fully stretched ladder of a fire truck. Even now the film can induce that suspension of criticism that Riefenstahl produced and which convinced millions that the devil on earth was a beneficent, spiritual leader who felt deeply the pleasure of his fellow participants.

Despite the crudity of the hero-making (so grotesque in view of our hindsight) and the staginess of the grander effects, the film won prizes for its artistry from the French who certainly did not admire its message. Previous praise of the film has emphasized the quality of editing, but few have cited its communication of joyous mass festivity and its subtle sensuality. The scene most often taken from *Triumph of the Will* to form documentaries of the period shows Hitler, Heinrich Himmler, and an aide—just the three of them—strolling down a wide boulevard to a solemn march, "I Had a Comrade." The camera's eye rises and its angle increases with almost heartrending majesty to reveal that the trio is distantly flanked on either side by perhaps 100,000 perfectly still, obediently ranked troops. With tender care and faultless aplomb, the three men approach a low, wreathed monument to fallen fighters for the movement. They salute and depart. This one scene sucks the observer into a powerful massed formation that evokes the power of determined masses and historical grandeur and prophesies a relentless destiny.

Another quality of the film is its evocation of a Nordic Eros. Leni Riefenstahl had a quality rare among women: a keen appreciation of muscular, male good looks. There are dozens of brief closeups of fine Aryan heads and shoulders which then flick to the head of Hitler who, we know, was no beauty. The sturdy mesomorphs and slender boys in the tent cities fondle one another in rough, affectionate horse play while jovial, fat cooks prepare barrels of wurst and pea soup. More perfect boys give each other haircuts and hold shaving mirrors for each other. Convulsed with laughter, a high spirited group blanket-tosses one of their number. Thirty boys are excitedly crushed, holding their neighbor between their knees as crouched, wet eyed, they sing old songs at dusk around a campfire. Through-out the film there is evidence of the editing to show in shifts so rapid as almost to be juxtapositions, the movement of masses and the individual, straining necks and clear, loving eyes of the handsome Germans in those masses. It appeared from evidence in the film and from other news from Germany that after decades of despair all Germans were experiencing happiness and were rapidly overcoming the spiritual despair and economic paralysis still oppressing the rest of the world. The most dis-turbing news coming irregularly out of Germany concerned her racial policies which were disrupting certain elements within the nation and were causing disgust abroad.

Anti-Semitism is, of course, not new. There have been out-rages against the Jews since the Diaspora. In the virulence of his hatred, Martin Luther rivaled Hitler. The writings of both depict the Jew as a leering beast invested with all sorts of sex-ual, economic, and philosophical deviltry. Of Hitler it has been authoritatively stated that "Hatred of the Jews was perhaps the most sincere emotion of which he was capable."[18] Long before the 1933 revolution the Nazi street brawlers had attacked Jews, the so-called "race" whom the leader had convinced them was responsible for such crimes as the defeat of Germany in the war, pornography, modernism in art, the exploitation of the German people by capitalism, and (the contrary) the exploita-tion of the German people by Communism. Anti-Jewish legisla-tion was enacted shortly after Hitler became chancellor and was an integral part of the terror and the *Gleichschaltung*.

A national boycott of Jewish business was proclaimed on

March 28, 1933, to go into effect on April 1, 1933. In the month of April "non-Aryans" began to be purged from the civil service and universities and shortly afterward from professions such as law and medicine. Germans were at first warned and then expressly forbidden to be seen with Jews in public. There were laws against intermarriage and a campaign to expropriate non-Aryan property. The Nuremberg Laws of September 15, 1935, deprived Jews and part-Jews of their citizenship and civil rights. Many Jews left Germany and, once abroad, reported indignities against their kinsmen. Police urged on the hoodlums. Newspapers abroad published pictures of road signs saying, for example,

Jews are not desired here.
Attention Jews: This is not the way to Palestine.
It is dangerous for Jews to enter this town.[19]

William L. Shirer records having seen a sign in Ludwigshafen that said

Drive Carefully! Sharp Curve! Jews 75 Miles an Hour![20]

Racial policy permeated all aspects of German life in the Nazi era. German sport was not excepted. On April 1, 1933, when the boycott of Jewish business went into effect, the German boxing federation announced that it would no longer tolerate Jewish fighters or referees. The new Nazi Minister of Education announced on June 2, 1933, that Jews were to be excluded from youth, welfare, and gymnastic organizations and that the facilities of all clubs would be closed to them. As early as July 1933 one Fritz Rosenfelder of Bad Cannstatt in Württemberg committed suicide after his expulsion from a sporting club he had organized and had directed for many years. The published reaction of Julius Streicher, editor of *Der Stürmer* was:

We need waste no words here, Jews are Jews and there is no place for them in German sports. Germany is the Fatherland of Germans and not Jews, and the Germans have the right to do what they want in their own country.[21]

After July 1933 non-Aryans could no longer be life guards in Breslau and eventually all swimming resorts were off-limits to Jews "for their own protection." A sign in the center of the rustic Bavarian ski resort, Garmisch-Partenkirchen, announced, "Jews: Your entry is forbidden!"[22] On July 29, 1933, the Jewish Boy Scouts of Pirmasens had their organization dispersed and their funds confiscated. Bavarian officials dissolved the local Makabi (a Jewish sporting association) and Jewish war veterans' athletic organizations. Jewish teams were first forbidden to compete with Aryan teams and then forbidden to go abroad to compete. A police sports association was forced to expel all the members of its ladies' auxiliary who had competed with a team of Jewish women. By the beginning of 1935 all private and public practice fields were denied to Jews.

I have noted earlier that the Weimar Republic had fostered sport. A partial rationalization in the upper levels of the Republican bureaucracy for the public expenditure on sporting equipment was that sport could be a substitute for the military training severely circumscribed by the Treaty of Versailles. With the advent of the Nazis, subterfuge was done away with. The Nazis' glorification of teamwork, comradeliness, and physical fitness was amalgamated with aggressive patriotism. The members of the sporting clubs and the emotionally charged work battalions (who, incidentally, served for very little pay) were told that they were performing quasi-military functions, preparing for the armies of retribution. The Nazi philosophy of sport, in fact, attacked the notion that "politics has no place in sport."[23] Nazi athletic theory was also deeply racist.

An important, if not profound or scientific, theorist of sport was one Bruno Malitz, a sports leader for the Storm Troopers, who wrote a treatise on athletics which Propaganda Minister Goebbels declared a book that all Germans should read and that was sent to all the sporting clubs in Germany.[24] Malitz believed that all clubs should be *"völkisch deutsch."*

Frenchmen, Belgians, Pollacks, Jew-Niggers have all raced on German tracks, played on German football fields, and swum in German swimming pools. All kinds of foreigners have been having a marvelous time at our expense. The sporting promoters have thrown great sums of money about so that the international connections of Germany with her enemies shall be made yet closer.[25]

Taking his lead from the Führer's rhetoric, Malitz declared,

Jewish sports leaders, like the Jewish plague, pacifists, the "reconcilers of peoples," Pan-Europeans . . . have absolutely no place in German sport. They are all worse than rampaging hordes of Kalmucks, worse than a flaming conflagration, famine, floods, drought, locusts, and poison gas—worse than all these horrors.[26]

In early July 1935 the Blue-White Tennis Team of Dresden won the middle-German championship, thereby qualifying for the next round of eliminations for a national title, but were deprived of their victory after they were questioned by a local party official (*Gaudienstwart*) who determined that they had not sufficiently "understood National Socialist ideology."[27] All the various German sporting associations had been merged into and subsumed by the Reich Federal Sports Association—a characteristic example of the *Gleichschaltung*. On August 6, 1935, this Nazi association ordered that the month of September 1935 would be set aside by the sporting clubs for the discussion of the Jewish question.[28]

Before the imposition of the racial laws, there had been some 40,000 Jews (out of a total Jewish population of 500,000—i.e., less than 1 per cent of the total population of Germany) associated with some 250 sporting clubs. This figure does not include the Jews or *Mischlinge* (racial mixtures) assimilated into Gentile clubs. Within two years all, including the best, of these sportsmen were barred from practice or competition. This policy was bound to affect the composition of the German Olympic team as

well as violate certain traditions of international Olympism. Jewish athletes from the beginning had participated in the Olympics. Ironically, at the first Games in Athens, two of the winning
German gymnasts, the Flatow brothers, were Jews.[29]

When members of the International Olympic Committee
learned that Dr. Theodor Lewald, the Christian president of the
German Olympic Committee, was about to be removed from his
post, there was consternation among his many friends outside
Germany . Indeed, Lewald's warm international friendships
were largely credited as winning the prize of the XIth Olympiad for Berlin. Lewald was one of many distinguished-looking
paladins of international muscularity who had modeled their
attitudes toward Olympism after the writings of Baron Pierre de
Coubertin. Like the now aged founder, Lewald was lively and
cheerful. He was short, had an aggressive white mustache, a
puffed-out chest, a firm handshake, and the twinkling, easily
wetted blue eyes of a leader who accomplishes much by charismatic persuasion. He had helped organize German Olympic
teams since 1904 and 1906 and had been head of the German
Olympic Committee since 1924. One of Lewald's contributions
to German physical education had been to expand the concept
of athletic education beyond the narrowness of "Vater" Jahn's
patriotic gymnastics. He intended to have Germans compete
with Anglo-Saxons in team and individual events without embarrassment. In a tragic vignette characteristic of the shrill
excitement of the early *Gleichschaltung*, some zealot (or perhaps a settler of an old score) revealed that Lewald was a
Mischling—his paternal grandmother had been born a Jew.
Her good sense in converting to Christianity at the age of seventeen did nothing to remove a poisonous racial taint. A hubbub,
due to letters from Lewald's friends overseas threatening the removal of the Games from Germany, arrested this particular
purging. Lewald was kept on as an "adviser" for the German
Olympic Committee for the XIth Olympiad. The technical op-
erations of the Berlin Games were actually delivered to the

capable hands of Dr. Carl Diem who, like the majority of his countrymen, accomplished prodigies while in the thralls of the *Bewegung*.

Contrary to the prescriptions of Coubertin, German Olympism became absorbed by and eventually an ancillary of German politics. The *Reichssportführer* or director of all German athletics was Captain Hans von Tschammer und Osten. Born in 1887. Tschammer und Osten had taught French and English as a youth and had become a follower of Hitler very early— in 1922. It was claimed that he rode a horse with some grace. He knew nothing about sport, but was a loyal *alter Kämpfer*. Tall, clean-shaven, with heavy black eyebrows and perfect posture, the *Reichssportführer* rarely appeared in public unless he was in brown riding britches, high leather boots, peaked cap, and decorations—the uniform of an officer of the Wehrmacht. In addition to his duties as a bureaucrat in the Reich's Ministry of the Interior, Tschammer und Osten was installed as President of the German Olympic Committee. As an administrator and ideological cheer leader, he had the difficult task of forcing the small universe of German athletics to purify and energize itself in keeping with the philosophy of the Third Reich. Shortly after the Nazi seizure of power the Olympics of 1936 had been singled out as an opportunity to show the world what the new Germany was capable of.

As in other aspects of German life, German sporting excellence had been damaged by some distinguished defections. One of the first to leave was Alex Natan, a sprinter who had been part of a German quartet that equaled the world record for the 400-meter relay in 1929. He fled to England.[30] Rudi Ball, Germany's best hockey player, emigrated to France. When the campaign for Aryanization of sport began in earnest in April 1933, the status of the engineer, Dr. Daniel Prenn, was in doubt until the new *Reichssportführer* was named. Short and stocky, Prenn had been Germany's best tennis player since 1928 and was Germany's best hope for the impending Davis Cup matches. Foreign correspondents sought him out, but he kept quiet. Then on April 24, 1933, the German Lawn Tennis Association announced that "non-Aryans cannot play in representative matches or in official league contests." A rider specified, "The player Dr. Prenn (a Jew) will not be selected for the Davis Cup team in 1933." Prenn became a British subject and continued to play tennis there.[31] The German tennis officials also declared that thereafter, "German players will be required to use German tennis balls. English tennis balls will be used only until the German plant, now under construction, is able to meet the demand."[32] As was the case in analogous aspects of intellectual endeavor, leading athletes in several sports who were not Jews began to announce their withdrawals for reasons of sickness or training infractions that were not officially connected with the racial policies, but which, in fact, were very likely the effects of crises of conscience. At least we can hope that this was so.

The most celebrated instance of racial discrimination against an athlete centered on the great fencer, Helene Mayer. Miss Mayer had been born of a Christian mother and a Jewish father, Dr. Ludwig Mayer, in Offenbach in 1911. It is still not known for certain whether she had been raised as a Jew or a Christian. She began taking fencing lessons when a child and won the German foil championship when she was just thirteen years old. Her father died in 1931. She left for Los Angeles in 1932 to compete in the Olympic Games there. Helene then decided to remain behind and study international law at the University of Southern California. She later switched to languages.

Miss Mayer looked like the very model of an Aryan brood mare. She was upright, statuesque, and weighed about 150 pounds.[33] She had green eyes, a rather beefy face with a strong jaw, and ropes of blond hair which she kept efficiently wound about her head in a hausfrau manner. Helene had won a gold medal for Germany in the 1928 Olympics and was the world foil champion in 1929 and 1931, though she had taken only a fifth place in the Olympics of 1932. In late November of 1933 it was with astonishment that Helene Mayer and the world's sportswriters learned that the Offenbach Fencing Club had expelled its most famous member. For some reason the German Fencing Association announced at the same time that the action of the local club did not affect her membership in the national federation.[34] The eminence and particular location of Miss Mayer at the time of the onset of the Nazi racial policies made her an apt heroine for a *cause célèbre* centering on the meaning of vague Olympic ideals that had been evolving for forty years.

At the time, the trickling stories of an upheaval in the little world of German sport were but footnotes to the major concerns of a politically and intellectually demoralized world. Still, we should remember, despite the stories of injustice within Germany, the new Germans seemed to be unique in the decisiveness with which they were shaking the economic miasma paralyzing all other nations. Economists, harassed and discouraged bankers, and politicians learned that the Nazis were using wildly speculative fiscal techniques and conquering the depression. Businessmen could not escape the fact of the upsurge in German exports due to the re-imposition of aggressive selling methods. Travelers returned with tales of the euphoric Germans who were giving themselves up to the pervading milieu of hard work, hard play, and enchanting festivity.

3
Sportsmanship and Nazi Olympism

Preparations for the eleventh modern Olympiad took place, both in Germany and abroad, in an international political climate that was turbulent and grimly portentous. The Games of 1932 in Los Angeles four years earlier had provided festive diversion for many disillusioned Americans. The Los Angeles Games, however, had been prepared when it was far from evident that the economic crisis would be as severe or as disruptive as it turned out to be. In the years 1930 and 1931 few nations had made radical attempts to halt the deepening crisis.

The international economic and political expectations were very much different in 1934 and 1935 when not only Germany but the whole world was preparing for the Games in Berlin. Though we now know that the worst of the slump had passed, at the time the statistical basis for optimism was inconclusive and correctly appraised by only a few experts. It is important to note that the various national recoveries were to a large extent attributable (and even then widely recognized as such) to the interference of the national state into domestic affairs. The state, often reluctantly, began to direct labor, banking, and international commerce—activities that the conventional wisdom had barred from heavy-handed civil interference. The conventional wisdom (and by this I mean a view of politics and economics based on philosophical assumptions that became current in the eighteenth and nineteenth centuries) had decreed that these forces should be freely determined by the world's millions of voters, buyers, sellers, and producers. However, nations recovered from the pervading economic and consequent psychological corrosion most dramatically to the extent that they did not respect the conventional liberal assumptions, those abstract ideas about the necessary course of political action that had been the guides for Europe's elites since the French Revolution.

The Germans were not the only people who submitted to radical experiments in the face of peril. In the United States the steel industry was operating, for a while, at one tenth of its capacity and primary producers such as miners and farmers were suffering keenly from a halving of world commodity prices. The Americans finally submitted, in late 1932, to the New Deal which was pledged to economic leadership far more vigorous than the role heretofore assigned to the federal government. The traditionally stable British political system was maintained by granting emergency powers to the national government which frequently bypassed parliamentary procedure. Even France, which had a balanced industrial and agricultural economy that partially isolated her from the worst of the international economic crisis, was torn by internal political dissension—dissension that paralyzed her and prevented French action against the international political swashbucklers unleashed in the middle 1930's. Even the sealed-off, supposedly autonomous Soviet Union (which will remain outside the narrative scope of this book since she did not participate in the Olympics) was badly damaged by the decline in commodity prices, since she had to export twice as much wheat and other raw materials in order to obtain machinery for her second five-year plan. The Soviet purges of the late 1930's were the Russian variety of a

world-wide epidemic of convulsive political experimentation
and consequent adjustments.

In Germany the economic and political confusions due to the
depression moved to a climax early in 1933 and then were
roughly eliminated or at least masked after the National Socialist revolution. Super-politics—totalitarian politics—were the
antidote. The tales of the refugees from Germany and articles
quoted from the Nazi newspapers such as *Der Angriff* and
Der Völkische Beobachter revealed to the world that the German solution to the crisis was planned and put into effect by
aggressively disregarding many traditional concepts of justice
and, indeed, by contemptuously flouting firmly held, abstract
ideas produced in the Western tradition—ideas about the nature of man and society. Liberals were horrified. Many romantic
intellectuals and many disillusioned or frightened political figures, however, were enchanted with the tales of economic and
political success coming out of energized Germany and were
not opposed to ending the confusion and agony in their own
lands in a similar fashion. In several nations that were traditional supporters of the modern Olympic Games, Nazism and
indeed a certain enthusiastic, though slovenly, kind of Nietz-
schean, anti-philosophical, political philosophy became chic.
Here and there one heard pragmatical praise for Adolf Hitler.
After all, crazy as his program might have sounded in the 1920's,
it was working in the 1930's. So, in spite of the fact that, in their
preparations for their Olympics as well as in other aspects of
life, the National Socialists were violating established rules of
domestic and international behavior, protests from outside Germany were unusual.

In Great Britain, traditionally a refuge for political perse-
cutees and the place where such German-Jewish athletes as
Daniel Prenn and Alex Natan fled shortly after the revolution
of 1933, totalitarian projects as antidotes to the inactivity of the
traditional politicians were having a vogue.[1] In his newspaper
articles Winston Churchill praised Benito Mussolini and Adolf

Hitler as preferable to the specter of Communism—then considered the likely ideological haven of the desperate masses of unemployed. Walter MacLennon (also Baron Citrine, a Trades Union official and consulting member of the Government) wrote a pamphlet, "Under the Heel of Hitler: The Dictatorship over Sport in Nazi Germany."[2] MacLennon's trumpeting for a campaign of formal protests against the Nazification of German sport made little impression on the English. The British Olympic Committee, itself composed principally of the titled aristocrats whose moral assistance Baron Pierre de Coubertin had always preferred, was frightened by the prospects of a Red revolution and was inclined to reject any political calls to action by an avowed leftist. The British Olympic Committee devoted itself to the task of locating funds for a large team for 1936.

The turmoil in French political affairs was felt by the French Olympic Committee which was traditionally dependent upon a government subsidy. Financing was not granted until the very last moment and the boon was based upon a cold calculation. When the Popular Front of Premier Léon Blum voted for credits to support a large French Olympic team, the expense was justified as a gesture for reciprocal participation in France's own grandiose adventure in internationalism about the same time. France would spread a feast for the world at her ambitious Universal Exposition of 1937 in Paris. The fact that Blum was himself a socialist and a Jew besides indicated a certain lack of alarm in the Third Republic over the implications of Nazi racial doctrines as evidenced in Germany's policy regarding sport.[3] Expressions of disgust and tentative movements for the formation of a boycott of the 1936 Olympics were voiced in Sweden, the Netherlands, and Czechoslovakia.[4] The Spanish Republic refused to grant credits to their Olympic Committee and Spain, like the Soviet Union, had no team in Berlin in 1936. In view of the fact that small countries such as Finland and Hungary had long used their performances at the Olympiads as means of increasing their international renown, one could hardly expect that their politicians would express official protests, much less threaten non-participation. Still, the only really enthusiastic greetings of the preparations for the 1936 Games came from Japan and Italy. Indeed, Italy and Finland were the first to accept Dr. Carl Diem's invitations to the Berlin Olympics.

Japan had long since embarked on a national sports program the results of which were demonstrated at Los Angeles in 1932. Japanese eagerness to make a mark at Berlin was intense, since the nation was in the control of military adventurers who viewed sport as a paramilitary activity. Like Hitler and his lieutenants, the Japanese leaders were keen to use the sporting fields as stages for advancing the prestige of the nation. The Japanese were also determined to demonstrate sporting sophistication in order to obtain the Olympiad for Tokyo in 1940. Mussolini's Fascists also favored a patriotically oriented sports program and saw in National Socialist Germany a sort of sister regime. Italian preparations for the eleventh modern Olympiad were costly and characteristically enthusiastic.

The American reaction to the *Gleichschaltung* or forced coordination of German sport was quite another matter. The Americans actually produced a serious and frightening (for the Nazis at least) protest movement. Since the protest movement tells us much about American intellectual life at the time and since the protests influenced the 1936 Games, the American objections to Nazi sport deserve some description and analysis. It should be emphasized here that the passionate devotion to Olympism—or more specifically, the view that despite the political obstacles, the Olympic Games had to go on—had been deeply impressed upon all the high-minded followers of Baron Pierre de Coubertin. For the elderly bureaucrats of international sport, the progress of the Olympics was somehow linked with the orderly spinning of the globe. Olympic officials, American and otherwise, had tended to think like the ancient Greeks: that chronology itself may have depended upon the orderly progress of the quadrennial agonistic displays of the world's best.

American newspaper readers in 1933 were able to read on

their sports pages of the imposition of the Nazi racial laws. For high-minded American sports bureaucrats a shocking incident had been the removal of Dr. Theodor Lewald from his post as president of the German Olympic Committee because of his *Mischling* or partly Jewish ancestry. The International Olympic Committee met in Vienna on June 6, 1933. American Olympic officials were stalwarts in a campaign to remove the Games from Germany if she did not cease to discriminate against her Jewish athletes. They demanded the firm reinstatement of Dr. Lewald. On June 7, 1933, Lewald, who had been given the post of "adviser" to the German Organizing Committee for the Olympiad, himself announced from Berlin that his government had authorized him to promise that Germany would observe all the Olympic resolutions and that "as a principle" Jews would not be excluded from German teams.[5] Brigadier General Charles E. Sherrill, a crisp looking, bristle-mustached, American member of the I.O.C. and a former outstanding sprinter (he was credited with being in 1888 the first to use the crouching start for the dashes) demanded proper manners from the Germans. Sherrill later wrote to Rabbi Stephen S. Wise in New York:

It was a trying fight. We were six on the Executive Committee, and even my English colleagues thought we ought not to interfere in the internal arrangements of the German team. The Germans yielded slowly—very slowly. First they conceded that other nations could bring Jews. Then, after the fight was over, telephones [sic] came from Berlin that no publication [sic] should be given to their Government's back-down on Jews, but only the vague statement that they agreed to follow our rules. . . . Then I went at them hard, insisting that as they had expressly excluded Jews, now they must expressly declare that Jews would not even be excluded from German teams. All sorts of influence was exerted to change my American stand. Finally they yielded because they found that I had lined up the necessary votes.[6]

Sherrill, in order to have concrete proof of the Germans' compliance, requested that Helene Mayer, the championship fencer from Offenbach then living in Los Angeles, be invited to join the German Olympic team. Five days after the concession by officials in Berlin, Hans von Tschammer und Osten, Hitler's *alte Kämpfer* and now *Reichssportführer* who had just replaced Lewald as president of the German Olympic Committee, declared to a meeting of German sports officials: "You are probably astonished by the decision in Vienna, but we had to consider the foreign political situation." Tschammer und Osten also declared his satisfaction with the on-going racial cleansing of the German sporting clubs.[7] At that moment, since Jews were being barred from practice and from the sporting clubs whose members alone had access to the Olympic trials, Jews were, of course, being barred from the trials for the German team.

At a meeting in the United States of the Amateur Athletic Union (A.A.U.) on November 21, 1933, the delegates, with but one exception, voted for a boycott of the 1936 Games unless the position of Germany vis-à-vis her Jewish athletes be "changed in fact as well as in theory." Gustavus T. Kirby of the American Olympic Committee had proposed the resolution and was vigorously supported by Avery Brundage, then president of the American Olympic Committee.

Brundage had long been a figure of some importance in American sport and in American business. Avery Brundage had competed in the 1912 Olympics in Stockholm when he was twenty-five years old and was sixth in the decathlon which was taken by the great American Indian, Jim Thorpe. Thorpe, one of the greatest athletes of all time, was far superior to anyone else. At the same Olympiad Jim Thorpe also won the pentathlon (old style—it then consisted, like the decathlon, only of track and field events) taking first in four of the five events. Thorpe's record in the decathlon stood for fifteen years, though when it was learned that he had played bush-league professional baseball in 1909 and 1910, his medals were taken from him and his name wiped from the official record books.

Significantly, in the long and sincere campaign of American sports writers to restore the medals to Thorpe, who eventually became a broken drunk, Brundage was an influential judge adamant for the strict upholding of the principles of amateurism. In 1914, 1916, and 1918, years when there were no Olympic competitions, Brundage was voted the Amateur all-around Champion of America. In 1915 in Chicago he had founded the Avery Brundage Company, a construction and real estate firm which became the foundation of his growing financial interests. Brundage's energy, affability, devotion to sport, and rigid code of personal behavior were apparent when he began to campaign to centralize the bureaucracy of American amateur sport in the 1920's. He was in close touch with aging Pierre de Coubertin who throughout his life had made eloquent pronouncements in favor of purity in athletics. Like almost all the bureaucrats of international amateur sport, Brundage was convinced that the founder was a genius and a saint. Perhaps Brundage's touchiness over the issues of lucre or sharp practices in the world of athletics was moral compensation for his survival in the shark-infested waters of American big business. Avery Brundage became and remained a very rich self-made man.

Brundage was first elected president of the American Olympic Committee and of the American Olympic Association in 1930. For years he had had the backing of the National Collegiate Athletic Association (N.C.A.A.) and the Amateur Athletic Union (A.A.U.). Bickering within the Balkanized world of American amateur sport declined under his leadership and the conscious moral separation of American amateur athletics from professional sport became greater than similar gaps in any other sporting nation. American sports journalists have long included in their number a few very clever writers and many cynics. The organizational isolation of amateur sport from professional sport has seemed to them artificial and, in many cases, hypocritical. Brundage personified much of the frigidity and false cleanliness of American amateurism and obliged the sportswriters by occasional rudeness and pious pronouncements that were both nettlesome and newsworthy.

It was only during the preparations for the 1936 Games that Avery Brundage first assumed major controversial prominence. After the anti-Nazi resolution of the A.A.U. of November 1933, the American Olympic Committee continued to postpone acceptance of the German invitation. As the facilities for the Games in Berlin became another prime public works project of the National Socialists and as Germany as well as other countries selected and trained their teams, well-publicized suggestions appeared here and there that the United States ought to boycott the Nazi Olympics. Nervously and with a fanfare of international publicity, the German Olympic Committee finally announced in June 1934 that twenty-one Jewish athletes had been nominated for the German training camps. Understandably suspicious, the American Olympic Committee dispatched Brundage himself to Germany to make an on-the-spot investigation.

Upon his return, Brundage revealed himself to be one more important personage dazzled by the order, relative prosperity, and joy that most travelers observed in Germany in those years. On the basis of his interviews with Jewish leaders (who, one hostile journalist noted, were always met in cafés and were always chaperoned by Nazi officials) Brundage concluded that the Germans were observing the letter and the spirit of Olympism. And on the basis of his recommendations the American Olympic Committee voted to participate in the XIth Olympiad. This particular decision did not, however, dispose of American suspicions of the Nazis. The body that supervised the Olympic trials, the A.A.U., was still on record as opposing American participation. Furthermore, its president, former Judge Jeremiah T. Mahoney, a Catholic deeply troubled by the aggressive paganism of the Nazis, was forming a "Committee on Fair Play in Sports" to channel and make more effective the growing domestic alarm over the news about Nazi atrocities. For, despite Brundage's claims to the contrary, trustworthy stories of religious and racial persecutions continued to leak out of Germany. For example, it was learned that, though twenty-one Jews were "nominated" for the Olympic training camps, none were "invited" to attend.[8]

By the summer of 1935, American hesitation had dragged on for two years. A modern Olympiad was an extremely complex affair to organize. It was far too late to arrange for elaborate or even acceptable staging of the Olympiad anywhere except in Berlin where everyone knew that grandiose preparations had been underway for some time. Most American Olympic officials had accepted Coubertin's commandment that, whatever the obstacles, the regular march of the modern Olympiads must somehow take place. Brundage and those loyal to him therefore took the position that: (a) the Germans were keeping their promises to behave and (b) Olympism was so important a movement that its modern opponents, however high-minded they claimed to be, had to be silenced, since they were placing in peril an institution that was far more important than their petty egos. One consequence of such determination was that Commodore Ernest Lee Jahncke, who was of German ancestry, an upholder of a less pragmatic Olympic ideal, and one of the three American members of the International Olympic Committee, was squeezed from his position on that body. As an emergency measure, Brundage was also making tentative preparations to form a rump organization, parallel with the A.A.U., that could hold the tryouts for the 1936 American Olympic team.

In 1935 several other matters tended to produce a crisis atmosphere around preparations for the Olympic Games scheduled for the next summer. At Nuremberg in 1935, Hitler strayed from his usual policy of staging the party rallies as merely ceremonial cult rituals. At a great meeting at Nuremberg's *Kulturvereinhaus* on Sunday evening September 15, 1935, Hitler brazenly proclaimed the "Nuremberg Laws" which deprived German Jews of their citizenship and the protection of the laws of the Reich and which established social policies (e.g., forbidding intermarriage and making it illegal for German girls to work as servants for Jews) designed to preserve "the purity of Aryan blood." Naturally these extraordinary pronouncements attracted journalistic attention and were generally viewed with horror in the United States.

As this rally was taking place in Nuremberg, General Sherrill, a member of both the American and International Olympic Committees, was on *his* tour of Germany. He sailed from Europe on the *Normandie* and landed in New York on October 22, 1935—a day after Jeremiah T. Mahoney released a long public letter to Theodor Lewald, charging the National Socialists with a list of abuses against Mahoney's view of what was a sacred Olympic ideal.[9] As he was interviewed for his reactions to Mahoney's letter Sherrill stated:

I went to Germany for the purpose of getting at least one Jew on the German Olympic team and I feel that my job is finished. As for obstacles placed in the way of Jewish athletes or any others in trying to reach Olympic ability, I would have no more business discussing that in Germany than if the Germans attempted to discuss the Negro situation in the American South or the treatment of the Japanese in California.

Sherrill also ominously hinted that the imprudent level of Yankee concern with the internal policies of Nazi Germany could very well lead to a wave of anti-Semitism in the United States. The General condemned the boycott leaders and claimed he knew many American Jews who themselves opposed any boycott and feared "that it would be overplaying the Jewish hand in America as it was overplayed in Germany before the present suppression and expulsion of the Jews were undertaken."[10] The next day, Frederick W. Rubien, secretary of the American Olympic Committee, presented his position. He announced:

Germans are not discriminating against Jews in their Olympic tryouts. The Jews are eliminated because they are not good enough as athletes. Why there are not a dozen Jews in the world of Olympic calibre.[11]

Other American Olympic officials were competing with Brundage for the attention of the sportswriters. Sherrill was more emphatic when he claimed that "there was never a prominent Jewish athlete in history."[12] He hinted that the power center of the agitation against the Olympic Games was close to President Roosevelt, namely, two Jews, one of whom was the Secretary of the Treasury, Henry Morgenthau, and another he would not specify, only claiming that his family had long since Anglicized its surname.[13] By this time Sherrill was the most flamboyant polemicist against the agitators. It did not help his reputation for wisdom when he spoke (and was widely quoted) before the Italian Chamber of Commerce in New York and praised Mussolini as "a man of courage in a world of pussyfooters" and declared, "I wish to God he'd come over here and have a chance to do that same thing." [14]

The American protests frightened the Nazis. Just before Sherrill left for his tour of Germany, an American correspondent predicted "concessions" at the last moment.

In such a case they will be found in categories in which Germany stands slight chances of success because a German-Jewish victory would raise serious problems. Croquet and chess have been suggested as suitable categories.[15]

One actual concession was the case of Rudi Ball who was invited back from his exile in France which he had entered as a refugee in 1933. He rejoined the German ice hockey team. In addition, Sherrill had, as he claimed, succeeded in getting another Jew on the German team. The candidature that he had been particularly exercised about was that of Helene Mayer, the half-Jewish fencer, who lived in Los Angeles. While in Germany in the summer of 1935, Sherrill had, in fact, hounded the Nazi sporting officials, since they had not yet invited Miss Mayer despite their promises of two years before. The blonde fencer had already issued a statement that she would be pleased to represent Germany, since she had done so in two previous

Olympiads and because she was eager to visit her mother and two brothers. Finally Tschammer und Osten invited the girl and attempted to side-step some embarrassment by declaring Miss Mayer to be "Aryan" (indeed, she looked like an advertisement for one) despite her mixed parentage. Rumors immediately became current that Helene Mayer was being forced to compete for Germany out of fear for her family. Many American Jews tried to dissuade her from competing. Once she accepted the invitation, however, she eschewed politics and called Rabbi Wise "a meddler."[16] Two other German Jews who were known to be of Olympic caliber, the high jumper Gretl Bergmann and the sprinter Werner Schattmann, were indirectly refused a chance at Olympic berths by being denied the opportunity to participate in the tryouts for the German Field Sports Championships, which were really pre-Olympic qualifying trials.

In the United States the pressure to boycott the Olympics gathered strength from sectors of public opinion that were neither Jewish nor notoriously pro-Semitic. The *Gleichschaltung* had also required the merging of all Catholic and Protestant sporting organizations into the Nazi system. The Berlin Olympics became an issue upon which aroused Christians and militant liberals could meet for the expression of their fears and disgust. The liberal Catholic magazine *Commonweal* felt that the "Nazi youth organizations are flagrantly and purely pagan" and took the position that to support the 1936 Games would be to "set the seal of approval on the radically anti-Christian, Nazi doctrine of youth."[17] The National Council of the Methodist Church passed a resolution against holding the 1936 Games in Germany.[18] The American Federation of Labor declared itself against American participation in the German Games because the Nazis were anti-labor and because there was "nothing noble" in the persecution by sixty million Germans of 600,000 Jews— 100 to one was not fair odds.[19] Many city councils, trade unions, and civic organizations passed resolutions against honoring the

Nazi festival with an American presence. The American National Society of Mural Painters voted that no member of their organization would take part in an exhibit of painting that the Nazis were giving in connection with the XIth Olympiad.[20] Many American newspapers including all the New York dailies opposed the continued preparations for choosing a Yankee team. New York's governor, Al Smith, telegraphed his objections to Brundage. The sportswriter Damon Runyon wrote that "Germany's pagan putsch makes its acceptance of the real Olympic oath either an impossibility or a hypocrisy."[21] Many other sportswriters including John Kieran of *The New York Times* were shocked at Germany's "poor sportsmanship." Ed Sullivan of the *New York Daily News* noted with astonishment, "I read in the papers yesterday that Germany now proposes to wipe from the war records the names of Jewish war veterans who were killed or maimed in her defense."[22] As the A.A.U. prepared for its meeting in December 1935 it had before its executive board resolutions from organizations representing memberships of 1,500,000 and petitions containing the signatures of 500,000 persons who opposed the staging of the 1936 Games in Germany.[23] There was a mass meeting against American participation in Madison Square Garden on December 3.

It should be noted once more that those favoring (indeed, at the same time forming) a strong American team also assumed a high moral stance. Like their boycotting opponents, they too could decry the decline in international trustworthiness and, while doing so, defend the Olympics as being superior to the maneuvers of local politicians—German, American, or whatever. Unlike the half-cocked and passionately vocal organizers of the boycott movement, the defenders of international Olympism claimed they were supporting a movement that encouraged tolerance and peaceful understanding. Brundage and his supporters posed as being far above petty chauvinism—a position that did not prevent them from occasionally praising the visible accomplishments of the Nazis and from slurring the adherents of Mahoney's Committee on Fair Play as being "Reds" or even "Communists."[24]

Both sides gathered rhetorical ammunition for a great debate at the national convention of the Amateur Athletic Union which opened in New York in early December. The proponents of a boycott were armed with resolutions to that effect from regional associations of the A.A.U. The delegates met tensely, but the expected battle was never really joined. The executive committee of the A.A.U. met at the Hotel Commodore on Sunday, December 8, to listen to five hours of speeches for and against participation. The moguls of American amateur sport were hungry and tired when time for a vote came. The executives (who had weighted voting rights) defeated the proposed resolution against sending an American team by 2½ votes. The narrow majority then succeeded in passing a motion in favor of participation, adding the specific rider that their affirmative action was not to be "construed to imply endorsement of the Nazi government."

The expected debate, then, was never presented to the membership of the A.A.U. and the inspired defenders of a less Olympically disposed sporting ideal were not permitted oratorically to clarify their position. Brundage and his lieutenants were immovable in the face of accusations of parliamentary double-crossing and unscrupulous floor maneuvers. Then, in rapid succession, the press learned that Jeremiah Mahoney, the most prominent publicist favoring an American boycott and president of the A.A.U., had resigned from his position, that Brundage had been nominated for that post and almost unanimously elected and that, having combined in himself the offices of the American Olympic Committee and the Amateur Athletic Union, Brundage at once urged the voluntary resignation from their posts of all the officers of these organizations who were "anti-Olympic."[25] It should be emphasized here that, at the time, the question among the delegates and the membership was *not* whether racial persecutions should be approved of, but who should be believed: Brundage who denied their existence or Mahoney who said they were rampant in the world of German sport. Naturally, the wreckage due to clashing reputations left a great deal of bitterness among amateur sportsmen in the United States.

The boycott movement did not just end there. The president of the Maccabi World Union, an international organization of Jewish sporting clubs, wrote a public letter to Count Henri Baillet-Latour, president of the International Olympic Committee, saying that, while he could not question the decision of the I.O.C. to keep the Games in Berlin and while he sympathized with a desire not to mix politics with sport,

We cannot as Jews accept lightly the situation created by the Olympic Games being held in Berlin. I, in common with all other Jews and many non-Jews, look upon the state of affairs in Germany from the point of view of general humanity and social decency. We certainly do urge all Jewish sportsmen, for their own self-respect, to refrain from competing in a country where they are discriminated against as a race and our Jewish brethren are treated with unexampled brutality.[26]

This plea led to no wholesale boycott by Jews of the Olympics. As we have seen Rudi Ball and Helene Mayer rushed to join the German team. Many Polish, Czechoslovakian, and Hungarian Jews were on their homelands' Olympic teams. In fact, one Hungarian, Ilona Schacherer-Elek, was Helene Mayer's nearest competitor in fencing. A few famous Jewish athletes avoided Berlin. Judith Deutsch, an Austrian swimmer of world record caliber, boycotted the 1936 Olympics. French Jews who eschewed Berlin were bobsled champions Philippe de Rothschild and Jean Rheims and a famous fencer, Albert Wolff.[27] However, in Great Britain Harold M. Abrahams, of a prominent family of Jewish civil servants and noted athletes, most vociferously headed off any movement for a boycott.[28] Abrahams had won (and established an Olympic record) in the 100-meter dash at the 1924 Olympics in Paris.

At the time, Americans appeared to possess a near monopoly on moral outrage, even though the movement to boycott the Olympics was in the end ineffective. An anti-Nazi campaign to urge the withdrawal of Negro athletes scarcely got off the ground, but at least the indignation was expressed. On August 23, 1935, the *Amsterdam News* (published in Harlem) urged Negro athletes, "to display that spirit of sacrifice which is the true mark of all greatness." No doubt some American athletes ignored the Olympic trials out of strong feelings about certain trends in Germany: many were doubtless conscience-stricken as they struggled to do their best in the trials that would produce the eventual Yankee team. The campaign for a boycott also surely provided meritricious explanations for some athletes who failed to make the American team in 1936. There were, in fact, several Jews on the American team: Sam Stoller and Marty Glickman, who were sprinters and members of the 400-meter relay team, David Mayer, a weight lifter, Sam Balter, a basketball player, Max Bly, a bobsledder, and Hyman Goldberg, who was on the team for an exhibition of baseball in Berlin. While most of the world's sports fans were distracted by the preparations and the actual unfolding of the German Olympics of 1936, Judge Mahoney and many other morally offended Americans and Europeans were arranging to hold some "People's Olympics" or "Workers' Games" in Barcelona (which, we remember, had been Berlin's rival to host the XIth Olympiad) as a protest against the Nazification of international sport.[29]

For those who were eager for a splendid American presence in Germany in 1936 the debate over whether or not the United States should participate was not without helpful results. Avery Brundage who, besides his several other posts, was also chairman of the American Finance Committee for the Olympic Games, observed that "the active boycott by Jews and Communists" was in some ways "beneficial." The pressure for chastisement of the Nazis aroused the resentment of the athletic leaders, the sportsmen, and patriotic citizens of America and induced them to work harder, and to contribute more. It destroyed much of the ignorance and apathy present in prior years.[30]

In any case, despite the fact that the depression was by no means past and the sum asked for, $350,000, was a record for an American team, all the bills were paid and Brundage was able, in the end, to give a surplus of $50,000 to the American Olympic Association.

Pre-Olympic trials had begun before the A.A.U. finally voted to consent to authorizing an American team for Germany's Olympics. The finals of the ice hockey tryouts were, in fact, taking place in New Haven, New York City, and Rye, New York, just as the Brundage steamroller squashed the boycott movement at the A.A.U. meeting in early December 1935. Final trials to select the teams for the winter Games then proceeded in several locations in the United States. The speed skating finals were in Minneapolis in January 1936. Lake Placid hosted most of the skiing events except for the jumping trials which were held in Salt Lake City and the combined downhill slalom eliminations which were in Mount Rainier National Park, Washington.

Trials for the varied program of the summer Olympics were similarly dispersed all over the United States. The yachting candidates were determined in San Pedro, California. The finals of the equestrian competitions were at the army's cavalry base at Fort Riley, Kansas. The swimmers and divers met in Providence, Rhode Island, Chicago, and in Astoria, New York, for the women's events. Most of the final track and field tryouts were in New York City early in July of 1936, but there were two final trials for the marathon (which by that time had attained the status as possibly the most prestigious event of the Olympic program) in Boston and in Washington, D.C. Decathlon finalists met in Milwaukee. Women track and field candidates learned whether they would go overseas in Providence, Rhode Island, on

July 4, 1936. The dispersion of these well-publicized trials of course provided a wide geographical base for the local committees raising funds for what eventually became the largest American Olympic team yet assembled. Since Negroes were accepted for the American team, no trials could take place in or even near the deep South. A sports fan from Georgia or Alabama eager to move the minimum distance to see some Olympic candidates would have to travel to Baltimore or Cincinnati to see the pre-Olympic finals for, respectively, baseball and the 50-kilometer walk—sports which at the time attracted no Negro entries. The American Olympic Committee awarded some 3,000 certificates to contestants placing in the preliminary, sectional, semifinal, and final tryouts. The American team for the winter Olympics eventually consisted of 76 athletes and 14 officials. Of the 384 athletes and 87 officials selected for the summer Olympics, 383 were on board the *Manhattan* ("the Largest Steamer Ever Built in America") on Wednesday, July 15, 1936, when tugs pulled the confettied and streamered great ship out of New York Harbor.

As the *Manhattan* steamed east almost all of her 800 passengers who were not athletes or trainers were reporters or sports fans also on their way to the sporting festival in Germany. An exception was the young American diplomat George F. Kennan who "dodged the motions of the gum-chewing supermen, and a variety of hefty Amazons."[31] Certain decks had been set aside for workouts and those present felt they were traveling on a floating gym.

Harold Smallwood, a sprinter, had a shipboard attack of appendicitis. Winds and cold rain produced dozens of colds, but still the huge American team arrived cheerful and eager the morning of July 24 at Hamburg where they happily submitted to well-rehearsed welcoming ceremonies by the city authorities there. They then took trains for Berlin where there were more elaborate ceremonies in the afternoon. Further genial speeches, band music, and even a corridor of torch-bearing German youths greeted the American team when they arrived, tired, at the Olympic Village fifteen miles west of the center of Berlin and about ten miles from the sporting complex.

The lavish production at Los Angeles had been for some 1,500 athletes. Berlin was preparing for 3,500. After the Germans, the Americans had the largest team. Despite the continuing economic slump and the uncertainty of international politics (or, on the other hand, perhaps as psychological antidotes to them) other nations also sent large teams. Like the citizens of the ancient Greek city-states, all the world's patriots were eager to grasp at the prestige to be gathered by their Olympic victors. The Germans had overconscientiously prepared welcomes to impress, even overwhelm their visitors. For example, when their own misscheduling forced the French team to appear at the Olympic Village at 1:30 A.M. they were still greeted by corridors of Hitler youths holding torches high and playing waltzes.[32]

The man most responsible for all these preparations was Dr. Carl Diem. He was born in Würzburg on June 24, 1882. As a teenager in the 1890's he was a middle- and long-distance runner at a time when track events as practiced among the Anglo-Saxons were almost unknown among his countrymen who were quite devoted to gymnastics. Diem founded his first sporting club, Macromannia, in Berlin when he was seventeen. He was a burly, short man and a perfect miracle of channeled energy. After 1900 his special track event was competition army field pack marching. He led the German expeditions to the Athens Games of 1906 and to the Olympics of 1912 in Stockholm, 1928 in Amsterdam, and 1932 in Los Angeles. For twenty years after 1913, Dr. Diem was the secretary of the German government's Commission for Sport and Recreation (*Generalsekretär des Deutschen Reichanschusses für Leibesübungen*) and during this time he founded and built the principal German school for recreation teachers, *Die deutsche Hochschule für Leibesübungen*, in Cologne. Diem traveled a lot and knew many languages. The

Turkish government consulted him regularly concerning its recreation programs. He designed athletic architecture and athletic festivals in Germany. All the while Diem was engaged in
his promotional work he was producing a stream of scholarly
and theoretical writings of the highest quality. Only a fanatically
uncritical admirer of Pierre de Coubertin would dispute the
claim that Carl Diem is the greatest sports historian and most
profound theorist of sport education of this century. He was
expertly knowledgeable about the ball games of the pre-Columbian Indians, field hockey in ancient Egypt, Mongolian polo,
and the starting lines for the sprinters in ancient Greek stadiums.[33]

Like most prominent bureaucrats in the amateur athletics
movement, Diem was an almost slavish admirer of Coubertin.
Perhaps this reverential attitude toward the founder was a
without-which-nothing prerequisite for admission to international sport's inner councils. Diem had even investigated the
Italian origins of the Frédy-Coubertin family and solemnly
collected and edited the baron's frequently derivative and often fatuous utterances about the philosophical bases of sport.
Like Coubertin, Carl Diem cheerfully and paradoxically believed that pure sport was really for the world's elite though it
should also enliven and inspire the masses to higher accomplishments. Like Coubertin, Brundage, and most other directors of
the many national Olympic committees, Diem doubted not
that sport could both inspire the most passionate patriotism and
soothe aggressive tempers and was therefore a contributor to
the harmony of nations.

A calamity for young Carl Diem had been the canceling, due
to the Great War, of the VIth Olympiad, intended for Berlin
in 1916. The war wiped out years of his architectural planning
and detailed scheduling of the events and festivities. Through
the 1920's, Diem and Lewald (who resembled one another—
and both were near doubles of Count Henri Baillet-Latour,
president of the International Olympic Committee) succeeded

first in getting German teams readmitted to Olympic competition in 1928 and then repeatedly presented the case for an Olympiad in Berlin. After all, the facilities intended for 1916 were ready for use. The two men were delighted when Baillet-Latour on May 13, 1932, announced the award of the 1936 Games to Berlin rather than Barcelona. During the summer of 1932 Diem became a perfect demon of released energy running about Los Angeles collecting data about the American experience so he could learn from the Yankees and surpass them. Late in 1932 Diem returned to troubled Germany to get ready for the climax of his life.

The extreme complexity of the planning required to stage adequately an international festival heralded long in advance as the most lavish and biggest ever, was not so great as to daunt Carl Diem. Diem issued the invitations, scheduled the many parts of the program, and acquired the land and appointed the architect for the German Olympic Village. The facilities left over from 1916 were quickly shown to be generally meager in view of the Hollywoodian architecture and landscaping provided in 1932 by the Californians—who, of course, had to be surpassed. Diem got the Führer to lease until 1943 the Berlin Racing Association's very extensive land holdings which adjoined the twenty-year-old Olympic stadium.

To tout the coming festival, the Ministry of Propaganda was in charge of more general kinds of international and domestic advertising. Diem himself established an "Olympic Games News Service" which issued its first press notices on February 17, 1933. In January 1934 the News Service began issuing a monthly newspaper which "was sent to every administrative and sporting center in Germany and abroad that was in any way connected with the Olympic Games as well as to the international press."[34] At first the bulletins were published in five languages, but, as the circulation reached its peak of 25,000 the languages were increased to fourteen. Another monthly, *Olympic Games 1936: Official Organ of the XI Olympic Games*, began its run of fifteen issues in four languages in June 1935. A daily *Olympia Zeitung* appeared in thirty numbers between July 21 and August 19, 1936. Diem edited them all and fretted about technical details:

How many telephones should be provided for the Reichs Sports Field; which should be local and which connected with a central office; where a light system; where a microphone and where a loudspeaker? How high should the flag poles be; how high the steps; how should the seats be covered and how should the galleries be floored? How should the temperature of the swimming pools be regulated; how can it be kept clear and transparent? Should the box for the referees and judges be connected with the entrance for athletes? Where are elevators for transporting food? Which countries for hot and which for cold food? What about garages, work shops, the surface of the running tracks. . . .[35]

Dr. Diem assigned artists the tasks of designing the medals, the award certificates, a new gold chain of office for members of the International Olympic Committee, special postage stamps, advertising posters, press passes, and entrance tickets. Half the tickets for any particular competition were reserved for Germans; half for foreigners. For tourists from abroad he obtained reductions of 60 per cent in rail fares and a 20 per cent reduction in air and steamship fares on German carriers. One of his committees was charged with arranging a world festival of youth consisting of thirty "future exponents of the Olympic ideals" from each nation in the world.[36] The hosts for this particular rally that eventually assembled 11,148 participants were devoted cadres of the Hitler Youth who together with their guests led a "simple camp life" in tent villages in the Grunewald as they all attended the Games.

Diem also introduced some technological innovations into the projected sports meeting. Since the new stadium would hold more than 100,000 people, there was an urgent need for a strong loudspeaker that would not produce interior echoes. The German electrical industry complied, improving the loudspeaker devised for the Nuremberg rallies. The *Physikalisch-technische Reichsanstalt* produced three new scoring devices. One was a much improved photographic apparatus to determine the placings at close finishes of the track and swimming events. Another was a combined scoring board and primitive computer for showing the decisions of the judges of springboard and platform diving. A third invention was designed to minimize the effect of dramatic action in the fencing matches. A fencing judge had to combine a minute knowledge of the refinements of the contest, perfect concentration, and the keenest eyesight with a deep, incorruptible cynicism. In international competition a jury had often been swayed by "a fast thrust, executed with a triumphant shout and followed by a confident attitude usually indicated ·by an immediate dropping of the guard or removal of the mask"—this, even though the exultant competitor may have been hit by a counter movement.[37] *Brio* was almost wiped out of the 1936 fencing competitions by the introduction of an impartial electrical touch-recording device.

A new showplace in Berlin and a sort of tour de force that combined German hospitality with German method was the Olympic Village in Berlin. In 1932 the Californians had provided isolated, simple housing for the athletes who had come to America to compete. Diem established a new standard. The army engineers were in charge of erecting the German Olympic Village. Its builder and organizer, Captain Wolfgang Fuerstner, had been in charge of the Wehrmacht's sporting program. Like so many other functionaries who at this time directed programs intended to impress the foreigners, Fuerstner was given almost a free hand relative to the financial and other resources he could draw on. The village itself was situated in a birch forest and near some small lakes beyond the western suburbs of Berlin. Besides the meeting halls and commons, there were 160 houses of brick, stone, and concrete. A house held 24 to 26 men in double rooms each of which had a wash basin, a shower, and a toilet. Two stewards speaking the athletes' language were quartered in every house. Just before the athletes arrived the whole area had been landscaped and the peaceful lake provided with coveys of snow-white ducks. All this was intended to obliterate the signs of rapid construction.

Like the participants in the Nuremberg rallies, each of the thousands of athletes, coaches, and officials at the village had long before been given a series of colored slips that plainly cited the house, room, and bed he was to occupy. He also had color-coded books of meal tickets indicating for him and for the staff of the village the food he would get and details of his special care. The athletes were told of the precise kinds of transportation they would use from the village to the sites of the various events. The British official report afterward recalled the terrific melee on the first morning of the Games when 3,000 men tried all at once to board the buses for the *Reichssportfeld*, the central athletic complex. There would have been no confusion "provided the competitors carried out the instructions issued by the German authorities with regard to departure."[38]

The international camaraderie that the Nazis were eager to demonstrate to the photographers and journalists who were directed to the Olympic Village was, in fact, achieved. Planning, painstaking care, and the alert sensitivity of the domestic staffs had, among the male athletes at least, made for an atmosphere of easy sociability. Shotputters met to compare notes of technique; weight lifters publicly flexed. Tourists gathered to observe the seriousness, strenuousness, and amazing agility of the Japanese swimmers as they limbered up. No one publicly objected to the incessant noise making and ebullient horseplay of the Italian soccer players. In the evening athletes from all over the world gathered in the common rooms for reading, card games, or to watch movies of events that had taken place that day. The gymnasts were especially grateful for the daily films that permitted them to see what the judges had seen shortly before. Fuerstner had provided barbers, medical care, and even dentists. The Ministry of Propaganda offered for free distribution a picture of a Chinese athlete suffering some complicated dental work that would have been terribly dear at home. Tasteful bulletin boards had indexes of masseurs including special ones for the cyclists. The Americans had American mattresses; the Swiss and Austrians had their familiar feather comforters; the Japanese had mats on the floor. Around the quiet, idyllic lake at the village was a tree-shaded jogging track. On the lake, for the use of the Finns, was a faultless, torrid sauna the benefits of which they eagerly extended to others.

The care and feeding of the almost four thousand men from fifty nations at the Olympic Village was entrusted to the stewards' department of the North German Lloyd combine whose network of passenger ship lines covered the whole world. There was no common menu. Each national cuisine was reproduced for the guests of new Germany. Following are some observations made afterward by the head of the stewards' department at the Olympic Village:

France: The French sportsman is also an epicure, paying less attention to practical nourishment than to tasty and varied dishes. English steaks prepared Chateaubriand fashion with white bread and red wine preferred for weight lifters; all kinds of meat requested, this being prepared in the form of steaks, filets, cutlets, roasts, and ragouts; delicacies such as mushrooms, anchovies, corn on the cob, green peppers, etc. popular; stewed fruit with every meal; vegetables steamed in butter but without sauces; cheese, fruit, and coffee after the principal meals.

Germany: The weight lifters received beefsteak Tartar, chopped raw liver, cream cheese with oil and considerable quantities of eggs, often four per meal. Light refreshment before training and more substantial food afterward. The athletes required normal meals, steaks, cutlets, pork chops, roast beef, and fowl being principally requested. Large quantities of fruit; vegetables being prepared with flour; potatoes but practically no rice; tomatoes and salads popular; milk with grape-sugar and fruit juices preferred as drinks; various kinds of bread with large quantities of butter. . . .

Great Britain: Moderate eaters; grilled meat "medium" done, especially popular; three to four eggs, oatmeal, tea, milk, fruit, and toast for breakfast, Horlick's malted milk; plainly cooked vegetables.

U.S.A.: Beefsteaks as well as lamb and veal daily for lunch and dinner; no form of fried meat except fowl; underdone steaks before competition; for breakfast, eggs with ham, bacon, oatmeal or hominy, and orange juice; large quantities of fresh or stewed fruit; no kippered herrings; vegetables and baked potatoes with principal meals; sweet dishes including custards and ice cream.

The stewards' department also noted that the Chileans loved "large quantities of marmalade," the Czechs preferred pork fat in the preparation of all meat dishes, the Finns, besides their rye bread, were especially appreciative of the blueberries, the Hungarians asked for macaroni and sour cream for an "extra." Several East Indians were vegetarians. The Japanese wanted soy with everything and brought with them some of their more exotic condiments and preserves. The Peruvian weight lifters ate as many as ten eggs a day. The athletes from the Philippines refused spinach and cauliflower, but demanded one lemon per day per person. Many athletes were devoted to the quaffing of great quantities of orange juice.[39] The American consensus afterward was, "The best place to eat in Berlin was the Olympic Village."[40]

Of course, the housing for the male athletes in Berlin was devised not only for their benefit, but for purposes of putting the new regime in a good light. The women who competed were much less observed and much less comfortable. The forty-nine American female athletes and officials were taken to the women's dormitory, Friedrich Friesen Haus, a utilitarian dormitory near the *Reichssportfeld* that was surrounded by a high, wrought-iron fence. Once there, the women of all nations were isolated and put under the strict supervision of the Baroness von Wangenheim, a humorless Prussian with tiny eyes and great jowls below which she wore a thin string of very fine pearls. For some time there was no heat in the rooms and the food was inadequate both as regards quality and quantity.[41] The Baroness was unresponsive to frequent requests for improvement in living conditions.

Another center for the athletes was at the old castle of Köpenick which housed the rowers. The horses and men who were to compete in the equestrian events had arrived earlier in Berlin and had quarters far outside the sprawling capital. The sailing events took place near Kiel, 200 miles to the north, and the participants there just arranged for local housing on their own.

There is a strange postscript to add about the devoted administrator who oversaw the planning and construction of the Olympic Village. As was mentioned earlier, Captain Fuerstner was director of the German army's athletic program. It happened that he was also one of the few non-Aryan "blind spots" that the Wehrmacht was permitted by the Nazis. A few weeks before the foreign athletes arrived, Fuerstner was suddenly and inexplicably replaced at the Olympic Village by a certain Lieutenant Colonel Werner von und zu Gilsa. Then he was dismissed from the army—a personal calamity the loyal officer had never considered possible because of the frequent testimonials he had received for his good work. Though he, like the *Mischling* Dr. Theodor Lewald, was grossly demoted to being a piece of smiling window dressing, Fuerstner publicly voiced no displeasure and continued to serve nominally as second in command at the village until after the Games were over. Then, after a banquet honoring von und zu Gilsa for his services to the Reich in making the 1936 Olympics a success, Fuerstner killed himself with a single shot when he returned to his army barracks. The German press was at once instructed to explain that the officer had died after an automobile accident, but the truth leaked to foreign journalists. This unforeseen vignette required some sort of cover-up and retribution. General Werner von Blomberg, the Minister of Defense, arranged for a well-publicized funeral with full military honors.[42] For some weeks afterward the walls of the deserted Olympic Village were a favorite place for the Nazi zealots to scrawl obscene slogans against "the Jew Fuerstner" and against the Jews in general.

High-ranking Nazis were, of course, keenly aware that Germany was being watched by travelers for corroborating incidents of racial atrocities. There was, in fact, a confrontation between Hitler and Count Baillet-Latour, the Belgian *grand seigneur* who was president of the International Olympic Committee and who, publicly at least, made strong pronouncements that the Nazis were keeping their promises not to offend the sensibilities of their foreign guests. While motoring to Garmisch-Partenkirchen to open the winter Games, Baillet-Latour was astonished to see many vicious anti-Semitic posters along the German highways. As soon as he arrived at Garmisch he demanded and obtained an immediate audience with the Führer and through Paul Schmidt, the interpreter, they argued. Such ornaments were impossible preludes for a festival for all races and nations, shouted the great aristocrat. Hitler declared he could not alter "a question of the highest importance within Germany . . . for a small point of Olympic protocol." Baillet-Latour asserted that it was "a question of the most elementary courtesy," assumed an air of intransigency and threatened a cancellation of the winter and summer Games.

Though stymied a bit at first, Hitler began to talk glibly, exciting himself more and more while staring at a corner of the ceiling. Soon he seemed oblivious to the presence of his companion and it was almost as though he was in a sort of trance. Schmidt ceased translating and waited for "the crisis" to pass—being familiar with this kind of scene.

Then the chancellor fell silent for several tense minutes. The Belgian was silent too. Suddenly Hitler blurted, "You will be satisfied; the orders shall be given," and brusquely ended the interview by leaving the room. When Baillet-Latour returned to Brussels by car, he saw no signs. The offensive placards were taken from the roads until the Games were over.[43]

4
Three Preludes

The impact desired by the Germans for the beginning of the IVth winter Olympics was dulled by the blizzard of wet snow that began during the opening ceremonies on February 6, 1936. Great quantities of heavy flakes were just generally blurring. The comings and goings of the purring, great Mercedes-Benz limousines of the Nazi officials and Hitler were muffled in the flocked air. The chilled lips of the players in the marching bands could not produce the cutting blare and dazzle from the brasses. For the 15,000 spectators in the ski stadium soft snow obscured the nationalities of the athletes, the colors of the five-ringed Olympic flag, and the swastika armbands of the Nazi hosts. Snow fuzzed the diction of the speeches coming from the ubiquitous loudspeakers, made pastels of the reds and black of the Nazi banners, and turned almost mystical the figure of the Führer. Damp snow was mixed with newly turned earth to form mires around the hobnailed trampings of the sightseers. All through the events of the first days of the winter Games in Garmisch-Partenkirchen, the visitors were distracted by the whining of rocking autos stuck to their axles in the slurry formed by loose soil and clay and the ever present, fresh snow.

The officials of the winter Olympics in Bavaria had provided excellent facilities to impress important visitors. Like Nuremberg, the sacred site for the annual party festivals, Garmisch, though to a smaller extent, received a great deal of attention from architects and army engineers whose plans were realized by the willing backs of the *Arbeitsdienst* or labor corps. Ageless nature had provided the twin Bavarian villages with a variety of natural ski runs nearby, but in order to give a sort of focal importance to the jumping events, a new hill with a mathematically perfect slope was expressly built to end close to the center of the press and administration buildings. The new buildings were substantial and permanent.

Reporters found that they had the best seats from which to observe the uniformed Nazi officials and the athletes. Foreign officials and sympathetic journalists were equipped with heavy, strongly engraved identity cards that instructed all authorities "to give their assistance to the holder during his stay in Germany."[1] The Ministry of Propaganda had a ready file of slick photographs that were especially useful, since pictures snapped on the spot were dappled with snow flakes. There were diagrams of earthworks and trestles for the bobsled runs, photos of the smiling Führer, and ranks of doctors and nurses before a rustic (though new) building holding the sign "*Gesundheitsdienst*" (Health Service). Another photo showed a large stack of propane cylinders on each of which was stenciled the legend, "*Für olympisches Feuer.*" Taking an idea from the festival makers at Los Angeles, the fire would burn in a large ceremonial urn at the ski stadium for the duration of the Games, February 6 through 16. For those who took their own pictures, there were darkrooms. The press headquarters had banks of linguistic secretaries. Signs over the English-speaking stenographers said "Without Expense" and "You Dictate—We Typewrite."

Two groups of individuals failed to come away from the winter Games with happy impressions. Nor had there been much effort to seduce these persons in the first place. The vastly larger of the groups was made up of the majority of those present—almost all of them Bavarians. There was just not enough room for the crowds, sometimes numbering 75,000 or even more, most of whom would drive up for the day from Munich. The frequent parades of athletes and, more important, the arrivals and departures of Hitler, Hermann Göring, and Joseph Goebbels demanded the expedient, no-nonsense devising of cordons and corridors. Stern, beefy S.S. guards shoved and barked to observe schedules rather than good manners. Also present were hundreds of alerted, camouflaged army trucks, loaded with armed soldiers and commanded by decorated officers in low, racy staff cars. On their frequent and unexplained maneuvers, the army convoys and special guards detachments splashed slush and hustled the cars of tourists roughly aside. It was far more comfortable for millions of other Germans to listen to eyewitness accounts of the Games over the radio. They also knew they could wait a few days for the newsreels and a little longer for the promised special film of the winter Olympics.[2]

A much smaller group omitted from the fun of the winter Games was disenchanted long before it arrived at Garmisch: these few individuals were veteran cynics alarmed at the skillfulness of the tableaux the Nazis had prepared. Such visitors were the American journalists Paul Gallico of the *New York Daily News*, Westbrook Pegler, then a sports reporter of the *New York World Telegram*, and William L. Shirer, a foreign correspondent posted in Berlin. Since the hostility of this trio was already known, there were specially detailed groups of S.S. men who neatly headed them off when they intended to enter the stadium—most effectively when Hitler was present. Pegler infuriated Goebbels when, rather than telling his New York readers about *völkisch* heartiness and good will, he contrasted the ostensibly peaceful purposes of the Olympics with the jarring maneuvers of some 5,000 to 10,000 hard-looking, disciplined troops.[3]

On the other hand, a few wealthy American businessmen

had been given spacious quarters in a *gemütlich* Alpine chalet. Such accommodations were scarce. Their eager grasping of the festive gifts of the Nazis so alarmed Shirer that he invited Douglas Miller, the commercial attaché at the Berlin embassy who was "especially well informed about Germany to enlighten them a little." Shirer was the host at a luncheon staged for this purpose. Miller could scarcely utter his *caveats* since the ebullient guests were so eager to tell *him* what things in Germany were really like.[4]

Besides being expensively staged, the IVth winter Olympiad was on a scale of participation that far surpassed any of its three predecessors. Over one thousand athletes from twenty-eight nations competed. As usual, the largest number of entries was in the skiing events. In that age which was so successfully streamlining airplanes, passenger cars, and even refrigerators and table radios it is curious that the many photos of the time show even the speed skiers in floppy knickers and billowing parkas—all good wind catchers. To the surprise of no one, Scandinavians, particularly Norwegians, were the overwhelming victors in the ski events. A group of four Italians provided their rooters with a unique occasion for abandoned rejoicing when their team won a special demonstration called the "military ski patrol." For the first time at an Olympic meet, there was a combined downhill and slalom race for women. The winner was Cristel Cranz, a daring German girl, whom the coach of the American women's team believed might not have been beatable by many German males.[5] Two Germans also won the gold and silver medals in the men's combined downhill and slalom. The American skier who came nearest to winning a medal was Richard Durrance who was tenth in the men's combined downhill and slalom. Fourth in this race was the Norwegian, Birger Ruud. I mention him because Birger Ruud had won the jumping event in Lake Placid in 1932 and went on to win again in 1936 before a crowd of 150,000, the largest number of spectators to assemble at Garmisch for the winter Games.

Another Norwegian, Ivar Ballangrud, almost overwhelmed the other competitors in the speed skating events. Unlike the skiers, Ballangrud was pared narrow by gray tights that reduced his wind resistance to a minimum. He took the 500 meters, the 5,000 meters, and the 10,000 meters, but (nobody is perfect) had to accept the silver medal in the 1,500 meters. The races were run in timed pairs and he was just one second behind another Norwegian who was first. Ballangrud, surely one of the most remarkable of all Olympic victors, has been entirely forgotten. Fame is fickle. A few Austrian and some Dutch skaters were in the first ten places. The American who won a bronze medal and the lone Japanese who was just behind him to take fourth in the 500-meter skating race were exceptional.

The Americans had sanguinely appeared in Bavaria with a winter team second in size only to what the Germans themselves assembled. The Yanks finally made some mark in the bobsled events. The runs themselves became badly cut up and one of the impressive sights for the privileged overnight guests in Garmisch was to watch the *Arbeitsdienst* crews working high up in the mountains by torchlight in order to repack the ice blocks on the curves. An American pair from the Keene Valley Athletic Club won the gold medal and the "Sno Birds" of the Lake Placid Club were third in the two-man bobs. A Swiss pair was second. Swiss teams were first and second in the four-man bobsled race. For all these events the times were bad and ugly spills were frequent.

Despite the burden of responsibility the athletes and coaches felt due to the costs of their training and transportation and despite the tensions due to the heightened patriotism generally in the air in the middle thirties, there were remarkably few disputes over rules or questionings of the decisions of the judges. An exception was the unquenchable row over the qualifications of the British ice hockey team. It was known some time before February 1936 that two members of the English team, though born in Britain, had played on Canadian teams. They were also under a barrage of unsubstantiated accusations that they had previously been professionals. According to the rules of the International Ice Hockey League, they were eligible for the British team, but their presence was vigorously protested by Canadian hockey officials (Canada had won every Olympic hockey championship since hockey was first established as an Olympic event in 1920) and by the Americans who were demonstrating that high moral stance almost uniquely theirs at the time. At the last moment, in the interests of international amity, the Canadians sullenly withdrew their protest and settled down to the series of matches to acquire the goals that rank the teams. Ironically, indeed almost diabolically, the winning order was: the United States third, Canada second, and Great Britain first. The two Canadian-Britons who were the issues in the dispute performed brilliantly and were crucial factors in the extraordinary outcome.

Another outstanding ice hockey player was Rudi Ball, the Jew who had been invited back from his exile in Paris to play for the German team. Somehow the Germans drew the Americans in their first match to lose 0–1 and then met the British in the second match for a 1–1 tie. They therefore lacked the goals that would have brought them a medal-winning place. The German team was very good and Ball himself blithely behaved as though nothing had happened. He took no notice of the fact that Nazi officials pointed him out as a refutation of the lies of those few journalists unsympathetic to the cultural resurgence of the new Germany.

A series of contests that generated exceptional excitement at Garmisch were the figure skating championships. Despite the facts that there were fine athletes in the other sections of the program at Garmisch-Partenkirchen and that these athletes turned out some great performances, only the few fancy skaters seemed to draw the admiration, heartbreaking envy, and love that are the rewards and burdens of the sporting world's charismatic stars. To the surprise of no one, Karl Schafer, the

Austrian who had won at Lake Placid, was again an Olympic victor as a male solo. Schafer was tall and had a rather long, lined face which he set in a mien of studied indifference. He was far ahead in the school figures, his specialty, and wisely stuck to a conservative program in the free skating where he revealed his wit and elegance in a series of rapid dance steps. Second to Schafer was the German Ernst Baier, another serious, muted perfectionist in the most theatrical of Olympic sports.

A dazzling figure whom the dark and plain Ernst Baier set off perfectly was his partner in the pairs skating, Maxie Herber. Maxie was blonde, small, and slim, was dressed in pale satin, wore a tiny black beret, and smiled completely, like a movie star. Ernst and Maxie combined science and art and everyone knew it. Months before their appearance in front of the nine judges of nine different nations at Garmisch, they had had a movie made of their already established set of figures and turned the film over to a composer who then fit the notes of an orchestra to their every movement and gesture. The pair specialized in close synchronization of movement. Rarely touching, the dark male hovered over the speeding Maxie like the adoring shadow of a gorgeous, weightless gem. The result of their care was an apparently effortless response to fresh music. The spectator got the feeling of a light-hearted fantasy plus a degree of assurance and faultless rhythm never suspected possible by two skaters. The pair produced the impression that they were something new under the sun.

Then, a curious occurrence! Two Austrian children, fifteen-year-old Ilse Pausin and her sixteen-year-old brother, Erik— mere names on a list—took to the ice in an astonishing program that was the opposite of that of the methodical Ernst and Maxie. They chose as music a Strauss waltz with plenty of those seductive, throat-constricting accelerandos and retardandos. With a youthful verve, they flitted ecstatically across the rink like magic dragonflies. This was supremacy of another sort and the tempo of the new performance caused the spectators to respond emotionally with volleys of applause in an attempt to influence the ranking. There was really nothing to be done. Despite the hissings and grumbling of the predominantly German crowd, the nine judges were compelled by their own judgment to give the gold medal to Maxie and her consort. The schoolchildren were second; no one else was even close.

What is there new to say about Sonja Henie? Long before she made her appearance in the Bavarian Alps, Sonja had been the queen of ice, the empress of winter. She was Norwegian figure skating champion even before she entered her first Olympics in 1924 at Chamonix when she was eleven years old. Chagrined that she came nowhere near world supremacy in 1924, the child returned to Norway to study ballet and to skate seven hours a day. In 1927 she won her first world championship (of ten consecutive ones) and at St. Moritz in 1928 was Olympic champion—a position she retained at Lake Placid in 1932. Petite, with waving blond hair, round cheeks, button nose, and brave brown eyes, she was cute as anything and her stage presence communicated physical supremacy and aristocratic status. As an ornament to his crown, King Haakon of Norway adored her. She hobnobbed with royalty and was accustomed to command performances. By 1936 she had shed all girlishness. She alone of all the dowdy Norwegian athletes was clad in close-fitting white satin. Sonja wore a snug cap of white feathers, often flourished a fur muff, and bore a corsage—doubtless from an eminent male admirer. Thousands wished to be near her in order to view one of history's great personages. Her public appearances were triumphant processions. Her progress from practice or to banquets was inevitably accompanied by the moving hubble-bubble of massed whisperings of her magic name.

Sonja Henie's expected triumph was marred by the appearance of Cecelia Colledge, a modest, fair, English girl. In the compulsory figures, Miss Colledge acquired instant notoriety as a cheeky underdog for, almost miraculously, she astonished everyone by finishing just three points behind the legendary Norwegian. Of the two, the lovely newcomer was the first to perform her free skating and during her powerful spins, whirls, and jumps she had the stadium of 11,000 in an uproar of tumultuous admiration. A nervous mood reigned. Expectant thousands prepared to witness in public an epoch-setting royal deposition. Wringing of hands and dead silence as the reigning queen appeared on the glistening ice. No one could recall having seen her nervous before. Then, melting the cold with a fabulous smile already a decade old, Sonja Henie gave the best performance of her career.[6] Her coda was a risky, double "Alex Paulson jump" stopped by a graceful split. The at first reluctant thousands gave themselves up to the vocal admiration of incontrovertible supremacy. The judges agreed and Sonja Henie won her third gold Olympic medal. Valiant Cecelia was, of course, second.

The twin villages of Garmisch-Partenkirchen had not been long opened up for the really big business of winter sport. The Berlin bureaucrats distributing public works provided large-scale architecture for the performances of the athletes, sympathetic journalists, and for important personages. There were no facilities for extracurricular excursions. There were only a few small hotels and dormitories and no halls for festivities. As a consequence the entertainments that had to accompany the winter Games were held in nearby Munich.

It was in Munich at the Hofbrauhaus that *Reichssportführer* Hans von Tschammer und Osten clicked big beer mugs amid flash bulbs at his special *Bierabend* for hundreds of officials and journalists. For those who were in positions to express gratitude for such attentions, the Nazis offered a great many other banquets and festivals in the merry Bavarian capital. In Munich's attempt to extend a vaguely comprehended "Olympic spirit" beyond the athletic and into Munich's famed "artistic" ambiance, there was a special evening of Olympic music and ballet. Richard Strauss, then seventy-two years old and the most famous living German composer, had written the music for a "fantastic dance" called "The Olympic Rings." The ballerinas Liselotte Köster, Daisy Spies, Ursula Deinert, Heidi Höpfner, and Margot Höpfner, clad respectively in flimsy red, yellow, black, green, and blue costumes, mimed the significance of the five rings on the official Olympic flag.

When the winter Games ended, each competitor received an envelope, really a portfolio, containing an engraved banquet invitation, an entry ticket to a ball, and a whole booklet of colored tickets for such things as refreshments and a trip on a special train that was met in Munich by a brass band. This particular dinner and ball was for 2,000 people. Periodic amusements roused the flagging guests from eight in the evening until after three the next morning. Citations of several acts deserve to be lifted from their decades-long oblivion in the German *Official Report*. At 9:00 P.M. there was a tableau, "*Die Meisterspringer von Gudiberg (Ein olympisches Spiel mit Gewitter und 300 Darstellungen)*" followed by a "*Schneeflocken-Ballett.*" Midnight was introduced by a "*Mitternachtswirbel! (eine Ode an die Weisswurst)*" and at 2:00 A.M. the no-doubt sleepy two thousand were revived by a gay "*Cancan zu Zwölft.*"[7]

The actual closing ceremonies that took place at Garmisch-Partenkirchen were distant in tone from knee-slapping Bavarian *Gemütlichkeit* and clearly drew from the Nazi experience at the Nuremberg rallies. Just before dusk the medal winners assembled at the ski stadium and, in rapid succession, Hitler himself congratulated the victors who, if they were Germans, gave him the expected salute. As the darkness gathered, massed skiers, all carrying torches, flew down the slopes of the surrounding mountains. There was a gigantic display of fireworks and as the athletes made their farewells a ring of powerful searchlights aimed vertically into the night sky threw beams that formed a slim, immensely high colonnade of light.

The winter Games were considered a success or at the very least, worthwhile, by the Nazis since (with the exception of the supposedly insignificant dissidents noted) they convinced foreign observers that the directors of the New Order were administratively capable and were sincere, gracious hosts.[8] But still, over the sporting events, the attendant festivities in Munich, and the appraisals afterward there hung a certain miasma, perhaps a suspicion that all was not well. The atmosphere of strain and anxiety at a large athletic meet creates nervousness. "Garmisch had this atmosphere doubled and trebeled."[9] A certain lack of perfection may have been due to the fact that Dr. Carl Diem, the master sports historian and sports administrator, was too immersed in preparations for the summer Games and was not in the south to censor certain inept entertainments or to do such things as quiet the incessant "Achtungs" of the loudspeakers. Diem, by exercising his taste and prestige, might have been able to curtail the admission of heaving masses of coarse Bavarian day-trippers and the arrogance of the army regiments.

In any case, it seems strange that an outstanding Olympic victor such as Ivar Ballangrud (whose accomplishments bear comparison with those of almost any athlete the next August), the figure skaters, Maxie Herber and Ernst Baier, and some others have not lived as heroes in the history of sport. The two durable heroes of the IVth winter Olympiad were Sonja Henie and Adolf Hitler. Only the undisputed empress of winter and the increasingly secure master of the Third Reich possessed the magic required to fascinate the masses at Garmisch and had the rank of "stars" in the world at large. The two were demonstratively together a great deal. They fed on each other's staged smiling ("was it *his* corsage?")—she in clinging white; the Führer with slicked hair and wrapped in a massive black leather overcoat deliberately burnished to a higher sheen than the similar coats of his hangers-on.

During the Games Hitler refrained from political pronouncements and posed only as the genial patron of the athletic festival. He posed as somewhat less godlike than usual though he exuded confidence. But we know now that inwardly Hitler was extremely unsettled, for as the Norwegians skied to victory, the bobsleds careened down the slopes, and Maxie and Ernst skated like dreams, the master of Germany was laying plans. Hitler was getting ready for one of the most desperate gambles of his career and for what was to be a turning point in history.

By the beginning of 1936 Hitler felt he had the internal security to return boldly to a neglected tenet of *Mein Kampf*—that the odious and humiliating punishment of Versailles of June 1919 had to be obliterated. To do so, Hitler would have to break up the French dominated system of mutual defense which had been reinforced (with the assenting participation of the Weimar Republic) by the treaties of mutual security signed by the Western European powers at Locarno in December 1925. Before March 1936 Hitler had made only a few tentative approaches to the diplomats of Poland, Italy, and England to woo their countries from French domination. On March 16, 1935, he had, however, with much fanfare formally denounced the disarmament clauses of the Treaty of Versailles, reintroduced conscription, and announced a program of rearmament. Still, these provocative actions took place in an atmosphere of accommodating sentiment, the intensity of which varied greatly in the ruling councils of such nations as Great Britain, Belgium, Holland, Poland, and France. The gentlemen who were in charge in Europe's higher councils felt that though he was badly brought up and certainly unorthodox, the new boss of Germany was in no danger of unleashing his as yet modest army and, even though his protests were expressed illogically, excitedly, and even sometimes in bad German, Hitler's claims of post-Versailles persecution were just. Besides, those statesmen who might have decisively stopped Hitler were themselves distracted by their own serious domestic cares and seemed afflicted by a partial paralysis that prevented them from acting against Japan in the campaigns in Manchuria or against Italy's unapologetic aggression against Ethiopia. The League of Nations was dying. Hitler would give it a near killing blow.

The Rhineland was a long band of German territory thirty to seventy miles wide that bordered Holland, Belgium, Luxemburg, and, more than any of the others, France. Articles 42 and 43 of the Versailles Treaty required that this territory be entirely demilitarized—that is, it could harbor no troops or fortifications—as a buffer between Germany and her possible victims. Article 2 of the Locarno Treaty had specified that the remilitarization of the Rhineland was to be treated as a *casus foederis* (cause to bring the provisions of the treaty into effect, i.e., a cause of war). It was no secret that these provisions were deeply galling to Hitler. As the genial Führer was playing a role for the world at Garmisch in February 1936, it was also no secret to the highest levels of French, Belgian, English, and Soviet governments that Hitler was eager to prove his mettle in the Rhineland. Terrified French politicians consulted with their generals, their bankers, and with British statesmen. In the morning of March 7, 1936, the diplomatic corps in Berlin was called to the Foreign Office to hear a strange set of German proposals for a series of pacts "to guarantee the peace in Europe for twenty-five years." Then in an extraordinary special meeting of the Nazified Reichstag, Hitler in a garbled and lengthy speech unilaterally repudiated the Locarno treaties and spoke convincingly of his sincerity for a firm basis for peace in Europe offering to sign solemn guarantees of his intentions. He eagerly posed as a model of good sense, but was clearly confused and agitated underneath. The uniformed claque of deputies (as astonished as anyone there) was finally brought to its feet roaring and stomping when Hitler announced that he was going to deneutralize the Rhineland. Even as he spoke, 35,000 German troops were moving over the border of the demilitarized zone to be received with rejoicing and some apprehension in all the Rhineland cities. The soldiers were jumpy and so were the Rhinelanders. All knew very well what might come of this amazing maneuver.

In France, particularly, there was a mood of shock. Their protection, the result of more than fifteen years of patient diplomacy, was destroyed. Once more, as in 1870 and in 1914, the French faced the prospect of ghastly humiliation and the possible slaughter of their youth by the detested Huns. The ministers in Paris spoke of a general mobilization of the large well-equipped French army—an action that would have unquestionably forced the Germans back, but would have also caused severe dislocations within France. An election was coming up. A calling up of reserve troops would drain the treasury and further weaken the franc, then trembling at the brink of another devaluation. French diplomats urged the British for joint action. Faced with widespread pacifism and a ruling class that was either largely sympathetic with the new Germany or perturbed over the recent French agreement with Bolshevik Russia, Stanley Baldwin, the prime minister, urged prudence and further consultations. The leading councils of the democratic powers in Europe were moved both by horror at what the Rhineland upset might mean and by a desire to hide their pusillanimity from their populations. Finally, using the excuse that the British would not agree to joint sanctions against Germany or join France in a counter-invasion of the Rhineland, the French leaders, after some agony, decided not to mobilize. Among the ministers in the capitals of the nations bordering on the new Germany, there was an eager searching of means to shift the responsibility for inaction. Since the contractual basis for European security had been almost wrecked, there was fear of a new wave of international anarchy. The legalistic excuse for the stalling was that Hitler's coup was not a "flagrant" aggression nor a "flagrant" violation of the solemn treaties so many politicians believed had kept the peace since 1919. In the meantime, more Wehrmacht troops settled in the Rhineland to total about 90,000. The architects in Berlin ordered the construction of German fortifications opposite the Maginot line.

It was only after 1945 and the publication of memoirs and the records at the Nuremberg trials that historians learned the extent to which the Rhineland crisis caused a tumult within Germany itself. In 1936 Nazi propaganda apparatus was able to give the impression abroad that almost all Germans were solidly, uncritically loyal to their leader, that domestic success was total, and that onetime dissenters had been themselves overwhelmed by that success. There were, in fact, loose ends everywhere in the Reich, most especially at the highest levels of the Third Reich's administration. Nowhere, perhaps, had the *Gleichschaltung* met with less coordinating success than among the senior officers of the army. The Prussian generals were revolted by the political indoctrination courses designed for the army and adhered to an ancient tradition that the Wehrmacht must be above the petty pushing and shoving of internal politics. In the meantime, Hitler's crony, Heinrich Himmler, was seeking to undermine the General Staff while building his own elite legions of S.S. (*Schutzstaffel*) guards. To a man the traditional generals had been appalled at Hitler's demands for a Rhineland invasion so early. The available French forces were better equipped and the French generals had strategies and mobilization plans that would have destroyed anything the Germans might put on the field on such short notice. The German army had no reserves and the generals preferred, if the Rhineland adventure was to be launched at all, to move when conscription and the rearmament program would make their victory certain. Hitler alone perceived the depth of the spiritual disarray in Europe's high political circles and on March 2, 1936, demanded the design of a Rhineland campaign from his Minister of Defense, the most cooperative of the great generals, Werner von Blomberg. The rest of the General Staff were informed of the hasty plans only on March 6. Horrified, the generals felt as though the madman was staking his fortunes on a single number of the roulette wheel and convinced him "to use as weak a force as possible in order to cut losses to a minimum in case of a French counter measure."[10] The next day, March 7, the alarmed German military attaché in London, himself a member of the General Staff, cabled to Berlin that the Cabinet was in an uproar and that the chances of British military intervention were at least 50:50. Upon receipt of this telegram, even the compliant Blomberg lost control of himself and clamored for permission to withdraw the units that had at that point only occupied Saarbrücken, Trier, and Aachen.[11] Afterward even Hitler confessed:

The forty-eight hours after the march into the Rhineland were the most nerve-wracking in my life. If the French had marched into the Rhineland we would have had to withdraw with our tails between our legs, for the military resources at our disposal would have been wholly inadequate for even a moderate resistance.[12]

That Hitler was profoundly agitated by the pessimism of the generals was indicated by the grandiloquent and inconsistent peace guarantees he wildly offered to all Europe on March 7 just as he was starting what was, as the Locarno Treaties specified, an unequivocal *casus foederis*. Internally frightened, he held firm. The hours and days passed. There were no sanctions, no calling up of the reserves, no general mobilizations. Only the Germans marched.

The significance of the Rhineland crisis within Germany was that Hitler lost all his respect for the courage and political judgment of the generals he inherited from the old regime and, correspondingly, felt an enormous surge of confidence in his own genius. The generals themselves were not aware of his distrust and continued to protest subsequent risks taken with the forces under their nominal commands. With one spin of the wheel, this total neophyte in diplomacy and military affairs had completely reversed the European balance of power in Germany's favor. An article on Hitler in a British journal had the title, "What a Man!"[13] A lasting result of the Rhineland affair was therefore to increase Hitler's faith in what he described, in a speech of March 15, 1936, as his own *"schlafwandlerische Sicherheit"* (sleepwalker's self-assurance) in foreign affairs.[14] Though he fervently proclaimed to the attendant world that Germany's historic griefs had been assuaged, he was even then preparing his intuition for greater tests.

When the Führer had addressed his Reichstag members, most of whom were in military dress, on March 7 to inform them of his plans for the Rhineland, he pleaded for permanent peace and also expressed, once again, his concern for his people.

Today I have therefore decided to dissolve the German Reichstag so that the German people may pass judgment on my leadership and on that of my associates. During these three years Germany has regained her honor, refound her faith, conquered the greatest economic distress, and finally inaugurated a new cultural advance.[15]

Goebbels let loose a whirlwind election campaign, intended almost as another example of nation-wide festivity, to draw from all the Germans feelings of enthusiastic participation and eager yearning for a proper outcome. The campaign reached its climax four days before the voting when Hitler broadcast his speech from Essen at the great Krupp factory, Germany's largest munitions manufacturing center. At the moment he approached the microphones of the Reich's radio network, blasting sirens from more than 100,000 loudspeakers throughout the nation issued the order that loyal Germans must interrupt their work and stand still when their leader mounted the rostrum of the Krupp plant for his speech. In *his* major speech, Dr. Joseph Goebbels proclaimed, "Hitler is Germany!" The uncluttered ballot of March 29, 1936, was printed in a large, Gothic black letter font. An "X" in the one circle provided meant approval of the National Socialists' *"Reichstag für Freiheit und Frieden"* (Parliament for Freedom and Peace) and all unmarked ballots were rejected as void. Hitler got 98.79 per cent of the vote. Within little more than three years he had reached a position in Germany and possibly in Europe that the legendary wizardry of Otto von Bismarck had never accomplished by means of the scheming and risks of three decades.

The extent to which the events of March 7, 1936, marked a turning point in history were perceived by few at the time. Even the generals of the Wehrmacht could not have foreseen what the accretion to Hitler's confidence in his destiny would subsequently produce. Only a few diplomats, bureaucrats, and military strategists outside of Germany realized that since the legal basis for peace had been irreparably mutilated, there now had to be a military basis for restraining what might well develop into an especially virulent epidemic of German ambition.[16]

Another prelude to the XIth Olympiad was an event which was almost (but not quite, for Hitler and Goebbels were engrossed in the drama) beneath the notice of the generals, cabinet ministers, and diplomats, but one which, because of the attention given it by the world's sportswriters, altered the climate of public opinion and, quite possibly, the outcome and subsequent appraisals of the Olympic Games in Berlin. Far more than was the case in the Rhineland crisis, the readers of the sports pages were impressed by the first Schmeling-Louis fight of June 19, 1936. Here we must enter the shark-infested seas of professional sport, the pugilistic backwaters of which certainly contain more pseudoevents, artificial reputations, and convoluted crookedness than all the other aspects of athletics that have been made rotten by the corrosive power of large wads of money. The most enchanting and therefore the most corruptible aspects of boxing and the fiestas most carefully observed by those hawk-eyed cynics of the journalistic profession, the sportswriters, are the so-called heavyweight title bouts. And the person who is the target of lucre and the focus of spotlights of fame is the reigning heavyweight champion of the world.

The universe of prize fighters, their hangers-on, and their fans first gave serious attention to Max Schmeling in late 1928. During the years that concern us, the center of that universe was somewhere on a stretch of 49th Street between Broadway and Eighth Avenue in New York City. Here was where the young toughs strutted before the promoters, were interviewed by reporters, and were watched by the big-money men. Since the person who controlled the public appearances of most of the champions in every division of professional boxing was one Mike Jacobs, this stretch of real estate with its various, "sporting clubs," gymnasiums, bars, and other locales for kibitzing was known as "Jacobs' Beach." When Max Schmeling arrived in New York the title of the heavyweight division was open, for Gene Tunney (champion 1926–1928) had just retired undefeated from the ring. Boxing as a sport had until that point scarcely penetrated beyond Britain (original home of so many of our sporting pastimes) and the United States. So when Schmeling claimed to be the German champion, the response was, "So what?" He was big, though. He took punishment well, had a right fist like a pile driver, and acquired one of the cheekiest managers in the business, Joe ("Yussel the Muscle") Jacobs (no relation to the promoter, Mike).

Joe Jacobs contrived to insert twenty-four-year-old Max into the elimination tournament to find a new king of the ring and Schmeling in several fights in 1929 smashed the faces and reputations of rising rivals. The German resembled Jack Dempsey in looks and in his bobbing and weaving style. His crude German-English was as comic as the imaginative Yiddish-English of his hovering shadow, little "Yussel the Muscle." The incongruous pair inspired good journalistic copy and in turn the reporters of the ring awarded Schmeling the sobriquet, "the Black Uhlan." Finally Joe Jacobs consented to arrange a bout between the erratic American, Jack Sharkey, and Max for June 12, 1930. The winner would assume the empty throne of the heavyweights.

In the first round both started fast, but Sharkey fired lefts with such speed that Max only landed a few blows to Sharkey's head. The second and third rounds were occasions for Sharkey to weaken Max and as the fourth opened the eager fans saw that Sharkey was trying hard to put the big German away. The crowd was on its feet as, in a neutral corner, he gave Max a hard right under the heart and then with a shot that took all the big American's strength, Sharkey threw a half-hook, half-uppercut that was apparently aimed at Schmeling's waistline. Where that fabled blow landed is one of the enigmas of Clio, the muse of history. Its locus has been disputed in haberdasheries, saloons, and shoeshine parlors ever since. What followed immediately was a scene of the wildest disorder.

Schmeling dropped to the rosinated canvas, his face contorted, his gloves at his genitals. Never a shrinking violet, "Yussel the Muscle" vaulted into the ring and began screaming, "Foul! Foul!"[17] just as the referee (who clearly saw no foul) began to count. The bell saved the fallen Max at "Six." Intimidated and bewildered, the ref circled the now riotous ringside, seeking corroboration for Joe Jacobs' claim. Upon hearing from one judge (the other denied the foul) that he had indeed observed the low blow, the referee, despite the fact that Sharkey's manager and second and other partisans were also running everywhere hysterically screaming, "No foul! No foul!" decided at once that Schmeling was the technical winner. The tumult and din permitted no conventional announcements, so he rushed to Schmeling's corner and perpetrated one of boxing's deathless, tragicomic scenes when he raised the mitt of the limp, battered body supported only by Max's seconds. Schmeling had won the world championship on the basis of a foul and while sitting down!

The aftermaths of this bout were numerous. Though the New York State Athletic Commission did not then take the championship from Schmeling, they ruled that henceforth boxers would be required to wear a tougher athletic supporter for the whole groin area and that no championship fight could be decided on the basis of a single low blow. Now moneyed and, as ever, well managed, Schmeling continued boxing and took some of the depression's fat purses. He resolutely, however, refused to meet Sharkey again. Pushed to the limits of endurance, the Boxing Commission then declared his title void and awarded it to Sharkey. Joe Jacobs and Max at last consented to a return match on June 21, 1932. When the bell for the fifteenth round at Long Island Bowl rang that night the fabled right of Max Schmeling was still cocked and ready and he was dethroned not only legally, but in the eyes of millions. The "Black Uhlan" sailed to Germany where he married a movie blonde named Anny Ondra, bought a villa in the country and an apartment in Berlin, and took up trap and skeet shooting. However, he did not quit boxing for long. Despite his pleasure in comfort, he urged his little manager to finagle his comeback. Max must have developed a taste for substantial earnings, otherwise he would not have been keen to keep going after he was K.O'd. by Max Baer in 1933 and lost a twelve-round decision to Steve Hamas in 1934.

One trembles as he approaches a narration of the career of Joe Louis. He was born in 1914 of a poor family in Alabama. His mother took the children to Detroit where Joe worked as an auto mechanic and boxed at a boys' club. He showed a remarkable talent for punching hard and learning fast. These admirable qualities brought him some expert coaching and a series of ready victories, usually by knockouts, in amateur bouts near home. After Joe won the light-heavyweight championship at the A.A.U. Golden Gloves tournament in 1934, he immediately turned pro. He took his first purse, $50, in July of that year. During the rest of 1934 he put ten opponents to sleep and took decisions over two more. It was inevitable that his ensuing reputation would draw the attention of the impresario Mike Jacobs who saw that the boy got more of the coaching he cooly absorbed with such intentness and that he earned enough cash to make the down payment on a $25,000 house for his mother. Joe's unbroken list of victories continued. He was the talk of "Jacobs' Beach," first as "the Boy Bomber" and then as the "Brown Bomber."

The industry and its consumers, of course, were rotten with anti-Negro prejudice and had already been disfigured by a long "save-the-white-race" phase after the championship of Jack Johnson (1908–1915). The moguls had passed over skilled black fighters, but they could not ignore Joe. He was expert, a surpassingly handsome physical specimen, clean, abstemious, loyal to his mother, and serious. He never shot his mouth off. In short he was hailed as a credit to his race. His neatly tucked stance and economy of movement reeked of science. An admiring reporter observed:

Any romantic white person who believes that the Negro possesses a distinctive quality ought to see Louis. He suggests a gorilla or a jungle lion about as much as an assistant professor at the Massachusetts Institute of Technology.[18]

Joe's string of victories continued into 1935 at a slower rate, since Mike Jacobs was conniving to save the boy for those big-money bouts that required a great deal of strategic planning and weeks of ballyhoo. Still, Joe's opponents were the best that could be found. On June 25 at Long Island Bowl the youth met the Italian Primo Carnera who was more than five inches taller than six-foot-one-and-one-half-inch Joe. In the sixth round the giant was draped on the ropes, pleading with the referee for mercy. Louis's hammer-like blows wrecked Lee Ramage, Kingfish Levinsky, and the Basque, Paolino Uzcudun. As Joe Louis assumed the position of hero of heroes to American Negroes, the pressure to witness his performances became almost frantic. Mike Jacobs' prices for seats mounted. He attracted the big bettors and Joe Louis became mythic material as his saga became subtly intermixed with the adventures of a great nation pulling itself out of the depression.

Excitement before the fight with Max Baer (who, unlike Joe, made wisecracks and went to parties) was climactic. Unlike Louis, who had been badly battered a couple of times when a beginning amateur, Baer in forty-eight fights had never been off his feet. Baer was a dangerous fighter who was at his best when he trained hard which was almost never. No one had ever seen him in better condition than at the weighing-in on the eve of the fight. Mike Jacobs had squeezed 95,000 people into Yankee Stadium and (one of his greatest tours de force) got some 20,000 seats stamped "ringside." Nearest the ring were five state governors, the Republican National Committee, many millionaires, and a lot of people in show business whose agents ordered them to be there so their pictures would be in the next day's papers. Before the pair shook hands Baer was tense and noisy. Louis's sole theatrical gesture was the grand removal of his blue bathrobe with a vermillion lining. During the first round, Baer's lunging blows glanced off the well-covered Louis who looked like an evasive, tan crayfish. Then the carnage began. By the fourth round, Baer's nose squirted blood. His face was squashed. A hard punch to the temple brought the white man down to a strange squat where he peacefully took the count of "Ten." The paying spectators at Yankee Stadium were appreciative for having been given good drama. They danced around the radios on the hot streets of Harlem. The gamblers had given Joe two to one and estimated that $5,000,000 had been bet in the country.[19] The mogul of "Jacobs' Beach" announced that with the sale of movie rights he had staged the first million-dollar gate since 1923. It was nice to have money again.

The "Brown Bomber's" triumphs continued into 1936. Mike Jacobs cannily delayed matching him with Jim Braddock, the reigning champion, because it was good business to keep two big attractions in the public eye as long as possible and to build excitement (and accumulate demand) for the foregone conclusion. In the meantime, Joe Louis had to meet Max Schmeling who was on a comeback trail, having beaten Hamas and Uzcudun, both of whom had won over Schmeling before. Now thirty, Schmeling was also intently watched from Germany where his laborious recovery, analogous to the rise of Louis, was gathering patriotic and mythic significance. Hitler and Goebbels were fans and made public pronouncements on Max's German qualities. On March 20, 1936, Mike Jacobs announced at a press conference that Schmeling and Louis would fight in Yankee Stadium in late June, that part of the proceeds would go to the Free Milk Fund for Babies and he also designated the fighters' respective training camps for which admission would be charged. In preparation, Schmeling had been present when Louis fought

Paolino Uzcudun and had repeatedly watched movies of the Louis-Baer fight. As usual the sportswriters consulted the big gamblers for quotes on the odds. The usual ratio was eight to one, but when one sought Schmeling money, the odds offered in fact were no odds at all. Speculation centered on which round the "Black Destroyer" or "Black Widow" would choose to give the lethal sting to the German. In Germany itself there was avid interest, but no betting. As there were no dollars, there were no marks for Schmeling and to wager against a potential Aryan knight would be unpatriotic. The two met at Yankee Stadium on June 18 as planned, but the battle was postponed due to rain and Max's little manager, Joe Jacobs, harangued reporters, denying fiercely that his charge had looked up at the sky and mused, "I'm afraid that it's going to clear up."[20] The next night at ringside, before the fight, the German veteran had the jolting experience of witnessing an elderly well-wisher fall dead at his feet from a heart attack.

There was thus a portentous air about this fight from the beginning. At the referee's ceremonial warnings, some connoisseurs of the ring noticed that while Joe, as usual, looked impassively at the mat, Max seemed intently fixated on a spot on the left side of his partner's face. A choked anticipatory roar came from the packed stadium as round one opened. Louis took the first round, though the punches he landed on Schmeling did no damage and Max seemed to be watching Joe with the most extraordinary concentration. In the second round Max uncorked his legendary right a few times, bobbed a lot, and was tensely cautious, but allowed Louis to bloody his mouth and almost to close one of his eyes. Max later wrote of the third round: "I never see so many left hands."[21] But, after one of those left jabs, Joe had brought his guard back sloppily and Max got in a quick smash to the "Bomber's" jaw—a punch which Max later claimed decided the fight. Imperturbable Joe was shaken and furious and, as retribution, finished closing Max's left eye before the bell rang. Rage and savage teasing on the part of both in the fourth round and then, after the sluggish recovery of a left hook by Louis, almost unbelievably, the underdog laid another right to the head that sent the miracle of the age down to a dazed count of "Two."

What was this? The atmosphere in Yankee Stadium was now almost explosive. No one recalled having been in a fight crowd before where the tension was so shoutingly expressed, so wildly ferocious. Somehow, Max's managers shielded him from the partisanship in the mobs and convinced him that victory was in the bag, that he should be careful and wait for Louis to drop his left guard again. But to the hysterical thousands, the impression was that the two men struggled totally without restraint. The din was terrific, a continuous blast, and thereafter prevented the fighters from hearing the bells that ended the rounds. The German's murderous right after the gong ending the fifth round had the full power of Schmeling's furious body behind it and sent Louis near collapse to his corner. Joe belied his reputation for purity and kindled the ire of the judges by throwing two low fouls. In the meantime the mobs of yelling fans at the vast stadium lit by moviemakers' lights had shifted their allegiance to the German and were lusting for the kill of the black American.

Max became wary and ultra-conservative. After all, he had the sight of but one eye. After taking a painful foul in the eighth round Max got in another hard right to the jaw that put rubber-legged Louis on the ropes. Schmeling continued to pound punishment. Thrilled that they were witnessing a legend in the making, the ecstatic spectators were hoarse, delirious with joy. Louis was "just a hurt, bewildered boy . . . I got tired hitting him," Max recalled later.[22] The entire strength of the older man's physique went into rights that battered the handsome youth's head, face, and jaw. Finally, in the twelfth round after a final supreme lunge by Schmeling, Joe Louis, blinking and shaking his head incredulously, fell to the canvas and at once stiffened and tried to rise. At the count of "Seven" he was on his elbow, but got no farther at "Ten" and "Out."

On "Jacobs' Beach" and in the barbershops and saloons of America, analysts tried to draw cheering conclusions from the upset of the "superman." Joe Louis had proven that he could take punishment. Boxing as a whole would benefit since the "Brown Bomber's" future opponents would not be petrified in advance by terror. But really, Louis's fans were in despair. There were fistfights without gloves on Harlem's streets. One black girl took the defeat so hard she tried (unsuccessfully) to end her life with poison in a drugstore. The heart of Josephine Tandy, a sixty-six-year-old Negro woman of Madison, Indiana, stopped as the radio announcer described Joe's collapse in that twelfth round. At the same moment Robert Gantt, a sixty-year-old who was with a group of Negro partisans about a radio in Columbia, South Carolina, suddenly perished of angina pectoris. In all, twelve deaths in Canada and the United States were attributed to excitement during the fight.[23] In some places in America there was rejoicing, since a white man had so decisively crushed a black man who was too fine a boxer for the racketeers to keep from trying for the championship. It was about this time that, here and there in the United States, Hitler was rousingly cheered when he made his ever more frequent appearances in the newsreels.

During the first Schmeling-Louis fight excitement was also high in Germany where, because of the time difference, the fans had to listen to the fight in the early morning hours. At the conclusion Hitler at once dispatched a telegram, "Most cordial congratulations for your splendid victory," to Max and sent flowers to Anny Ondra. Propaganda Minister Goebbels personally cabled, "I know you fought for Germany; that it was a German victory. We are proud of you. Heil Hitler! Regards." The official German news agency announced, "Inexorably and not without justification we demand that Braddock [who was, we remember, still heavyweight champion] shall defend the title on German soil." *Der Angriff*, like its bosses, interpreted the outcome in political terms:

Schmeling, the German, did that for the Americans, for the same people who did not want to give him a chance, who mocked him, derided him. He succeeded against world opinion. And he says he would not have had the strength if he had not known what support he had in his homeland. He was allowed to speak with the Führer and his Ministers and from that moment his will to victory was boundless.[24]

A wax recording of the German announcer's blow-by-blow description was played repeatedly on the German radio and over the public loudspeakers. Austrians cheered the fight movies that were rushed from New York to Europe. An officer of the Zeppelin *Hindenburg* gave up his berth on the transatlantic airship so that the "Black Uhlan" might speed home to feast upon patriotic adulation. Once in Berlin, Schmeling, his mother, and his blonde wife were peppered with the lights of flashbulbs as they lunched with Adolf Hitler in the Reich Chancellery. In the United States a poll of sportswriters later voted that Schmeling's was the "best comeback of 1936."[25]

5
Festivals, Symbols

All Germans were intended beneficiaries of the Nazi festivals which had psychological and civic value. We have already observed that Hitler planned the film of the 1934 party rally to offer the joys of participation to the many millions who could not be on the spot. After the National Socialists had declared the XIth Olympiad to be a project of major cultural importance, complex and novel preparations were made so that as many as possible could participate spiritually in that celebration.

In the capital itself, Dr. Carl Diem, chief of the Organizing Committee of the Berlin Games and, in fact, boss of the whole show, mounted an ambitious exhibition of artifacts and displays that illustrated the origin and importance of the Olympic Games.[1] The Olympic Exhibition opened at the German Museum in Berlin in February 1935 and stayed there for six weeks. It then toured the major cities of Germany until September 1936. The displays dealt principally with the origin and progress of the modern Olympics. The Olympic Exhibition also displayed many photographs of Germany's best athletes performing their specialties and models and plans of the facilities where the athletic combats would take place. The inclusion of photo murals of ancient Olympia and the casts of Greek athletic sculpture illustrated Diem's desire as well as that of many other Germans, sentimentally to link the projects of German culture with the most vigorous culture of all time. For some, particularly the educated, urbane Germans, the prominence given to antique amphorae awarded at the Panathenian athletic meets, the sleek statues of perfect Greek youths, and the casting of the magnificent statue of the Olympian Zeus made from the original at the National Museum at Athens—all these objects lent a comforting classical patina to an event which increasingly was being heralded as the cultural debut of Nazi culture to the world. The Olympic Exhibition required a great deal of space and room. Its assembling and dismantling demanded patient care. Therefore, it could not be seen or possibly much enjoyed, if viewed, by the great bulk of the German people.

Though it was hardly at all publicized abroad, a perhaps more significant attempt to communicate the excitement of the Olympic Games to the Germans was the *Olympia-Zug* or Olympia Caravan. The *Olympia-Zug* was designed to describe the spiritual significance of the coming Games to the rural Germans. The caravan itself consisted of four immense, Mercedes-Benz diesel trucks. Each flew two swastika banners from poles set in holders at the sides of the windshields. Each truck hauled two trailers (making twelve units in all) that were as wide and as high as the road regulations at the time allowed. When the caravan arrived early in the morning in a provincial town, the trucks and trailers formed a circle, usually in the town's square. The squares were often picturesque and might be surrounded by cobbled streets and ancient, gabled public buildings. The trailers were expandable—i.e., they could be stretched laterally like an accordion, thus greatly increasing their interior area. Nine of the twelve units formed a ring of exhibition rooms; three held the materials for the raising of a tent in the center of the ring. Members of the crew of the *Zug* hired local roustabouts to help expand the sections of the exhibit, erect the covered passageways, and raise the large tent. Parts of the readily erected equipment of the *Zug* were fifteen high flagpoles making an outer circle around the tight Olympic encampment. At the tops of the poles grandly flapped the red, white, and black banners of Nazi Germany. Technicians in Berlin had planned ahead for the flow of traffic around the circle of exhibition halls which had glass skylights overhead. The center tent was the main auditorium where shifts of locals watched short sound movies. The price for entry was low. Besides there were provisions for plenty of free admissions. The New Order did not wish to exclude anyone German from the Olympic Games. The *Zug* with all its heavy equipment traveled some 10,000 kilometers—as far as some of the remote North Sea provinces and into the Bavarian Alps for its series of one- to three-day stands. A team of twelve guides kept the streams of gawkers moving through the exhibits which were usually crowded from morning until night.

A heralded message of the *Zug*, like that of the large Olympic Exhibition that toured the big cities, was that the new Germany was producing the athletic festival of 1936 for the world in order to show the world the vitality of the cultural vanguards of the twentieth century. The *Zug* was also touted as a smaller version of the exhibition assembled for the metropolises. In fact it was not. Classical trappings and historical tableaux were minimal. The display was really intended to inspire uncritical pride in the new Germany. True, there were pictures of Myron's *Discobolus* and of a Greek Hercules intended to evoke ancient athletics, but these bows to a dead culture could only bore the provincial burgers and peasants. There were some accurate models in white plaster of the ski slopes at Garmisch-Partenkirchen, of the Olympic Village, and of the new sporting complex in Berlin. Far more prominent was the propaganda for physical culture. There were photo murals of exemplary, smiling work battalions, usually doing some kind of dirty work like cleaning ditches or leveling hills and low-angle shots of the oiled, sinewy torsos of Nordic youths tossing medicine balls and panoramas of ranks of marching zealots at Nuremberg.

Other large photographs showed the Führer in earnest discussion with the Reich's sports leader, Hans von Tschammer und Osten. Swastika flags flanked pictures of the Chancellor and more swastikas were shown carried high by the joyous troopers photographed at the rallies. Legends, in the Gothic script favored by the cultural commissars of the Third Reich, explained that the pair were commenting on the construction of the athletic architecture in Berlin.

The new complex in Berlin was the most ambitious ever undertaken for purely sporting purposes. Construction had progressed rapidly and the vast complex of arenas, playing and practice fields, schools, offices, parking lots, and subway stations was nearing completion at Berlin's western edges. The huge focal stadium, though it was the largest built until that time, occupied just one twentieth of the area of the new sporting complex. The *Reichssportfeld*, as the area was called, was as big as Berlin had been in the year 1680. In addition there were other facilities in or near modern Berlin for the rowing contests, equestrian events, and for housing the athletes and the staffs for broadcasting and filmmaking.

The architect of the stadium, Werner March, was especially proud that, whereas it had taken 15½ minutes for the last spectator to leave the Olympic stadium in Los Angeles, at his larger stadium that figure had been trimmed by two minutes. Long afterward, Professor March recalled that when Hitler and he inspected the ongoing construction, the Führer's usual observation was that everything was too small.[2]

Even before the National Socialists had adopted the XIth Olympiad as a cultural vehicle, Dr. Theodor Lewald, at the time president of the German Olympic Committee, had supervised the design of the new, visual *Leitmotiv* intended to symbolize the first German Olympiad. Eventually this motif showed the German eagle hovering over, almost clutching Coubertin's five Olympic rings. For a while Lewald posed this two-part symbol over Berlin's Brandenburg Gate and then further complicated the design by adding beneath those three stories of meaning a symbol that had not yet been a part of Olympic iconography. Lewald's added candidate was the outline of a bell—to call the world to Berlin. The early mood of enchantment with trademarks later became more restrained. For German domestic use the usual Olympic motif was the eagle (which after 1933 had taken on an angular, distinctly dauntless look) over the rings. Abroad, the Olympic rings surmounted the Brandenburg Gate. The bottom quarter of Lewald's original four-tiered invention took off on a ceremonial career of its own as "the Olympic Bell."[3]

Lewald commissioned a noted German sculptor, Walter E. Lemcke, to design a great bell which would hold as integral parts of the casting, the slogans and motifs of Olympism that had been devised until that date. There would be the motto of Père Didon's lycée, *"Citius, Altius, Fortius,"* which Coubertin had taken as a suitable motto for international sport, and Coubertin's five intertwined rings. To indicate that this bell had been designed for a specific Olympiad, raised ridges outlined an eagle over the Brandenburg Gate. Since the sketches and first models were done in 1932, the eagle in this case was the modest, feathered, Weimar bird. In a ring of script around the sound bow, just above the lip of the bell, were inscriptions of "Berlin 1936" and the bell's message, *"Ich rufe die Jugend der Welt"* (I summon the youth of the world). The sculptor finished the plaster model in 1933 and the *Bochumer Verein für Gusstahlfabrik A. G.* declared its willingness to cast this bell as it had the one for Berlin's St. George's Cathedral in 1897. Including its yoke the whole bell was almost ten feet high. The casting required 16.5 tons of molten steel. Cooling, chasing, polishing, and tuning all took several weeks of work. It was pitched in the key of E minor and had rich overtones.[4] For the journey from the Rhineland to the capital the German National Railways donated the use of an immense tractor and a trailer which resembled a railway flatcar. They had a cruising speed of 12 miles per hour. This was the same rig that had transported the largest block of granite for the monument to President von Hindenburg at Tannenberg.

The Olympic Bell, trussed to a massive arch of gathered oak beams, was designed as a major symbol and, consequently, became a focus of civic rites. It began its journey from Bochum on the morning of January 16, 1936. The tractor and trailer stopped in Dortmund, Unna, Werl, and in Hamm which had recently renamed its picturesque town square Adolf Hitler Platz. The square was filled with infantry regiments. All the officials of the town welcomed the enormous bell. It then went on to Beckum, Wiedenbrück, Gütersloh, Bielefeld, and Oeynhausen, at each of which places it was the recipient of well attended solemn ceremonies of a quasi-religious nature. In Hannover there was a vast assembly of factory workers, delegations from the sporting clubs, Storm Troopers, and S.S. guards. Physical Education Director Dunkelberg extolled the bell as a symbol of the staunch will which now characterized the German nation.[5] Northward and eastward the bell's pompous journey continued: Braunschweig, Magdeburg, Burg, Genthin, Plauen on the Havel. It was necessary to make a detour after Eiche because of a low railway overpass. The ponderous vehicles with their enormous symbol arrived at Potsdam, the ancient Prussian royal city, on the birthday of Frederick the Great. Each step of the trip was marked with well synchronized and ever larger receptions. There were brass bands playing slow marches and ranked, evenly spaced thousands of patient Hitler Youths. Municipal officials gave patriotic speeches. Joseph Goebbels ordered that the later ceremonies exalting the trip must be broadcast to the entire nation. Crowds were required to greet the new symbol in Berlin and accordingly many thousands turned out to join in another one of the Third Reich's large assemblies.

An innovation for Berlin in 1936 was a ceremonial boulevard, dubbed by the Organizing Committee (in Latin) the "Via Triumphalis." The triumphal way went for some ten miles westward from Alexander Platz in the center of the old city, to the Lustgarten, along Unter den Linden, through the colonnaded Brandenburg Gate and down the Charlottenburger Chausee, eventually reaching the sporting complex at the western suburbs. The several huge squares and grand boulevards of the Via Triumphalis provided a landscape large enough for the assembly of really vast numbers of party functionaries and other groups of Germans. During the ceremony at the Kaiser Franz Josef Platz its manufacturers ceremonially presented the bell to Hans von Tschammer und Osten who accepted it on the part of the Ministry of the Interior which had nominal supervision of the Berlin Games. In his speech, Tschammer und Osten declared that the mighty tones of the bell "shall not merely summon the youth of the world but shall remind us constantly of those who gave their lives for the fatherland." In his speech Dr. Lewald alluded to the Germany of Wilhelm von Humboldt, Johann Gottlieb Fichte, Wolfgang Mozart, Johann Schiller, Ludwig van Beethoven, and Richard Wagner.[6] The heavy casting was then hauled to the sporting complex where it was later raised to the top of a slim 243-foot tower. The Glockenturm was the highest structure at the Olympic sporting complex. Its bell was to be connected to a winding wheel almost twelve feet in diameter that was in turn to be swung by an electric motor that was timed to produce deep gongs every thirty seconds.

The most celebrated detail of the bell came to be that band of Gothic script around the sound bow that declared that the XIth Olympiad would be in Berlin and, set forth the cheeky legend, "*Ich rufe die Jugend der Welt,*" which the Nazis in their publicity releases of 1935 (just as the American movement for a boycott was becoming well noted) translated as "I summon the youth of the world." The line was actually taken from Schiller who was an unobjectionable German, but, unfortunately for the bell's fame, in foreign advertising Hitler himself was posed with the bell on the covers of pamphlets and on posters and special postage stamps. It appeared as though the upstart was declaring that *he* "summoned" the youth of the world. Even aside from persistent tales of book burnings, racial atrocities, concentration camps, and the revival of executions by the guillotine and the ax, the arrogance of this figure and his command was nettlesome or even grossly revolting. When devised in 1932 the call had been conceived of as the proper expression for the Olympic spirit. In 1935 and 1936 the summons seemed like the arrogant manifesto of a peculiar regime where everything, even sport, was taking on the overweening harshness of totalitarian politics.

The publicity campaign managers in the Ministry of Propaganda were not insensitive to alarm abroad. By the spring of 1936 both Hitler and the bell had disappeared from the international advertising for the Berlin Olympics. Even within Germany the festivity-inducing, symbolic roles of the bell were greatly reduced after its arrival in Berlin. Goebbels apparently perceived that the crowds that had greeted its progress across northern Germany had been more obedient than sincere in their enthusiasm. Probably very few Germans were actually moved to spine-tingling awe by this finely tuned chunk of metal, this piece of synthesized Olympic festivity. The contrary was true of another series of arrangements made in Berlin by Dr. Carl Diem's Organizing Committee.

At noon on July 20, 1936, there occurred an eerie scene in a quiet vale in the Peloponnesus. With stately, measured steps, fifteen Greek maidens, clad simply in gathered folds of classical draping, their dark hair bound and drawn back from their serious faces, had just marched through the tunnel-like passageway that once was the entrance to the great stadium at ancient Olympia. When the girls arrived at the spot where marble slabs marked the starting lines of the sprinters thousands of years before, they placed a large, concave reflector in a wrought iron base. The reflector would focus the rays of the sun, high over the Alphios valley. The high priestess of the group bent to hold a kind of wand before the reflector and after a few seconds some fluffy material at the end of the stick ignited and flared into a vigorous fire. Carrying the flame aloft the firebearer and her attendants turned away and marched back through the passage into the Altis, or sacred enclosure of Olympia. They filed slowly past the ruins of the ranked treasuries that the classical Greek city-states had raised in honor of Olympia's gods and passed before the fallen gray column drums of the temple of Hera, Olympia's oldest monument. Finally the girls' leader transferred the flame to a brazier at the fire altar of the Altis. A Greek orator read a vaguely prophetical message from Baron Pierre de Coubertin which said in part:

We are living in solemn hours. Everywhere around us are occurring the most extraordinary and unexpected things. Like a thick morning mist there are taking shape before us the figures of a new Europe and that of a new Asia. It seems to me that, now more than ever, the crisis that we must face and debate is, above all, a crisis in education. I offer you my message—doubtless the last that I will have the chance to formulate. I hope your course is a happy one. It begins after all in a most illustrious place, under the aegis of an eternal Hellenism that has not ceased to light the way of the centuries and whose ancient solutions remain today as applicable as they ever were.[7]

A slender, well-made, deeply tanned boy with a strong, broad nose and thick waving hair came forward. He was wearing only close-fitting briefs. He ignited the tip of a silvery torch from the dancing fire at the altar, turned away, and with the torch held high, sped in the direction of Athens. This was the start of the twelve-day journey of the "Olympic Fire" which was to advance another 3,000 kilometers before it would grace the stadium of the new Olympians in Berlin.

The idea was entirely Dr. Carl Diem's. In May 1934 the International Olympic Committee approved of his proposal for an ambulatory, international fire festival. Though the ancients had nothing like the kind of relay that the German revel maker envisaged, they had used torches for some of their ceremonies. An early problem faced by Diem had been the question of the manner in which the fire should be conveyed in 1936. A classicist, Professor Karo, informed Diem that the Greeks carried fagots of narthex stalks, found especially in the highlands of Ephesus. The pith of these stalks burned persistently for long periods, but, the

Professor allowed, they would never last twelve days. No form of flammable material then in existence would work. Thereupon Diem and some German chemists devised a torch that would burn vigorously for but ten minutes, yet would be unaffected by wind, rain, or tumbles. The burning material was to be of incendiary magnesium. In addition each torch would contain two special fuses so that if the burning matter should fall from the torch, the fuses could continue to glow and automatically re-ignite some safety materials. The Friedrich Krupp Firm in Essen agreed to fashion chromed, stainless steel holders for the more than 3,000 torches necessary for the whole relay. Each torch with its holder was a little over two feet (27.7 inches) long and weighed 1.5 pounds.[8] At the tip was a highly incendiary substance for quick ignition at that moment when the flame was to be passed from one runner to the next. Complex and unequivocal planning was crucial for this addition to the already symbolically surcharged Olympic program. Diem had to negotiate with the Zeiss firm of Jena, famed manufacturers of optical equipment, for the mirror that gathered the rays of the Greek sun to start the flame. A certain Herr Carstensen of the Propaganda Ministry personally covered the route by car in September 1935 in order better to be able to prepare lively and accurate copy in advance for international distribution. The German diplomatic corps was ordered to obtain exemptions from customs regulations for the torches and the inflammable chemicals they contained. Diplomats also received pointed instructions to help them in their dealing with Eastern European officials as they devised suitably pompous and brief welcoming ceremonies for the torch as it passed through the capitals of Greece, Bulgaria, Yugoslavia, Hungary, Austria, and Czechoslovakia. Hitler himself became keenly interested in this project which was presented to him as a classical revival. Consequently, Dr. Wilhelm Frick of the Ministry of the Interior and Herr Bernard Rust of the Ministry of Education also became interested and the torch project had no lack of official aid. Diem himself began an enormous admonitory correspondence with the Olympic committees of the Balkan countries, demanding assurances of accuracy and verifiability for their claims of a line-up of runners. He gave specific suggestions for adequate protection of the sacred flame and for dignified local festivals.

When the Greek virgins (if Diem demanded proof, we have no record of it) first kindled the flame in the stadium at Olympia, they were in austere isolation. A different scene faced them at the sacred enclosure of the Altis when they deposited the newly-made fire at an altar there. A large proportion of the Greek bureaucracy had turned out in striped pants and frock coats, having made the rugged journey from Athens. Technicians of the German National Radio Company were already using their portable equipment to transmit commentary—for Greece itself had only primitive broadcasting facilities. There were several foreign correspondents who observed the proceedings from the enormous, shell limestone column drums of the fallen temple of Zeus. At Olympia and posted along the route were cameramen of a new Olympic Film Company, headed by Leni Riefenstahl.

It required 335 runners, each traversing one kilometer, to cover the distance through the mountainous Peloponnesus, north to Corinth, across the isthmus to Delphi, to Eleusis, and then on to Athens. Athletic organization had progressed but little in Greece after her modern Olympiads of 1896 and 1906. The sporting clubs of the larger Greek cities had to recruit as runners peasant boys who were deposited ahead by motor truck to receive the enduring fire. Modesty prevented these youths from running their sections of the journey in the light trunks of the first Greek runner (much less the classical and photogenic nudity urged by Leni Riefenstahl). They sweated, passing the blazing torches while heavily clad in festive regional costumes. At a short ceremony in the restored stadium at Delphi, the runners wore the white leggings, flared skirt, and tight vest of fustanella—the same costume Spiridon Loues had worn when he accepted his awards for his victory in the first marathon race in 1896.

In Athens in early July of 1936 the Greek king presided at a formal ceremony of welcome. A large fraction of the Athenian population almost filled the ancient Panathenian stadium of Herodes Atticus, reconstructed for the first modern Olympic Games forty years before. Oratory all through Greece "expressed the gratitude of the New Hellas to the New Germany for having instituted the Torch Relay Run."[9] The route from Athens to the border was the most difficult. Temperatures on the treeless plains of northern Greece sometimes reached as high as 122 degrees Fahrenheit. A series of cloudbursts near Salonika forced some youths to run their kilometers through hail, rain, and high winds. Still the flame burned on—as planned. In spite of the streams of rain the entire population of Salonika turned out to watch the transfer of the flame in front of their city hall.

At Kula on the frontier Lieutenant-Colonel Leonidas Pteris passed the torch to M. Tenin G. Georgioff, president of the Bulgarian Olympic Committee which had scheduled the traverse of that country. Festivities in Bulgaria were on a high standard— perhaps because the Bulgarians had only 238 kilometers to cover and 238 runners to recruit, as compared with Greece's 1,108. Villages delayed the transfer of the flame in attempts oratorically to play great roles for the outside world. The welcoming ceremony in front of Sophia's cathedral was before packed thousands and lasted an hour and a half. Jeweled, brocaded metropolitans of the Orthodox Church somehow contrived a religious ceremony out of the arrival, sojourn, and departure of a bogus symbol of classical paganism. A further incongruity was the prominence of the swastika banners of National Socialism before the headquarters of the Bulgarian church.

In Yugoslavia the runners sped past frequent signs of welcome with the five Olympic rings. The 575 Yugoslav runners were seldom alone, for, especially near the big towns, dozens of young and old men turned out in flapping white shorts and sleeveless white undershirts to flank the torchbearer. The torches held in readiness for the stretch near Jagodina malfunctioned and would not endure the three or more minutes necessary for a running kilometer and the runners were, for a while, carried on the running boards of automobiles, a strategy which also regained time lost due to Bulgarian rhetoric. Because of this peculiar departure rumors swept the world that at one point the flame had gone out. Diem denied the reports. Besides, a spare flame, also ignited at Olympia, was always nearby, shielded in a ship's lantern carried in the back seat of an accompanying Opel sedan.

A string of 386 Hungarians awaited at the kilometer markers along the paved roads leading to and from Budapest. However, the Hungarians were able to insert a detour through some isolated mining districts in order to bring Olympic greetings to the population there. "At Kecskemet, famous for its fruit, an altar was erected in the idyllic market square and adorned with Olympic rings formed of apricots."[10] Gypsies along the way sometimes seranaded the runners and a Gypsy chieftain, Magyari, contributed his presence to the ceremonies before the tomb of the unknown soldier in Budapest.

In Austria hastily devised measures were necessary to protect the 219 runners and their precious cargo. Unexpectedly large crowds of sightseers who seemed to be in moods of joyously sentimental exhilaration were parted by phalanxes of motorcycles and siren-bearing patrol cars so that the torchbearers could proceed as planned. Holding the fire high, an Austrian youth entered swastika-decorated Vienna at twilight. Searchlights illuminated the Heldentor which flew the flag of the Austrian Sporting Club and a banner with the Olympic rings. Mixed with the disorganized cheering were "Heil Hitler!" salutes. North of Vienna, mobs of happy Austrians had waited along the roads throughout the night to observe the spectacle of the speeding runners, making up time, with the deathless torch.

The last Austrian bearer of the holy flame arrived at the Czecho-slovakian frontier at the appointed time, 9:45 A.M., on July 30, 1936. The Czechs, too, were enthusiastic. All along the 282 kil-ometers on either side of Prague hastily organized delegations of sportsmen and police had to protect the advancing flame from the crush of rapt spectators.

After Hellendorf on the border where the flame began its trip through Germany, the demonstrations were both much larger and more orderly. The Germans had had more time to organize. Tschammer und Osten's *gleichgeschaltete* associations of Ger-man sportsmen had been warned that they had a hit on their hands and were in charge of overseeing the secure, though as festive as possible, transport of the Olympic fire to its goal. The local National Socialist party cadres assisted. The entire route through Saxony was lined with ranks of Nazi party organiza-tions, the members of which sometimes linked arms to keep the necessary corridors free of children and less disciplined sports-men. At Dresden the vast open area of the Königsufer was en-tirely packed with people who listened to fanfares by the Hit-ler Youth trumpeters. The city's famous church bells clanged as the flanked runner approached the center of the beautiful city. However, the churches played no part in the ceremonies in Dresden where, during the electrically amplified speeches that were also sent by radio to all Germany and the world, the fire from pagan Olympia burned at a new, classically inspired altar before the city hall. In Meissen drum rolls and fanfares re-sounded from all the towers of the town in honor of the daz-zling symbol of Germany's Olympic Games.

The arrival of the flame in the evening at Bad Liebenwerda was particularly impressive. The façades of the buildings of the town's old central square were floodlit and the assembled crowd of 20,000 held as many glowing candles. At 11:38 on the morn-ing of August 1 at kilometer stone 7.3, the boundary of greater Berlin, an athlete from the Berlin-Brandenburg district ac-cepted the flame at the tip of his stainless-steel torch and ran toward the center of the capital. Again the timing was faultless.

A special assembly was already in the later stages of formation at the Lustgarten where 25,000 brown-shirted Hitler Youths with sheathed dirks at their sides, thousands of youths from other lands, 40,000 Storm Troopers, and hundreds of thousands of miscellaneous spectators thrilled to fanfares and then gave a lone runner a thundering "Heil!" as he entered the enormous square. All watched reverently as the sacred flame rested for a while at another high, classically inspired altar. There was no confusion and no skepticism in Berlin. The routes of the torch-bearers to and from the Lustgarten were broad, immaculate boulevards between the vast numbers of respectful participators who greeted the flame with the Nazi salute. For those who could not glimpse the runners or perhaps not see anything at all (as, of course, must have been the case for many of those present) inescapable loudspeakers kept everyone informed.

The final portion of the long journey was down the cleared Via Triumphalis (actually the Kaiserdamm) and on to the main stadium at the *Reichssportfeld*. It was by this time the afternoon of the opening day of the Olympic Games. The very last member of the relay was Schilgen, a Berliner. Schilgen was tall and slender, had long golden hair and perfect Nordic features which were impassive in the face of the adulation of millions as he ran the last stretch to the Olympic stadium. As he ran, the graceful athlete who was fair and clad in white was flanked and followed by two symmetrical wings of dark-haired athletes dressed in black. The formation of seven runners was a sort of advancing "V." The inside legs of the six muted followers were perfectly synchronized to be in time with the right and left bounds, respectively, of the blond leader. Since the crowds were kept distant from the runners, the remarkable spectacle was rhythmically stirring as well as almost eerie in its splendor.

This last runner, the slender, flaxen-haired German, appeared suddenly to the eager spectators at the eastern end of the Olympic stadium. Heralded by massed trumpet fanfares, he ad-

vanced alone to a ledge high above a flight of steps. He moved
forward a few paces and paused to regard the vast concourse of
people. The torchbearer then tripped lightly down the stairs
and ran to his left halfway around the red cinder track trailing a
wisp of blue smoke from the torch which he held high in his
right hand. At the other end of the stadium he started deftly to
climb another stairway. At a large marble dais this new god
turned to the stadium and once more advanced and paused, the
cynosure of admiration and emulation. All gasped. Then turning
he walked to a colossal brazier atop a tripod. The noble figure
rose to his full height and slowly dipped the torch into the brazier where at once there sprang to life a tossing fire that would
signify that Berlin was the host city for the XIth Olympiad of
our era.

It was noted earlier that, though Berlin was to be the focus
for the Olympic Games, the National Socialists were eager that
the maximum number of Germans should have access to as much
Olympic ceremonial as could be offered to them. Potent examples of the Nazi functionary's concern for the festive enfolding
of the provincial Germans were rapid reinstitutions of the sen-
sationally successful torch run. The Olympic program for August
1936 included the customary schedule of yachting events. Since
the nearest open water was at the North Sea, the sailing races
were scheduled to be held at Kiel. Accordingly, 347 German
runners, all clad in white shorts and white jerseys, each ran a
kilometer toward Kiel at an average time of three minutes for
his stretch. The first torch was lit from the brazier at the Olympic
stadium at 6:30 P.M. on August 2. The flame arrived at Kiel at
9:26 A.M. a day and a half later.

The demands for Olympic fire were still far from satisfied.
The rowing and canoeing competitions were to be at Grünau be-
yond the eastern suburbs of Berlin and 37 kilometers from the
Olympic stadium. In an organizational tour de force, some of
Dr. Carl Diem's underlings arranged that there should be 537
partaking athletes. This heavy participation was accomplished

by having each torch carrier go just 200 meters and to be flanked by two titular torchbearers. This run took place on Friday, August 7, and, though short in distance, lasted four hours and forty minutes because of enthusiastically attended ceremonies at the stadium, at the Berlin city hall, and at Grünau after the flame was deposited at the Bismarck tower there. The last part of the route was, fittingly, over water and during this stretch the torch was held aloft by a youth in the forward number of a group of festively decorated Canadian racing canoes. Just ahead of the lead boat was a motor launch carrying a whirring movie camera and its crew.

Leni Riefenstahl's cinema photographers were all over Berlin in the next weeks. They were lodged in the hovering Zeppelins, atop towers, and in pits at all the competitions. The spectators at Grünau were once treated to an odd sight when a commandeered anti-aircraft balloon carrying one of Leni's men sprung a fast leak and descended gently to deposit a furious photographer, some costly equipment, and a lot of immediately worthless footage into the lake.

Independently of Leni Riefenstahl's project there were other, far more bulky cameras being set up at the sporting complexes. Some looked like long, white cannons. Some rode with their crews atop heavy vans containing whining electrical generators. All this photographic apparatus was intended to channel electronically devised pictures into eighteen new television halls (Fernsehstube) in Berlin, seating, in all, 3,000. There was also a receiver at the Olympic Village.

So the Berlin Olympics were the first sports events to be televised.[11] Unfortunately for those fans who relied on the innovation for their experiencing of the Olympic festival and unfortunately for the reputations of the Olympic organizers and electronic technicians of the Reich, the nature of the televised proceedings often had to be divined. At the polo games only black or chestnut horses offered their silhouettes. When the signal was good from the main stadium, spectral figures dressed like athletes floated and shifted (to the announcer's commentary) in a blotchy milkbath. It was a noble try.

Berlin itself had been cleaned and dressed for a whole series of festivals that had the common intention of convincing the Germans and their foreign guests that the new Germany was, as it claimed to be, a savior and a creator of culture. The four million Berliners, living in the fourth largest city in the world, had constant instruction from above that they had been entrusted with an obligation to demonstrate the excellence of German National Socialism to the whole world. Unlike the ambiance at the winter Games in Garmisch-Partenkirchen where there had been ineptness and some brutality to corroborate Nazism's skeptics, in Berlin in August 1936, almost no one escaped the impression that the new Germans were working hard, were playing hard, were at peace, and would stay that way.

All the Germans seemed desperately eager to be friendly. Hospitality was lavish. The enforcement of low wages and low prices provided the visitor possessing foreign exchange with some tourist's bargains. The Reich was pursuing a policy of blocked marks that permitted tourists to buy German currency at rates lower than the official exchange rate which quoted a mark at a value of about 40 cents. Accommodations in Berlin's great luxury hotels were rarely more than 15 marks per person. Clean, spacious hotel rooms without baths were available for about 5 marks. Efficient housing services could provide foreigners (who had first choice) with a bed in a pension or a private home for 2 or 3 marks a night.

One journalist reported that the Germans were "going without eggs" so there would be enough for the visitors.[12] Meals in the crowded restaurants, where one had to compete on an even basis with provincial Germans who had flocked to the Games, were also large, better than usual, and cheap. Prices outside Berlin at the same time were even more advantageous. The police of Berlin were reinforced by special functionaries of the Ministry of Interior who were deputized to seek out price gougers and to stun them with summary and Draconian penalties. The Reich printed a special schedule of prices for wurst venders who were to sell their wares, regardless of quality, by weight. Even sausages were ingratiatingly *gleichgeschaltet* for the Nazi Olympics of 1936.

Der Angriff, traditionally one of the most combative of the Nazi journals, instructed its readers:

We must be more charming than the Parisians, more easygoing than the Viennese, more vivacious than the Romans, more cosmopolitan than London, and more practical than New York.[13]

Travelers who came by train from Holland, Belgium, or France began to report that the German conductors and other railway employees were displaying effusiveness of almost comic opera proportions in their regard for comfort of foreigners. Some officials were apprehensive about the emotional tensions mounting in the Berliners. Were they apt to take it all too deadly in earnest? Seeking to supply a synthetic antidote to a notorious failing of the Teutons, the German Labor Front published an announcement declaring a "week of mirth and happiness":

The coming eight days will be days of jollity and cheerfulness. Prior to the strain of the Olympic weeks, Berliners should take stock of themselves, then with merry hearts and friendly expressions on their faces, receive their Olympic guests. None should miss the chance.[14]

Trend watchers in the new Germany could perceive no immediately hilarious reactions except on the faces of some of those who read the proclamation.

With a naïveté that was both touching and ominous, visitors were confidently assured that the boulevards, streets, and even the dingy by-ways of the enormous, sophisticated city would be utterly safe. International and local criminals were intimidated in advance. In 1935 the Prussian police had prepared a handbook for wide distribution that contained 1,000 descriptions, with photos and fingerprints, of known confidence men who might be tempted by the concentration of merrily distracted humanity in Berlin. Diem boasted that the book would "be valuable long after the Olympic Games for the prevention of crime everywhere in the world."[15] Many with known trouble-making proclivities were just rounded up and stashed in jail while the crush of foreigners was on. During the whole festival there were only 64 charges against pickpockets of whom 39 were foreigners "which shows clearly the part that international crime plays in such occasions." "As many as 702 boarding houses, 532 hotels, and 115 pensions of questionable reputation had to be supervised" by special detachments of the police. Begging had already been outlawed in Germany in 1933, so throughout the festival only 104 beggars were arrested. For the Olympic Games and the consequent influx of the famed and foreign, a special new branch of begging was invented which made the approaches under the guise of collecting autographs.[16]

Diem had posted interpreters about the city. The tourist identified them by little lapel flags. Some pennants promised more linguistic facility than could be delivered, but still the guides went to endless trouble to help a stranger. Foreigners were also encouraged to wear lapel pins to indicate their fatherland. Many Berliners, in turn, went about with a chart of the world's flags which they pulled out of their pockets when they spotted a lapel insignia they did not recognize.

Flags played a large role in the Nazi Olympics both where the athletic events were staged and away from the swimming pools, mats, apparatus, and various arenas. Berlin itself seemed hung with flags from one end to the other. The Via Triumphalis was entirely ranked with rows of really large white flags with the blue, yellow, black, green, and red intertwining rings of Olympism and with banners of equivalent size holding the black swastika. Main thoroughfares near the stadium also had long colonnades of high poles carrying banners. Private persons cooperated to decorate their houses. One saw some white flags with the Olympic rings before balconies and draped below windows, but overwhelming these symbols of internationalism was the red, white, and black of the National Socialist emblem—after all, Berliners had to be practical. The Nazi flags would find repeated uses long after the two-week period of the Olympic Games. On the railway tracks leading to the congested, decorated capital, it was not unusual to see a swastika spread across the side of a locomotive and the Olympic rings on the tender.

One saw the hooked cross of Nazism everywhere. A curious encouragement for the predominance of the swastika before Aryan private houses was the fact that Jews tended to fly the Olympic banner. Since the Nuremberg Laws of September 1935 forbade the Jews to display the new German flag, in order not to have their locations stand out by being unadorned, they flew one that was decorative and which, incidentally, signified peaceful internationalism. Some large department stores in the center of the capital flew whole symposiums of flags—excepting the flag of National Socialism—and in August of 1936 the Nazis did not seem to mind this.

Apropos of the German Jews and the Nazi Olympics, it is significant to note that months before the Games, Propaganda Minister Goebbels, who at that time was somewhat in the ascendant in the coterie surrounding the Führer, suggested and enforced a cessation of the anti-Semitic campaign. Of the Reich's two conflicting objectives, racial aggression and international prestige, the latter was uppermost. Goebbels had long been particularly revolted by the cheap vulgarity of Julius Streicher's *Der Stürmer*. Therefore, all over Germany the abrupt warnings barring Jews from the resorts and the dirty anti-Semitic slogans at the road sides came down. The clumsiest anti-Semitic sheets were banned from Berlin. The slots at the news stands usually reserved for Streicher's paper held, instead, *Das Schwarze Korps*, the organ of the S.S. guards. However, the efficiency of the *gleichgeschalteten* Germans was never perfect and one snoopy journalist found a copy of *Der Stürmer* on sale outside the *Gedächtniskirche*. It was a special "Olympic issue" and half

Members of the National Socialist workers' service packing the bobsled runs at Garmisch-Partenkirchen. (Office of Alien Property, National Archives)

A publicity photo of the band that would welcome the foreign athletes to the Olympic Village. (Office of Alien Property, National Archives)

A publicity photo of the new, synchronized automatic cameras to record close finishes. (Office of Alien Property, National Archives)

Limousines outside the Olympic stadium. These cars and their chauffeurs were at the disposal of international Olympic officials and other great personages. (Library of Congress)

Two athletes, models of German womanhood.

Joseph Goebbels examining the details of a "Sulky Rider" at the exhibition of modern sporting art. (Library of Congress)

A publicity shot. Greek patriots hail the passing runner in the early stages of the torch run.

Adolf Hitler and Leni Riefenstahl honor a group of German Olympians. (Presse Diffusion, Lausanne, Switzerland)

One of the television cameras. (Library of Congress)

Partakers in a rally for kayak paddlers await the filling of a lock. This was one of many special meetings of sports enthusiasts held in Germany as adjuncts of the Olympics of 1936. (Library of Congress)

Spiridon Loues, winner of the first marathon race in 1896. He prepares for his introduction to Hitler. Max Schmeling can be seen at the shepherd's left. (Library of Congress)

A Hollywood publicity photo of Eleanor Holm. This was taken from the *Berliner Illustrierte Zeitung.*

Jesse Owens winning the broad jump. (Library of Congress)

Gisela Mauermayer, the champion German discus thrower.

Cyclists at a "scratch" start. (Library of Congress)

The marathon runners Kitei Son and Ernest Harper rounding the halfway mark. (Library of Congress)

Marshall Wayne, gold medal winner in high diving.

The crack American 4 × 100-meter team that appeared and did not run. Sam Stoller and Martin Glickman, third left and far right, who were the only Jews on the American track and field team, were mysteriously replaced at the last minute. (Library of Congress)

Victory ceremonies of the pentathlon. The American silver medal winner, Lt. Charles F. Leonard, is in his sweatsuit. The German victor, Lt. Gotthardt Handrick, and the number three man, Captain Silvano Abba of Italy, give their respective salutes. (Library of Congress)

A large field of entries preparing for the 1,500-meter run. (Library of Congress)

The German weight-lifting team. (Library of Congress)

The victory ceremonies for the women fencers. Ellen Preis of Austria is third. Ilona Schacherer-Elek of Hungary holds one of the small potted oaks from the Black Forest that were given to each gold medal winner. Helene Mayer, the runner-up, salutes her Führer. (Library of Congress)

An aerial view of the Olympic stadium. The acquatic sports complex is partly visible to the north of the stadium and on the left. The great bell tower is at the far right of the Maifeld, which is partly obscured by the airplane's wing. (Library of Congress)

of its front page was taken up by a cartoon showing "a degenerate and brutal looking person labeled 'Jew' staring with envy and hatred at a German-looking victor crowned with laurel." Across the bottom was Streicher's slogan, "Jews are our Misfortune."[17] Visitors to Berlin who wished to talk to Jews or otherwise investigate the "Jewish question" in Germany were required first to contact officials of the Gestapo and were afterward trailed.[18]

However disquieting the anti-Semitic manifestations were in Germany in late July and early August 1936, all foreign observers could not escape the fact that the oppression of the Jews was much less vulgar and brutal than had been the case for three years previously. Jew-baiting had been ordered to cease from the very highest quarters. Evidence of persistent racialism might be and was, in fact, interpreted as vestigial rough edges of a superseded policy. It would not take much of an optimist to interpret the letting up of the pressure on the Jews as indicating a major shift in the policy of the regime. The shift might very well be a harbinger of greater relaxation of the pressures on the German people and consequently presage an enjoyment of the fruits of their constructive efforts. These sincere, hardworking, patient people had been enduring terrific frustrations since the revolution of 1933 and even long before.

Relaxed, happy, flag-draped Berlin—with all her rough edges —was, then, emphatically ready for the athletic festival and ingratiatingly eager to please her foreign visitors. Overwhelmingly, foreigners too were eager to please and few groups were distinct in their behavior. The American Negroes were, of course, exceptional sights who were pointed at, but they reported no rudeness or ugly incidents. The women from the Far East were also objects of curiosity. One of the pleasures of the Berliners late that summer was to seek out for admiration the soigné Japanese women who were, whether in kimonos or dressed in Western clothes, always brightly, though faultlessly clad. The Italian Fascists, present in very large numbers, were repulsive to a few. The notorious national tendency to enthusiasm was wrapped in conceit and arrogance. Groups of Mussolini's shouting, gesticulating partisans—both athletes and mere tourists—strutted arm in arm on Berlin's boulevards in fancy military dress as if the whole affair was a holiday for them alone.

As was the case at the winter Games seven months before, the Third Reich most devotedly pampered the journalists and the big shots. At the main Olympic stadium, which was huge anyway, the planners had arranged for compressed seating in order to accommodate a maximum number of spectators. The reporters, photographers, and radio announcers, however, had spacious seating just above the special loge for the Führer and other celebrities. Reporters, then, had the very best seats at the stadium. They were sufficiently separated so that one's arrivals and departures would not ruffle his fellows. In addition to the spacious seating for those who would narrate the festival to the world, at the main stadium alone the authorities had provided 50 telephone booths, 80 writing booths, and 63 typewriters. Near the center of Berlin a remodeled older building, now the Olympic Games Press Headquarters, held 300 more writing desks. There were free pads of paper, plenty of giveaway publicity shots, darkrooms, and secretarial assistance. Lengthy procedures for obtaining the embossed and colorful press cards and the rigorous routine for checking them were irritating, but, conversely, convinced the journalists that their estate was receiving deserved consideration.

At a complex festival like the Olympic Games, competitive sportswriters are able effectively to fasten upon "incidents" to attract their editors who are eager to raise circulation. It is the journalists' devilish, morbid seeking for disruptive and unforeseen occurrences at the Olympiads which infuriated athletic bureaucrats like Pierre de Coubertin and Avery Brundage. There were, in fact, lots of nasty things going on in Germany and, as it turned out, at this particular international sports festival. The greatly heightened patriotic pressure to win had to result in equivocal decisions by the less sober judges and fouls by youths obsessed with yearnings for victory. The Olympic Games of 1936 were full of lapses of protocol—and worse. Many were reported, yet so great was a countervailing pressure for amiability that few of the international "incidents" assumed large proportions until long afterward.

So on the evening of July 31, 1936, all Berlin was prepared and optimistic. Policemen were preparing to direct motor traffic on special routes that would not annoy the hundreds of thousands of pedestrians. The great scoreboards over the various arenas were tested and found to be operating perfectly. The messages of the loudspeakers (preceded always by harsh "*Achtung's!*") were proven to penetrate every part of all the sporting complexes. Leni Riefenstahl's photographers had loaded their movie cameras. One hundred vans had stored 20,000 doves in cages under the stands of the main stadium. There they rustled and cooed.

As for the athletes themselves, they endured the inevitable, gnawing anguish only they can know. Before them was a great contest—the greatest of them all. The next days would hold for many of the youths the climaxes of their lives. In their beds in darkened rooms they twisted and stared open-eyed at vivid reveries of failure. On the eve of a big meet, the scheduled competitors rarely envisage triumphs. In horrible tableaux, the world's best athletes, cursing the sweet sleep that escaped them, conjured vivid images of disaster. A strong girl, anchor in her relay on the way to an Olympic record, drops the baton in the final pass; a leading cyclist in the pack spills, taking with him many others who were innocent; a backstroker misses a turn; a gymnast pulls a sensitive tendon he had hidden from the coach; a horseman's nervous, thoroughbred mount balks before a difficult barrier; a yachtsman is fouled; a cramp causes a rower to fall over his oar. For the athletes, the nights in festive Berlin were usually passed in compulsively contemplating horrors such as these.

The next morning at the newest and biggest stadium in the

world the crowd of 110,000 had filled the concrete benches very early in order to arrange themselves for the most carefully thought out festival ever devised for an athletic meeting. Overhead the sky was overcast, threatening showers that never came. The gray stone of the vast stadium looked almost venerable and tender. The track, a band of red cinders, surrounded the cropped green grass at the center of the infield. Sharp, parallel lines of almost hypnotic intensity divided the great red swath into the lanes that would separate competing runners. The emptiness of the level center of the stadium was a striking contrast to the churning, expectant masses in the sides of the oval bowl. Hovering over the whole scene was the huge airship *Hindenburg* trailing the five-ringed Olympic flag.

For a while the opening ceremonies actually focused on the new Caesar of the modern era. Hitler accompanied by Count Baillet-Latour and Dr. Lewald left the Chancellery in his be-nickeled coach. They were followed by a long string of black, four-door Mercedes convertibles that were filled with dignitaries. All cruised slowly down the flag-bedecked and garlanded Via Triumphalis. More than 40,000 Storm Troopers and other Nazi guard corpsmen kept the ten-mile boulevard clear of the crowd twenty to thirty deep that lined the route. The cortege arrived shortly before four o'clock at the vast *Maifield* or Field of May, the parade and polo ground just west of the stadium. Hitler descended from his huge open touring car and walked across the grass in front of ranks of the competitors who were in formation for their own march into the stadium. The official entourage was to enter the stadium through a wide tunnel at the western end of the stadium. This dramatic entry had already been dubbed "the Marathon Gate." The focal trio of Germany's leader and the two principal Olympic officials was closely followed by the king of Bulgaria, the crown princes of Italy, Greece, and Sweden, and the sons of Mussolini. Then came the members of the International Olympic Committee who wore top hats, frock coats, striped trousers, and spats and had slung around their necks the specially designed (for the 1936 Olympics—another of Diem's expensive touches) gold "Olympic chain of office." More or less distributed among the other distinguished Olympic guests were Hitler's favored lieutenants. Most of his cronies were in military regalia and some wore steel helmets. Field Marshal von Mackensen paraded without the death's head on his black busby—one of the few times he had ever done so. Göring had on the sky-blue uniform of a Luftwaffe marshal. Goebbels wore a white business suit. Hitler strolled in high leather boots and was drab—though hardly inconspicuous —in the brown uniform of a Storm Trooper. The arrangement of the dignitaries was almost informal and they chatted of this and that as they passed under the stadium toward the expectant crowds who waited their leader. Hitler's emergence from the Marathon Gate was heralded by an electrically amplified fanfare of thirty trumpets. The most famous living German musician, Richard Strauss, dressed in white, energetically directed a huge orchestra and a chorus of 3,000 voices in "Deutschland über alles" and the "Horst Wessellied" and then gave a performance of a new "Olympic Hymn" which the aged composer, a culture hero of both Wilhelmian and Weimar Germany, had written especially for this occasion.

At one point in the officials' leisurely stroll toward the reviewing stand, characteristically named the "Tribune of Honor," a fair-haired little girl in a blue dress emerged from a group of standing onlookers and, with perfect self-possession, approached the center of attraction, curtsied, and handed Hitler a small bouquet of flowers. It was Dr. Carl Diem's five-year-old daughter, Gudrun. The music of orchestra and chorus played on as more than a hundred thousand people sighed tenderly. She then departed and merged again with the multitude, her appointed task accomplished. Then the fading notes of the music merged gently into the tolling of the colossal bell atop the Glockenturm at the Maifeld. Thus the historic role of Lewald's "Olympic Bell" which at last cast forth its long-prepared ceremonial command, "I summon the youth of the world!"

As the enormous clapper slammed every 30 seconds the officials composed themselves at the Tribune of Honor. Just as the bell's last reverberations were dimming the finest athletes of the world began their traditional march into the stadium to pass before the honored guests and the multitudes. Since Greece originated the Olympic Games in antiquity and hosted the first Olympiad of the modern era, her team, preceded by her flag-bearer, came first from the tunnel. Most Greek athletes wore dark blue blazers. Some were in fustanella. Then came the Egyptians wearing maroon fezes. Since it is *Aegypten* in the language of the hosts, Egypt was thus first in alphabetical order. Each of the variously and colorfully clad 50 teams of athletes and officials made a tour of the 400-meter track and then took a place in the closely cropped, green infield. Once a team took its place, an athlete immediately stepped forward to take a position in front of his fellows and stood at attention holding a sign declaring the country of their origin.

As always, the spectacle of the assembling of the athletes was emotionally moving. The especially well-synchronized timing and efficiency as well as the great number of performers in this parade made it especially so. Still, there were shadings in the performance which in turn led to opportunities for the excited spectators to show, by applause or more vociferous expressions, their political prejudices. These demonstrations, as interpreted by the reporters, produced a few of those *contretemps* of the Olympic Games—"incidents."

The march of the athletes in 1936 was complicated by an existing, though rarely used, "Olympic" salute which resembled the Nazi "Heil" except that the open hand, palm down, was held off to the side. In a few delegations the salute was plainly Olympic; among others the gesture was clearly a tribute to the new boss of Europe. The Austrians greeted Hitler in a Nazi fashion and moved the vast crowd to love and grateful applause. The small team of Bulgarians, who could hardly mean much to the Berliners, caused a sensation when they offered a smart Nazi salute and dipped their flag to trail its tip in the red cinders—all the while doing a snappy goose step. The Germans expressed their pleasure loudly, though this performance was, in fact, for the king of Bulgaria who was at the Tribune with Hitler. Then another generous, indeed almost fervent, ovation for the French team's 250 members, all of them clad in blue jackets, white trousers, and blue berets. Some Frenchmen later claimed that their salute was Olympic, but it looked like obeisance to Hitler, as with arms raised they passed the dais upon which the beaming recipient was placed. The prophet Coubertin was right! The Olympic Games would lead to the reconciliation of nations! Never was France more loved in Germany than at that moment! Then, unfortunately for their popularity, the next team, the British (*Grossbritanien*), wearing straw hats, executed a simple "eyes right" salute as they passed the Tribune of Honor. The Germans felt that this English understatement was a slight to the host, Hitler, whom the Germans had been told was the patron of the whole festival. Tens of thousands fell sullen.

As the debuts of the teams went on the response of the Germans present was controlled and observant, keenly tuned to symbolic gestures from the foreigners. The Italian Fascists, grinning, ebullient, and giving the salute which they originated, got a warm reception. The large Japanese team, wearing cloth, peaked caps, dark blue blazers, and white trousers that only occasionally fit, were unable to produce the impression of spontaneous good will. Somehow the few Turks who emerged from the tunnel maintained the saluting position all around the track. The crowd was appreciative.

All the teams had been preceded by a flagbearer and all dipped their flags as they marched past the Tribune of Honor. That is, all except the team which was last in the alphabetical order, the *Vereinigten Staaten*, the United States. Three-hundred eighty-three Americans marched, led by Mr. Avery Brundage and their small, sturdy standard bearer, Alfred Joachim, a seven-time winner of the American all-round gymnastics championship. Joachim knew well that fitted within the tightness of established Olympic protocol was a more sacred American tradition dating from the inharmonious 1908 Games in London when, in a tart expression of Yankee arrogance, the flag-bearer then declared, "This flag dips for no earthly king." As the Americans marched past Hitler, the athletes gave him the "eyes right" and with their right hands placed their straw hats over their hearts, but Joachim, at once the focus of the multitude's attention, kept the stars and stripes where it had to be—proudly high. Light, fluttering applause (from the American spectators, no doubt), some shock (for could the Berliners be expected to be knowledgeable about fine points of American sporting customs?), and then some low whistles and stamping which were the local equivalents of Bronx cheers.[19]

Hitler had no time to show perturbation. Just after the first Americans passed him there began to emerge from the Marathon Gate the German team marching eight abreast in perfect order. They were all clad in white and wore (for some reason) yachting caps. At once the pressure was off Joachim as Richard Strauss's huge orchestra dropped the innocent march they had been playing and launched into the familiar phrases of "Deutschland über alles" and the "Horst Wessellied." Almost the entire stadium rose instantly to freeze into the "Heil Hitler" position and to stay that way. Thus the hundreds of American athletes completed their tour of the track and took their positions in the infield amidst a passionate, though somber demonstration of German patriotism.

After the German athletes took their appointed ranks on the green lawn, Pierre de Coubertin who was ailing and poor in Lausanne, was presented to the Olympic spectators in the form of a phonograph record. Over the loudspeakers his voice declared:

The important thing at the Olympic Games is not to win, but to take part, just as the most important thing about life is not to conquer, but to struggle well.

Then Dr. Lewald performed his most important duty, a purely formal one. He gave an irritatingly pompous speech. His eagerness to pander to the neoclassicism of his masters was revealed when Lewald, himself a victim of their racism, injected what was perhaps the sole discordantly racial note in the opening day's proceedings. At one point he declared,

In a few minutes the torchbearer will appear to light the Olympic fire on the tripod, when it will rise, flaming to heaven for the weeks of this festival. It creates a real and spiritual bond between our German fatherland and the sacred places of Greece founded nearly 4,000 years ago by Nordic immigrants.

He also proudly announced that the International Olympic Committee had the day before decided to establish Richard Strauss's "Olympic Hymn" as the official music for all future Olympiads. Theodor Lewald (who we recall was himself largely responsible for the Games being awarded in 1932 to his country in the first place) at one point turned rhetorically to the Führer, addressing him

respectfully and gratefully as the protector of these Olympic Games to be held in this stadium, built according to your will and purpose.[20]

This oratory, which lasted for twenty minutes, was by far the longest speech of the day. Its ironies must have been perceived by some of the observers present and it was not well received, though it did provide a rest from the heightened emotional tension of the crowd. All were relieved and tensely expectant when Lewald at last turned to the man most eulogized as responsible for this enormous international meeting. Hitler advanced to the microphone and, for once, was terse:[21]

I announce as opened the Games of Berlin, celebrating the eleventh Olympiad of the modern era.

Then the huge bowl of aroused humanity was immediately raised to a pitch of throat-binding, hair-raising excitement. All kinds of marvelous things followed one another in a relentless almost voluptuous piling on of stirring symbol and sensuous glory. At a great flagpole on the infield sailors sent up a huge Olympic flag with those five rings allegorically uniting the five continents and all the national colors. Other sailors along the skyline simultaneously raised the whole range of national banners on flagpoles around the high rim of the vast bowl. All the trumpeters in the stadium sounded a long flourish as distant batteries of guns pounded a twenty-one-gun salute. Below, around the edges of the central arena, Hitler Youths opened the cages and, on cue, 20,000 doves flapped and fluttered out, circling over the crowds in a spiraling, rising, slowly diminishing cloud. The 3,000 white-clad members of the chorus and the orchestra below them gave a performance of the new official hymn of Olympism and once more the German composer conducted.

It was just as Richard Strauss's authority commanded the massed voices to silence that there suddenly appeared above the east gate of the stadium, the solitary, fair youth who held high the sacred flame, kindled by the Greek sun, carried by 3,000 devoted runners from the altar at ancient Olympia. For a moment he was still as an involuntary, thrilled gasp of admiration escaped from that vast concourse of humanity. The boy ran lightly down the steps before him, bounded on to the cinder track and, looking straight ahead, ran before the Tribune. There, he was! A polestar, a fabulous, newly minted figure of mythology! At the other end of the stadium he climbed quickly up another stairway to the marble platform over the Marathon Gate. At that platform the heartbreakingly vivid emanation of classical antiquity again paused before the emotionally silent thousands. Then the last runner turned slowly and stepped to the high, ready cauldron. He rose to his toes and dipped his torch to the bowl and regarded the leaping flames for a moment. The new god turned, quickly ascended a few more steps, and disappeared.

The flagbearers of the participating fifty nations then advanced to form a semi-circle around a small raised podium which bore on its front a silhouette of the Third Reich's eagle clutching the Olympic rings. A muscular man, Rudolf Ismayr, the German weight-lifting champion, mounted the rostrum and to the horror of those symbolically sensitive regulators of Olympic protocol who were close enough to observe the scene, grasped the tip of a swastika flag, rather than the Olympic flag which was also nearby, as he read the Olympic oath into a microphone for himself and the others:

We swear that we will take part in the Olympic Games in loyal competition, respecting the regulations which govern them in the true spirit of sportsmanship for the honor of our country and for the glory of sport.

The flag carriers lowered their banners as 5,000 athletes raised their right hands in agreement. The orchestra and chorus began the grandiose "Hallelujah Chorus" from Georg Friedrich Händel's oratorio *The Messiah* which, incidentally, was the closest that the day's ceremonies came to the Christian ideology that had guided the West for centuries until that time.

Then, an occasion evoking history, nostalgia, and piquant charm. Out from the Greek delegation on the grass there emerged a very thin man dressed in the skirt, tights, and vest of fustanella. He carried some greenery. The old fellow had been observed earlier marching near the head of the Greek team. It was Spiridon Loues! With tears running down a dark face that was like a wrinkled prune, the hero of heroes at the Olympic Games of 1896 was led to the brown-shirted Führer whom he presented with a sprig of wild olive from the sacred grove on Mount Olympus, home of the ancient gods. Loues said,

I present to you this olive branch as a symbol of love and peace. We hope that the nations will ever meet solely in such peaceful competition.

Himself deeply moved, Hitler grasped the brown hand of the modest shepherd. As the chorus rose again for another per-

formance of the "Hallelujah Chorus" the teams and the emotionally aroused spectators began to file out of the Olympic
stadium.

Festivities at the stadium did not end there. In the evening
at 9:00 the bowl filled again for a "Pageant of Youth" devised
by Dr. Carl Diem. There were 10,000 participants. Row after
row of boy and girl gymnasts, planted on the brilliantly illuminated sward, swayed and stretched like animated tulips. The
science and precision of movements which, of course, owed a
great deal to the German experience with festivals of the *Turn-
erschaften*, were softened by flowing draperies. Then the best
ballet dancers in Germany executed perfect maneuvers to German classical music. The evening display closed with the choral
movement of Beethoven's Ninth Symphony. Beethoven, a titan
of romantic German culture, had set Schiller's classically redolent "Ode to Joy" to music:

> Freude, schöner Götterfunken,
> Tochter aus Elysium,
> Wir betreten feuertrunken,
> Himmlische, dein Heiligthum

The most enchanted participant in all these pageants was the
Führer himself. Though he had managed to be deftly and bo-
gusly installed as the patron of the Olympic pageant, Hitler
behaved with exceptional decorum. When he was away from
the Olympic festivities, the Berliners revealed that they had
been frustrated by their leader's reserve. In his four trips between
the Chancellery and the sporting complex, Hitler was the object of frenzied adoration. Germans unable to obtain tickets for
the stadium and numbering between a million and two million
flocked the Via Triumphalis in order to glimpse him. Between
the opening ceremonies and the evening "Pageant of Youth"
the newly paved square in front of the Chancellery was packed
with more thousands who waited for Hitler to appear at a balcony so they could express their adoration. Again and again dur-

ing this first day and afterward, Hitler was warmly congratulated for his performance by all the foreign notables, including representatives of Europe's royal houses and many members of the diplomatic corps who were known to have been frightened by Nazi ambition.

Berlin was taken up with congresses, rallies, receptions, and parties. The congress on physical education for the students from thirty-one lands, which was mentioned earlier, lasted a month. There was an International Sporting Press Congress which conveniently gathered in the 693 foreign and 730 German journalists who had been given press passes for the sporting events. One special performance for the sportswriters was an exhibition, ordered by Air Marshal Göring, of stunt flying at the Tempelhof airport in Berlin.

The airplane played a role at the 1936 Olympics. The Germans had succeeded in placing gliding, which was concurrently enjoying great popularity, on the program as an exhibition sport. One of the most sought-after foreigners in Berlin was the American Nordic, Charles Lindbergh. He became the man of the hour in Berlin after his speech to the Richthofen Pursuit Squadron. At the time troubled over the growing destructive potential of techniques for aerial bombardment, Lindbergh proposed a toast to the fighter pilots:

Here's to the bombers, may they get slower
And here's to the pursuit planes, may they grow swifter.

The *mot* was passed around Berlin. Never especially noted for his wit, Lindbergh became eagerly pursued by high-ranking Nazi officials. He toured the German plane factories. He also visited the Olympic Village and there sprinted around a practice track for photographers. The "Lone Eagle" was present at an airplane rally for participants from sixteen nations. German sporting officials had also arranged rallies for automobilists, motor cyclists, cyclists, and even one for canoeists, which was the largest of all.

Naturally the opening of each of the art and music exhibitions required festive accompaniment. The International Olympic Committee assembled for a ceremony in the main auditorium of the University of Berlin in order to mark the date of the official German request, six years before, for the honor of hosting the XIth Olympiad. On this occasion the gentlemen of the I.O.C. wore for the first time their massive, new gold chains of office. Dr. Wilhelm Frick, the Reich Minister of the Interior, had a reception in the Pergamon Museum, one of the Berlin showplaces rich in classical antiquities retrieved by the intrepid German archaeologists of the previous century. Frick's entertainment included a performance of the "Hymn to Apollo." This was the same melodic voice from the tomb that Pierre de Coubertin had presented in 1894 at his ceremonies when he intended to give classical respectability to his proposed establishment of international sporting festivals.

The new Germans were succeeding in presenting amiable faces to the world. We have already noted how Dr. Carl Diem had sought to intertwine both authentic and synthetic symbols of classical antiquity into what was, most importantly, a National Socialist festival. It is also interesting to note that Joseph Goebbels, who was far closer than Diem to the summit of power, though removed from the actual devising of the Olympic festival, worked some symbols of old Germany into concurrent festivals for burnishing the Nazis. Hitler's balcony greetings deliberately re-evoked the analogous appearances of the old German emperors before their throngs of servitors and subjects. The military parades and processions down the Via Triumphalis were partial revivals of the "Great Waitings" of the Hohenzollerns.

Goebbels and his wife entered the party-throwing lists in Berlin that August. In fact they gave the most costly party of the season. The guests were invited to the *Pfaueninsel*, a carefully landscaped and maintained island in the Havel near Potsdam. For generations the park had been a private playground for Prussian monarchs. There the dancer Barberina had performed for Frederick the Great. For the party of 1936 the army engineers had built a pontoon bridge connected with the mainland. The Goebbels' guest list numbered about 2,000 and included athletes, ambassadors, ministers, generals, admirals, writers, some members of Berlin's opera troupes, the International Olympic Committee, a couple of conspicuous German princes who had rallied to the Nazi regime and the most important and the least threatening of the *alte Kämpfer*. Also present were a number of movie starlets who were furtively pointed to as evidence of a notorious vice of the Minister of Propaganda. Goebbels himself was entirely gracious in white, double-breasted gabardine, one of the many light-colored suits he had on hand to set off his well-tanned face. Magda Goebbels was in white organdy. When the guests arrived they passed before a "guard of honor formed by young dancers dressed smartly as pages in rococo style who carried burning torches in their hands."[22] Thousands of lights were strung in the large old trees. Some of the lights formed patterns like gigantic butterflies. A display of fireworks was so noisy as to annoy some guests. Several dance bands played through the night. The food was excellent besides being plentiful—which was rare at a Nazi party—and champagne literally flowed in some little fountains with crowds around them. Very late, after some of the guests had already taken their leave, some of the tipsy starlets and girl pages broke the rules and began to fraternize with the rougher Nazi types. The resultant guttural laughter, slapping, and tickling offended a few of the more conventional society people present. Generally, however, the most distinguished group of individuals to assemble for a social function in Berlin since 1932 was convinced that Minister Goebbels could stage an elegant party just as well as his boss could present an athletic festival.

In Berlin's high society in 1936, the Goebbels had competitors. Göring gave a party in the garden of his house. For this occasion he had built a whole eighteenth-century village in miniature. There were inns, a post office, a bakery, and artisans' boutiques. The Marshal's private festival was marred by the exceptionally cold weather which portable coal heaters could not dispel. The dancers of the Berlin opera ballet shivered pathetically in their filmy costumes. Ladies who had intended to be dazzling in their light summer gowns sat with dripping noses, crabbily wrapped in overcoats. An entertainment for the startled guests was an exhibition of stunt flying by the World War I daredevil, Ernst Udet, who looped the loop and did barrel rolls frighteningly close overhead.

Joachim von Ribbentrop had just been appointed ambassador to London, the plum post in the German diplomatic corps. To celebrate his good fortune, he threw a party at his villa at Dahlem. Besides offering streams of champagne (he had earlier been a salesman for the French manufacturer, Pomery), he roasted a whole ox over an open fire.[23]

Within Germany in 1936 as well as at the parties and the athletic festival in Berlin there were plenty of rough edges and some vulgarity easily attributable to the ill breeding of the bosses of the new Germany. But no one refused the invitations and the foreigners as well as the Germans enjoyed themselves immensely. The festivals and their symbolism were significant steps that further entrenched the regime.

6
All Sports

We must give more attention to the 5,000 athletes. On any one day in the period August 2–16, 1936, winners were being determined at several sites in or near Berlin as well as on the North Sea. For purposes of narrative clarity I shall for a while impose a preconceived order of athletic events and report on a series of separate, specialized meets. Preliminary heats and trials can be discussed only exceptionally, but in an attempt at completeness, this long chapter will include some attention even to sports since dropped from the Olympic program as well as some esoteric activities such as shooting which draw critics rather than mobs of hero seekers.

In deference to the focus of worldwide spectator and journalistic interest, however, the bulk of the next several chapters will deal with the track and field events and, to a lesser extent, the swimming program. Much of Chapter 6 will be a crowded narrative. There is room for only a few tales of glory or of sinister maneuvers—though in both of these categories there were subjects aplenty in August 1936.

In a retrospective effort to give chronological and emotional dimensions to the Olympic Games of 1936, the last part of

Chapter 6 will renarrate the sporting program. The timing of the events had a great deal to do with the lasting judgment of the XIth Olympiad and we must move the muscled performers back into the world of patriotic collectivities. Chapters 7 and 8 will add the status of heroes, heroines, villains, and victims to some of the performers whose merited rhetorical rounding will have been so long delayed. But first all the sports, in a more or less artificially purified milieu:

Men's Track and Field

All these competitions, except for the 50-kilometer walk and the marathon run, took place at the Olympic stadium. The 400-meter oval track held seven lanes with eight lanes along the straightaway for the 100-meter dash. There were runways, circles, and courses for all the field events including six pits for the broad jump.

100-METER DASH. This competition opened in the presence of three co-holders of the world record, 10.3 seconds. These men were Ralph Metcalf (whom we remember as the gentlemanly silver medalist of 1932 at Los Angeles), Christian Berger of Holland, and Jesse Owens of Cleveland, Ohio. After a three-layered series of eliminations consisting of 12 "first" trial heats, four "second" trial heats, and semifinals, Owens and Metcalf found themselves matched in the final. But the winner was almost foreseen in advance, for Jesse Owens had again equaled the record in his first trial heat. In the final Owens clocked a record-breaking 10.2 which, even after pictures were produced by American photographers showing the stadium's flags as stationary, was disallowed because of the German officials' declaration that there had been a following wind. Metcalf, as in 1932 the *second* fastest man in the world, had stumbled after the gun in the final heat and was last at the start, but he had narrowed the gap between himself and Jesse Owens from two yards to one at the finish. Marinus Osendarp of Holland was third.

This is a good place to note that starting blocks had not yet been allowed for international, amateur competition in 1936; part of the equipment at every starting line was a series of little trowels to dig "toe holes." Footing was insecure and mishaps like Metcalf's were common.

200-METER DASH. In unusually cold weather and under threat of rain, Jesse Owens astonished the world by running the final of the 200 meters around a curve in the time of 20.3 seconds which broke Eddie Tolan's Olympic record of 21.2 and just missed the world record for the 200-meter straightaway by a tenth of a second. Owens pulled along with him another American, Matthew Robinson, who clocked 21.1 for second, and the fleet Hollander, Osendarp, who took third at 21.3.

400-METER RUN. The start of the final was staggered in the various lanes. Naturally the lineup as the race was underway appeared inconclusive until shortly before the finish tape was snapped. The victor was Archie Williams, a sophomore from the University of California at Berkeley. Williams's time was 46.5 seconds which was three tenths of a second less than the Olympic record set in 1932. Arthur Brown of Great Britain and James E. Lu Valle of the United States were second and third with times that were not outstanding.

800-METER RUN. This was one of the oddest races of the 1936 Olympics. John Woodruff, a freshman from the University of Pittsburgh, was "the man to watch"—for several reasons. He had been fastest in the semifinals. Woodruff also had one of the clumsiest loping gaits track fans had ever seen. He was huge and very dark and it was variously claimed that his strides measured nine, ten, and even eleven feet.

Despite the small starting field of only six in the final, Woodruff was hemmed in from the beginning and could not fight his way from behind the small, slow pack. Dr. Phil Edwards, a Canadian, led the first lap of the two-lap race. Seemingly disgusted, the American giant had slowed his pace until he was briefly, in fact, walking—last. Then he put on an ungainly sprint and, as the members of the pack did a great deal of barging among themselves, Woodruff passed *all* on the outside. A famous Italian, Mario Lanzi, pulled up near the finish to take second; Edwards was third. In the light of the existing records and the nature of the competition, the victor's time, 1:52.9, was poor, but a journalist estimated that Woodruff had run an extra 50 meters.[1]

1,500-METER RUN. The winner of the so-called "metric mile" was one of the cleverest strategists of the track events in 1936. Certainly, for the spectators, this was one of the most exciting races to observe during the Games. Of the twelve starters in the final, Glenn Cunningham was the holder of the record for the American mile and an Italian, Luigi Beccali, still in top form, was holder of the Olympic record. Cunningham seemed to be confidently setting the winner's pace until the gun lap of this race of 3¾ laps when a little man clad in black (he weighed just 133 pounds) with a full head of blond, kinky hair sped to the front for a sprint. Jack Lovelock had trained in his native New Zealand for three years for this minute (really only 56.8 seconds for his last lap) and allowed himself only the keenly satisfying indulgence of a glance back just before he broke the tape. Lovelock had, in fact, been in control the whole race and through it all gave that impression to the stands if not to his rivals. Cunningham's answering sprint brought him up second and incidentally caused him also to better the previously existing world record. Beccali, though he had been spiked early in the race, was third. Their respective times were 3:47.8 (the new world record), 3:48.4, and 3:49.2.

5,000-METER RUN. The focus of attention here was Lauri Lehtinen, holder of the world and Olympic records for the event and, we remember, one of the villains of the Los Angeles Olympics, where Lehtinen had tripped Ralph Hill. Ironically another Finnish favorite in Berlin, Ilmari Salminen, fell during the final and finished badly. Soon after the long race began the hero of the crowd became a small Japanese, Kohei Murakoso, who fought valiantly for the lead and held it several times during the middle laps. The winner in the end was Gunnar Hockert, another of the many pupils and heirs of Paavo Nurmi. He set a new world and Olympic record of 14:22.2. The Finns thus kept their Olympic championship for an event they had won every time but once (in 1920), since it had first appeared on the Olympic program in 1912. Lehtinen was second and a Swede, Jon Jonsson, was third. The pace was fast. Murakoso's fourth place time of 14:30 equaled Lehtinen's Olympic record set in 1932.

10,000-METER RUN. A fascination during this ordeal of 25 laps was the ghastly spectacle of the same Murakoso leading the large field of 31 starters and being hounded by a looming group of three tall Finns apparently chatting strategy. Near the end of the race, the Finnish consortium was abruptly dissolved and they each fought for the lead with the small Oriental. Ilmari Salminen, Arvo Askola, and Volmari Iso-Hollo, all Finns and all students of Nurmi, finished in that order. Almost in keeping with the plans of the Finns, courageous Murakoso was fourth. Salminen's time of 30:15.4 was short of Nurmi's 1924 world record by 9.2 seconds.

300-METER STEEPLECHASE. As an Olympic event this race consisted of an initial flat of 280 meters, a series of seven 390 meter laps, each with seven hurdles and a water jump, and a final flat of 68 meters. In 1936, training for the steeplechase was undeveloped and the competition was indifferent. The victor and world record setter with the then amazing time of 9:03.8 was Volmari Iso-Hollo, who had earlier taken a bronze medal in the 10,000 meters. Another Finn, Kaarlo Tuominen, was second. Alfred Dompert, a German, was third.

110-METER HURDLES. In 1935 an international committee's decision had radically altered the nature of the hurdles races. Before that time the barriers had been lighter and much more tippable. Also, three dumped hurdles brought disqualification and one could not establish a record if he upset even one. With the introduction of the weighted hurdle in the shape of an "L," the force required to down a hurdle was increased and the risk of injury consequently lessened. Post-1935 hurdlers were thereby relieved of a grievous psychological burden.[2] In 1936 Forrest G. Towns, a Georgian with a flawless rhythm of leg snap and arm-guiding action, set a new world and Olympic record of 14.1 in his semifinal heat. He won the final at 14.2. Donald Finlay of Great Britain and Frederick Pollard of the United States were second and third, in that order, in a rush at the finish line. Both were clocked at 14.4.

400-METER HURDLES. In this event the hurdles are lower by six inches than those used in the 110-meter event. The start is staggered. The barriers are placed at 35-meter intervals around the various lanes. The winning time was 52.4. However, the victorious American, Glenn Hardin, who was a powerful man on the flat, failed to equal his own Olympic record, set in a semifinal heat at Los Angeles in 1932, and was far short of his world record of 52.0 which he had set in 1934. John W. Loaring of Canada and Miquel S. White of the Philippines were close finishers for silver and bronze medals respectively.

400-METER RELAY. American quartets had won this prestigious event at every Olympiad since 1920 and they would have won the sprint relay when it first appeared on the Olympic program in Stockholm in 1912, except for a disqualification due to a trespassed zone.

The composition of the Yankee 400-meter relay team taken to Berlin was interesting because it contained Sam Stoller and Martin Glickman, the only Jews on the track and field squad. Sam and Martin had made their team because of their speed,

but their presence in Berlin inevitably had ideological implications due to the boycott movement in the United States and
due to the closely watched anti-Semitism of the host nation.

On the morning of Saturday, August 9, the day for their anti-
cipated qualifying heats and the final, Stoller and Glickman
were abruptly told that they had been replaced by Jesse Owens
and Foy Draper. Dean Cromwell, the coach for the event,
claimed that the threat of a "surprise" German team caused the
substitutions. The reporters knew that Stoller and Draper
were approximate equals with 100-meter "bests" of 10.3.

The new team from the United States was Owens, Metcalf,
Foy Draper, and Frank Wykoff, in that order. This quartet
equaled the old Olympic and world records in their trial heat.
At Owens' pass their lead in the final was five meters which
Metcalf lengthened to seven. Draper was ten meters ahead
when he passed the baton to Wykoff who snapped the tape with
a lead of fifteen meters thereby setting fresh world and Olympic
records with a time of 39.8. The final offered two instances of
that ultimate calamity for the relay sprinter. The fleet Osendarp
of Holland, anchor man of his team which was in second place
at his pass, dropped the baton, disqualifying himself and his
three teammates. The strong Canadian team also dropped the
baton at the last exchange, but recovered to finish fifth. Flawless hand-offs and grabs by the Italian team gave them second place with a time of 41.1. The much feared German team
was third with a time of 41.2.

There is little doubt that the team of Stoller, Metcalf, Glickman, and Wykoff could have won the event in Berlin, but this
foursome lacked Owens who made the new record (which held
for twenty years) possible. Accusations of vicious prejudice hung
over the American coaching staff for years. Whether or not the
accusers were justified, the substitutions were badly timed. The
bad taste exercised in this case was an indication that tougher
voracity for victory and new records was overwhelming customary standards of sportsmanship, international morality, and
the feelings of individuals. This kind of playing with athletes as

if they were insensitive animals was rare before 1936; much more common afterward.

1,600-METER RELAY. Only one member, Arthur Brown of the British four, had been good enough to take a medal in the 400-meter run. But the quartet (Frederick Wolff, Godfrey Rampling, William Roberts, and Brown) was well balanced. Their time of 3:09.0 was two seconds faster than that of the American quarter milers, none of whom had made it to the semifinals of the 400-meter run. The Americans were 2.8 seconds faster than the third-place Germans. In this race the British picked up a hero in Rampling whose time had previously not been outstanding and who in his leg of the race brought his team back from what appeared to be a hopeless position.

HIGH JUMP. The noisy, crowded Olympic ambiance is not often conducive to supreme performances in this event. The large field of starters (forty in 1936) and the time between jumps at the lower heights dissipates both the physical and the nervous energy of the best high jumpers. Still, Cornelius Johnson, a 6-foot, 5-inch college student from California, set a new Olympic record at 2.03 meters (6'8") which was two centimeters off his own world record. The next three places were tied at just two meters and the medals were decided by a jump-off which gave David Albritton and Delos Thurber of the United States second and third and Finland's Kalevi Kotkas fourth.

BROAD (LONG) JUMP. Jesse Owens, the holder of the world record of 26' 8¼", almost failed to qualify for the distance which the officials had set at 23' 5½". Not aware that competition had started, Owens ran through the pit once for practice. Astonished to learn that a judge counted his "warm-up" as a trial, he was distracted, and then fouled on his second attempt. On his third (it was his last chance!) trial to qualify Owens barely squeaked by to be one of the sixteen competitors.

The competition was extraordinary. During the finals the old Olympic record was equaled once and beaten five times. Near the end, Lutz Long of Germany precisely equaled the best that Owens had done. Then, on his last jump, Owens, combining his flawless grace and his inward competitive fury, leaped seven inches farther than he had done since arriving in Berlin. The new Olympic record was 8.06 meters (26' 5⁵⁄₁₆″). Afterward the champion and the blond runner-up walked arm in arm about the playing fields, ignoring the mobs and evidently musing to one another about fame, patriotism, and friendship. An unusually tall Japanese, Naoto Tajima, took third.

HOP, SKIP, AND JUMP (TRIPLE JUMP). Two days after winning the bronze medal in the broad jump, Tajima stretched for a new world and Olympic record in this event with an even 16 meters (52' 6″). Masoa Harada, a countryman of Tajima, was second. Jack Metcalf of Australia was third.

POLE VAULT. On August 5 at 10:30 P.M., twelve hours after the competition began, about 30,000 hungry spectators were still in the floodlit stadium. This despite the cold, drizzling weather. No old-time track fans could ever recall seeing such mass enthusiasm for a field event. The pole vault requires the most physically intricate maneuver in track and field competition plus an all-out effort. All the same, four men, exhausted and jolted (this was long before the introduction of the bending, whipping fiberglass pole) by the repeated trials, had cleared 4.25 meters. Then Earl Meadows of the University of Southern California flicked, but did not tumble, the bar at a new Olympic high of 4.35 meters (14' 3¼″). His rivals, Shuhei Nishida and Suoe Oe of Japan and Bill Sefton, a U.S.C. teammate, all failed in their attempts at that height. In the jump-off, Nishida and Oe shared the silver and bronze medals—they actually decided to slice them in two parts so each would have a share. Incidentally, in this contest, eleven men tied for sixth place.

SHOT PUT. On his next to last attempt, Hans Wöllke, a German policeman, heaved the 7.257 kg. (16 lb.) ball 16.20 meters (53' 1¾") to ease out the Finn, Sulo Barlund, who had been leading since the start. The bronze medal winner in 1936 was Gerhard Stöck of Germany. Though Wöllke's mark was a new Olympic record, it was far short of the world record of 17.40 meters (57' 1") set by the American, Jack Torrance, in 1934. Torrance was an Olympic competitor, but had injured himself before the Games and while in Berlin could only toss the iron ball a few inches farther than 50 feet.

JAVELIN. Gerhard Stöck, who was third in the shot put, took a gold medal in this event. Two Finns, Yrjö Nikkanen and Kaarlo Toivonen, were second and third. Stöck cast the 800-gram shaft 71.84 meters (238' 7")—far short of the best throw of the great Matti Järvinen who had held the world record for six years and whose best toss was 77.23 meters. Rather tragically, Järvinen had suffered a back injury on the eve of the 1936 Olympics and won only a fifth place with a throw of less than 70 meters. The javelin throw, incidentally, was the only field event at the Berlin Games for which new Olympic records were not set.

DISCUS. Even before August 1936, the heralded world's best discus thrower was Willi Schröder of Germany. He was just over six feet tall and therefore a little smaller than the usual champ in this event. However, Schröder compensated with the terrific centrifugal impetus of his spins, which, unfortunately, sometimes went out of control, thus heaving the tosser as well as the two kilogram (4 lb. 6⅔ oz.) dish out of the restraining ring. To his sharp embarrassment, the great German's best allowable mark in 1936 was more than five meters short of his world record of 53.10 meters (174' 2½") set in April 1935. Schröder finished fifth—just ahead of the only Greek to qualify in this Greek event.

The victor was Kenneth Carpenter with a mark of 50.48 meters (165′ 7¾″). Another American, Gordon Dunn, was second. Giorgio Oberweger of Italy was third.

HAMMER THROW. Until 1935 it was almost an assumption at international athletic meets that only Americans or Irishmen big as whales could throw the hammer (i.e., an implement consisting of a 6.80-kilogram head, a steel chain, and a triangular handle—the whole not more than 1.22 meters [four feet] long and not weighing more than 7.257 kg. [16 lb.]). Then Karl Hein, a German carpenter, after his last spin and release, thudded the hammer to a spot distant from him by 56.49 meters (185′ 4″) to break the 24-year-old Olympic record set by the Irish-born American, Matt McGrath. The heroic—and delighted and astonished—Hein was, however, short by more than a meter of Pat Ryan's world record which was established at a meet in New York in 1913. The next two places in Berlin were taken by Erwin Blask, a German, and Oskar Warngård, a Swede.

50,000-METER WALK. This heel-and-toe event first appeared on the Olympic program in 1932. In 1936 the start and finish were in the stadium, but the 31-mile, 120-yard route meandered far into the countryside west of Berlin. The patient victor of the field of 31 starters was Harold Whitlock, an auto mechanic from Great Britain, who clocked 4 hours, 30 minutes, 41.1 seconds. It was a more than usually difficult race for Whitlock. He had been sick at the start and only occasionally led in the first half. He was pushed at the end by Arthur Schwab of Switzerland and Adalberts Bubenko of Latvia, both of whom gasped as they crossed the finish line within two minutes of Whitlock's triumph.

MARATHON. After successive modern Olympiads, this gruesome display had acquired hoary prestige and was the center of the keenest spectator interest. The 1936 marathon was too dramatic for mere summary here and will be discussed in more detail in a later chapter. The winner and breaker of all previous records was Kitei Son, who marched with the Japanese team. Less than two minutes behind him was Ernest Harper of Great Britain and 19 seconds further on was Shoryu Nan of Japan.

DECATHLON. Who is the world's greatest all-around athlete? The question is re-answered every four years in a ten-part, two-day combat in which the competitors do the 100-meter dash, running broad jump, 16-pound shot put, high jump, and 400-meter run on the first day; the 110-meter hurdles, the discus, pole vault, javelin throw, and 1,500-meter run the second day.

The decathlon is a Scandinavian invention of the turn of the century. The nature, number, and order of the events has remained constant, but the scoring system has been changed frequently, since the standardized marks are based on the state of the ten Olympic records at that time. There had been several scoring systems before a new one was inaugurated early in 1936 and there have been several more since.

A celebrity in the German newsreels during the spring and summer of 1936 had been Hans-Heinrich Sievert, an outstanding performer in all the field events, who was heralded as the world's best athlete. But Sievert had been hurt in competition during the summer and, in Berlin, three Americans, Robert Clark, Glenn Morris, and Jack Parker, dominated the struggle from the beginning. Clark led after the first day. Morris, a twenty-four-year-old automobile salesman from Colorado, had caught up and passed Clark after nine events. Morris was tall, though he weighed just 185 pounds, which is rather slight for an all-around athlete. His stringy slenderness extended to his slightly pocked, though somberly handsome face. His small eyes were close together and exuded little joy in his effort. In any case, at the start of the 1,500 meters, Glenn Morris and the packed stadium had been told by the loudspeakers in several languages that he had to beat 4:32 in the "metric mile" to win the combined event. This was far faster than he had ever run the distance in his life.

That race was one of the dramatic peaks of the Olympics. Morris was already played out. His gait was graceless and as he forced his energies, his pensive face was torn with anguish. In the second lap the stadium thunderously booed and hissed a Belgian who cut in front of him. Deeply stirred, Morris passed to lead the field, but his strides were panicked and ugly. He did cross the finish first, though, and his time was the best he had ever done—4:33.3—or a little more than a second too slow. Hideous disappointment! And then the polyglot announcer confessed that his announcement had been a gross error; there had been some mistakes in the computations. It had not been necessary for Morris to break 4:32. He was the winner with 7,900 points and on the basis of any scoring system he had surpassed all records for the decathlon. Clark was a close second and Parker was third.

PENTATHLON. The modern pentathlon has little resemblance to the ancient Greek event for all-arounders. As it stands today the pentathlon is the conception of Pierre de Coubertin who sought support for his projects from the military leaders of all nations. And soldiers—cavalry officers particularly—have been the usual competitors. The whole program takes four days and consists of a 5,000-meter cross-country ride on a horse, fencing with an épée, pistol shooting, a 300-meter swim, and a 4,000-meter cross-country run. The series was originally designed to simulate the task of a military hero who had to deliver a message through enemy territory.

In 1936 the sections of the pentathlon were held in various places in and near Berlin. The forty-two men performed before few spectators and the competitions were managed by German officers in peaked caps, riding britches, and high, spurred boots. One of their number, a classically handsome, big man with light blue eyes, Lieutenant Gotthardt Handrick, was the clear victor. Though he had been the best in none of the five events (his muscular bulk held him to fourteenth in the cross-country run), Handrick was a fine rider, fencer, and pistol shot. Second was an

American, Lieutenant Charles Leonard, who had placed fifteenth in the riding and first in the shooting. The best rider was Captain Silvano Abba of Italy who won the bronze medal.

Women's Track and Field

Track and field events for women had been on the Olympic program only since 1928. In 1936 there were just six events, all of which took place in the main stadium.

100-METER DASH. In the second preliminary heat, Helen Stephens, an eighteen-year-old farm girl from Missouri, won over her nearest rival and was clocked at 11.4, an amazing time which (like the 10.2 mark of Jesse Owens) was disallowed because of a following wind. Still, in the final, Miss Stephens beat the then holder of the Olympic record, Stanislawa Walasie-wiczowna (American journalists called her Stella Walsh) of Poland, by nearly two meters and set a time of 11.5 which stood as a new world and Olympic record. Two tenths of a second behind the Polish girl was Käthe Krauss of Germany who was third. It is worth noting that Miss Stephens' time was better by half a second than the time made by Tom Burke, winner of the 100-meter dash in the 1896 Olympic Games.

80-METER HURDLES. The new electric cameras had their triumphant usage in the trial heats and in the finals of this close competition. In the final, the four leading girls across the finish line were all hand-clocked at 11.7 seconds. Then, the international quartet stood about wringing their hands and sporadically attempting to appear casual as they and the thousands of spectators waited for the film to be developed. The loudspeaker stated that Trebisonda Valla of Italy was victorious. The next two places were given to Anny Steuer of Germany and Elizabeth Taylor of Canada.

HIGH JUMP. The first three places were tied at 1.60 meters (5′ 3″). A jump-off gave Ibolya Csák of Hungary first, Dorothy Odam of Great Britain second, and Elfriede Kaun of Germany third.

Dora Ratjen, the German favorite in the event, disappointed the coaches by placing fourth. Later it turned out that "Dora" was really Hermann Ratjen, who claimed after the war that he had been pressed into transvestite service for the Reich by some Hitler Youth leaders.[3]

JAVELIN. No woman came close to Germany's Tilly Fleischer who on her fifth throw established a new Olympic record at 45.18 meters (148′ 2¾″). Another German, Luise Krüger, was second and Marja Krasniewska of Poland was third.

DISCUS. The winner of this event was foretold, since Gisela Mauermayer held the world record for the women's discus which weighs 2 lbs. 3¼ oz., or half the weight of the men's discus. Mauermayer was also remarkable for her dignified beauty both in motion and at rest. She had long blond hair which she wore in a bun, and exceptionally fine features set off by straight black eyebrows. Gisela smiled delicately and often. Despite her appearance of modesty, this glorious woman set a new Olympic record with a mark of 47.63 meters (156′ 3³⁄₁₆″), which was almost two meters farther than the best of Jadwiga Wajsówna of Poland and more than eight meters farther than that of third place Paula Mollenhauer, also of Germany.

400-METER RELAY. German women were dominating their track and field competitions. In a preliminary heat their superbly conditioned and practiced relay team smashed all previous records with a time of 46.4 seconds. At the last exchange of the final in the event, the third girl had a ten-meter lead over the Americans. Ilse Dörffeldt, anchor in the relay, was poised with all her strength and will to maintain her lead over the American star, Helen Stephens. At the pass from Marie Dollinger, Miss Dörffeldt furiously dashed, then staggered stiffly and grotesquely to a stop. Horror of horrors! She shrieked with grief as her hands rushed wildly to her head in an effort to block out the unanimous gasp of disgust from her assembled countrymen. On the way to a gold medal for herself and her three teammates, she had dropped the baton! The four girls met and embraced as they abandoned themselves to public hysterics.

Helen Stephens crossed the finish line at 46.9 seconds and beat her British rival by eight meters. A team of Canadian girls took a close third place as the stadium churned in a tumult of fury and sympathy.

Men's Swimming and Diving

All the swimming and diving events and the water polo games took place at the aquatic sports complex just north of the main stadium. The facilities were closely modeled after those used in Los Angeles in 1932. The stands held 20,000 spectators, but in and around the water sports complex on terraces and walkways, where they were victims of splashes from the pool, was room for perhaps 10,000 more. There was scarcely room for the place judges who attempted, stopwatches in hand, to clock accurately the swimmers in the eight lanes. In the light of the ranking of victors at Los Angeles, everyone except the Germans expected the aquatic contests to be exclusively a duel between the big, affable Californians and the small, intense Japanese. There were few surprises.

One of the upsets was Ferenc Csik, a student from Budapest, who was the winner of the 100-meter freestyle. Until Csik appeared in Berlin, he was known as just another good swimmer. Somehow he survived in the trials and semifinal heats and then parted the waters in the final with a time, 57.6, that was far better than he had ever achieved before. This time, however, was off the world record of 56.4 and just short of the fresh Olympic record set by Masanori Yusa of Japan in a semifinal heat. Yusa was second in the final and another Japanese, Shigeo Arai, was third.

Jack Medica of Seattle took the 400-meter freestyle with a time of 4:44.5 which was an Olympic record, but was short of Medica's own world record by almost six seconds. Medica was hard pressed by Shumpei Uto. Another Japanese, Shozo Makino, was third.

Medica and Uto were competitors again in the 1,500-meter freestyle where their order of finish was maintained with Medica this time winning a silver medal and Uto taking a bronze. The victor, with a time of 19:13.7, was Norburu Terada of Japan.

As he arrived in Germany for the Olympics, 18-year-old Adolph Kiefer of Chicago already possessed the world record of 1:04.8 for the 100-meter backstroke. Then in Berlin he rapidly established three successive new Olympic records in his trial heat, his semifinal heat, and his final race which Kiefer won at a time of 1:05.9. Another American was second; a Japanese was third.

The vociferously partisan and irrationally optimistic German crowd that overflowed the swimming stadium had a favorite in Erwin Sietas who was celebrated and dreaded as one of the few swimmers around who was capable of sustaining the new, spectacular, butterfly breast stroke for more than a few brief sprints. However, the best time that Sietas ever registered was in the final of his event and this time was still four tenths of a second slower than the best time of Tetsuo Hamuro who touched first at 2:42.5. Once more a Japanese had demonstrated that fierce determination to succeed that took so many of his teammates to the victory ceremonies. At *these* ceremonies the innovating Sietas was second; another Japanese was third.

Disciplined will and the devoted absorption of the lessons of alert coaches carried a quartet of Japanese freestylers on to world and Olympic records in the 800-meter relay which they won with the astonishing time of 8:51.1. A celebrated American team took their silver medal 11.5 seconds after the last Japanese touched the finish and a Hungarian four took their bronze medal 9.3 seconds later still.

The Americans and the Japanese had among themselves for years been .creating their own sphere of swimming competition. Between 1932 and 1936 their teams crossed the wide Pacific for meets during which the coaches of each nation closely watched their opponents for improved techniques. Some German spectators in Berlin had been curious as to why some Yankee swimmers were wearing the rising sun of Nippon on their clinging tank suits (which at this time still rose in straps over the shoulders). The explanation was that the suits were left over from the supply used at an earlier meet with the Japanese. The American team was short of money and these costumes were quite serviceable.

The Japanese divers had been fastidiously coached in technique, but the fierce resolve that hauled the swimmers to victory was self-defeating in diving. Here stage presence and, particularly, a gallant air are essential to supremacy. Occasionally a skilled and plucky Japanese diver would lose his composure and launch into an intricate vault almost as though it were a broad jump. Intensity would foul elegance and project the diver toward an irretrievably sloppy entry and, consequently, inevitably low point awards from the judges.

Marshall Wayne, a yellow-haired, bronzed, tall, poised youth from Miami, was a kind of champion in the department of male beauty in Berlin in 1936. He had long legs, a small waist, and huge shoulders and he approached the demonstrations of his skill with a noble nonchalance. The crowded spectators at the diving contests were sometimes unruly. They had been led to believe that German experience in gymnastics plus their new coach (imported from America in 1934) would lead them to sweeps of the medals. But Marshall Wayne could silence the stands. His approach to the springboard compelled admiration.

Wayne and Richard Degener of Detroit were near equals in

the springboard competition, but Degener in his optional one-and-one-half somersault with a full twist came as near as anyone could recall to perfection while Wayne, in the same dive, was a little off. That decided the medal ranking. Another American, Al Greene, took the bronze medal and produced what the Yankee journalists greeted and proclaimed as a "grand slam."

A "little slam" was what happened when Americans got a first and a second place. This occurred in the high platform diving. Here Marshall Wayne was supreme in performance as well as looks. The American Elbert Root was second. A German, Hermann Stork, was third.

Women's Swimming and Diving

The European female swimmers were more nearly of world class than their male counterparts were.

In the finals of the 100-meter freestyle, Hendrika Mastenbroek of Holland and Jeannette Campbell who (despite the name) was Argentinian were both clocked at 1:05.9, though the judges gave the gold medal to the eighteen-year-old Dutch girl. The bronze medal went to Gisela Arndt of Germany.

Miss Mastenbroek set her first Olympic record with her dash. She set another Olympic record in the 400-meter freestyle which she won at 5:26.4. A Danish girl was second. Lenore Wingard, the American who was awarded third, will never know what her time was, since *both* third place judges forgot to start their watches—a rather characteristic occurrence in the swimming races for females where places after the first were judged and timed by intruding incompetents.[4] There were many disputed finishes.

The recently invented and feared butterfly made an appearance in the trials for the 200-meter women's breast stroke. Its dreaded practitioner was a Miss Lenk of Brazil. But the innovator's sorties above the water were brief. Miss Lenk's flits caused her to exhaust herself utterly and she had to be dragged weeping from the water after failing to qualify in her trial heat. The first three places in the final went to Hikedo Maehata of Japan with a time of 3:03.6 (she had set an Olympic record of 3:01.9 in her trial heat), Martha Genenger of Germany, and Inge Sorensen of Denmark.

During the 100-meter backstroke races the focus of public interest did not approach the water. The focus was on the elegantly dressed, glamorous, and rather noisy Eleanor Holm Jarrett, holder of the world and Olympic records in the backstroke. But she was sitting in the stands! The answer to the question, "Why is she talking and gesticulating to reporters rather than swimming?" had nothing to do with a female complaint. The explanation must wait until a later chapter.

Mrs. Jarrett empathetically shrieked, "C'mon Alice," for an American girl to press on for victory in the final of the backstroke. In vain. Helped by a novel somersault turn, Dina Senff of Holland had broken the 1932 Olympic record of Mrs. Jarrett in a trial heat with a time of 1:16.6. Miss Senff then took the final with a poor time and her teammate, the versatile Mastenbroek, was second. Very close behind in third place was Alice Bridges who had not been sufficiently pressed on by the tumult in the stands.

At a later meet in Düsseldorf, Dina Senff went on to break Mrs. Jarrett's world record with a time of 1:13.6. The meet was held on October 25, 1936, a fact that was duly recorded on page 285 of the official American report of the Olympic Games of August 1936.

What a contrast in the two finest female divers! The Californian, Marjorie Gestring, was beautifully proportioned and healthy looking. But she carried a doll as mascot and talked of how proud her father must be. She was just thirteen years old and wore functional, black tank suits. Mrs. Dorothy Poynton Hill preferred fitted lamé. She had bright blond hair, plucked her eyebrows, wore waterproof lipstick, and even at the poolside (where the others were barefoot) she ambled on fanciful high-heeled sandals with straps about the ankle. Mrs. Hill's publicity stills resembled those of a film heroine of solid reputation. Two styles of deportment; comparable wills to victory; similar excellence in performance.

In Berlin the older woman kept the crown she had won as the world's best platform diver in Los Angeles. Her polished strength also brought her a bronze medal in the springboard diving. In the springboard event, however, the victor was the unaffected child in clinging black, Marjorie Gestring.

The springboard class was the occasion of another American "grand slam," for Katherine Rawls had taken the silver medal. Since Velma Dunn, another American, was second in the platform diving, Käthe Köhler of Germany was the only non-American to take a medal in the diving events for females.

Gymnastics

All these competitions were held in Dietrich Eckart Stadium, a new structure that had been fitted into a natural bowl in a wooded ravine at the western edge of the vast sporting complex. This new stadium had a stage and, before the stage, an arena with lots of apparatus that permitted competitions for several events to take place at the same time.

A group of Germans had won at gymnastics in 1896, the first modern Olympiad, and these contests had always been dominated by Central Europeans—indeed, this was their historic conception of what sport actually consisted of. Among the 25,000 spectators, English, Japanese, or French were rarely heard.

Over the years the international program of events as well as the scoring systems had changed. In 1936 the events for men consisted of free exercises, flying rings, the side horse, parallel bars, horizontal bar, and the long horse with compulsory work and individually devised routines in each class. To complicate the scoring further, there were winners in each of the six classes, an all-around individual championship, and an all-around championship for the national teams of eight men each. Perhaps the preceding paragraph should be re-read.

A Czech, Alois Hudec, was the world champion on the flying rings and Aleksanteri Saarvala of Finland was supreme on the horizontal bar, but almost all the other world class gymnasts were Germans or German-Swiss. Karl Schwarzmann, the older, stern-faced German who was unsurpassed on the long horse and was among the first four in three other events, was the all-around champion. Schwarzmann's high scores also helped carry his German team to the all-around championship. The Swiss were second; the Finns third.

Eight nations sent teams to Berlin for the first Olympic competitions for women in individual and team gymnastics. As individuals the girls competed in the side horse, the balance beam, and the parallel bars (which for women are of uneven heights). The teams of eight also competed, as groups, in two drills—one with hand apparatus (i.e., large inflated balls, wreaths, or exercise clubs) and with the hands free.

In 1936 only team medals were awarded. The placings were in the following order: Germany, Czechoslovakia, Hungary.

Fencing

In no other sport was the field of entries so cosmopolitan. There were 300 contestants from 31 nations. The matches were held in two gymnasiums and an amphitheater in Berlin and there were eight additional strips laid down on some hard clay tennis courts near the main stadium. The eliminations went on for two weeks; it was not unusual for a fencer to begin early in the morning, not to return to his quarters until after his last match late at night. Customarily it had been a combination of experience and histrionic ability—qualities that accrue after many years of competition—that produced the very best fencers. However, in August 1936 the stamina required to stay alert for so long made for a shift toward youth—even more so than in other sports. The adaption of electrical touch apparatus also may have lessened the effect of dramatics, confidence in which comes usually with age.

In Olympic fencing for men it is customary to award medals in the foil (flexible, rectangular blade—small guard), épée (rigid, triangular blade—large bell guard), and saber (thin, triangular blade—large guard—points and cutting edges may be used to score touches). The medals are awarded both for individuals and for teams. Giulio Gaudini was victor in the foils; Franco Riccardi took the épée; and both men assisted their fellow Italians to take a gold medal in the team competition. Endre Kobos of Hungary won the saber event. Italians, Hungarians, Frenchmen, and Germans—approximately in that order—dominated all the fencing bouts after the first eliminations.

In Olympic competition the only fencing event for women is the individual foils. A series of elimination matches left a field of eight tough continental ladies, including three of the greatest fencers of modern times. One of these was Helene Mayer, the statuesque blonde and Olympic victor at Amsterdam in 1928. Under pressure from the American Olympic Committee the Nazis had admitted Miss Mayer, a non-Aryan, to their team. Another great fencer was Ellen Preis, the Austrian who had been the Olympic victor at Los Angeles in 1932. The third was a young strategist, Ilona Schacherer-Elek, a dark non-Aryan and European champion of 1934 and 1935 who fenced for Hungary. All reporters at the time remarked that each of the three had never appeared to be in better form. Their matches were fought in the amphitheater that was packed (as the fencing contests rarely were) and breathlessly quiet. The atmosphere was one in which the tension of competition was shot through with an undercurrent of race, politics, and personal destiny.

It was the fate of Helene Mayer, who for so long had been a *cause célèbre*, to play the role of star in two of the most keenly observed contests of the 1936 Olympics. One match was with Schacherer-Elek. In their match early in the finals the young

Hungarian perceived her opponent's weakness. By means of irritating affectations, she succeeded in making Mayer nervous. The results of their three encounters were 3:2, 4:4, and 5:4, leaving the Hungarian ahead on the basis of points. Subsequently, in her encounters with opponents who had a less devastating combination of skill and cruelty, Mayer picked up points faster than Schacherer-Elek. They were tied before the bout between Mayer and Preis, a contest that perhaps was the most dramatic fencing match of the age.

The Austrian and Helene Mayer, who until now had been beaten only by another non-Aryan, were in deadly earnest. In an atmosphere so tense that the crowded spectators were almost too choked to express empathetic satisfaction or dismay, the two great athletes lunged stormily or dodged with uncanny agility. Almost miraculously, the scores for their three confrontations were 2:2, 3:3, and 4:4. A draw! However, points decided the placing of the victors. And there were no further matches of any pair of the three women. In the end Ilona Schacherer-Elek was the Olympic victor in Berlin. Ellen Preis took third. As handsome Helene Mayer accepted her silver medal in the victory ceremonies before the full stadium, she held her fine profile high and offered the multitudes in her homeland a faultless "Heil Hitler!" salute.

Equestrian Events

The equestrian program, like the modern pentathlon, has usually depended upon entries from army officers. In 1936, for example, the American team was, in fact, the team from the cavalry school at Fort Riley, Kansas.

At the Berlin Olympics there were three separate equestrian events. Dressage is an exhibition of riding in which elegance and control are critical. A much more rigorous part of the program for men and mounts is an "all-around" event lasting three days and consisting of an exhibition of the horse's training, a cross-country time-trial of 21 miles over difficult terrain, and a jumping test. The third event for horses and riders is a timed jumping competition called the *prix des nations* which is carried out on the last day of the Games in the infield of the main stadium. In each event of the three-part equestrian program there are individual and team awards. In order to win a team award, each of the three horses and three riders that started must finish all sections of each event. The judging and scoring systems are based on faults and are sufficiently complex and erudite to bypass here. As might be expected at a time of heightened military alertness, there were far more entries for the equestrian events of 1936 than at any previous Olympiad.

Competition was keen and overlaid with a barely masked patriotic ardor. The cross-country route was not only unusually rugged, but seemed almost viciously contrived. Still, the etiquette of the teams required polite forbearance. Most of the foreign teams were bitterly resentful, particularly over the hideous and often fatal combined obstacle and water jump, No. 4. Here there were ghastly spills that ended with wet flailing, thrashing in the mud, and frantic attempts of the furious riders and terrified horses to regain footing. The route destroyed the composure of exquisitely trained combinations of horse and rider and wrecked the aspirations of many.

One hero of the Germans was Baron Konrad von Wangenheim, a cavalry lieutenant. He had dislocated his left arm in the three-day event and insisted that he be permitted to ride with his arm in a sling in the *prix des nations* in order that his team not be disqualified. He rode well, but at an obstacle early in the course, he was unable to tug at the reins of his mount, Kurfürst, to wheel sharply to the left and Wangenheim crashed and rolled on the ground. Nearly fainting with pain, the Prussian officer remounted and rode fidgety Kurfürst over the remaining obstacles amidst frenzied cheering.

It turned out that the section of the Olympics for horses and riders was a triumph for the new Germany. The Germans had never before done remarkably well in international equestrian contests. In 1936 there were teams from 18 nations. But for their Olympics the best of Nazi Germany's horses and riders had long before been devoted to careful and systematic preparation. Silver and bronze medals were scattered among Poles, Dutchmen, Swedes, Americans, Portuguese, and Englishmen, but the stunning result was that German cavalry officers and Prussian gentlemen won all the individual gold medals and the championships in all the team events as well. During these competitions, incidentally, a special kind of distinction fell to the Austrian General Artur von Pongracz who rode in the *prix des nations*. Though he failed to place, the general was warmly applauded, for at 72 years of age he was the oldest competitor in the 1936 Olympics.

Rowing, Sculling, and Canoeing

The rowing and sculling events were held over the 2,000-meter (13 yards less than 1¼ mile) water course at Grunau where the Organizing Committee of the XIth Olympiad had generously provided stands for some 30,000 spectators. Many more than this number, however, crowded the area near the races:

Like so many of the sports on the modern Olympic program, rowing is an English invention in which the English had been supreme in the nineteenth century and Americans excelled in the twentieth. Historically, the Canadians had also done very well. This Anglo-Saxon domination was upset in 1936 when strong individuals appeared from such unlikely places as Poland, Argentina, Denmark, and even Switzerland—which gave rise to jokes about the "Swiss navy." At Grunau the gold medal in the double sculls was taken by a British pair, Leslie Southwood and Jack Beresford. Beresford was himself a sort of special hero because this was the fifth Olympiad in which he had participated as competitor. In the prestigious race for the eight-oared shell, the University of Washington's team beat out the Italians and the Germans by less than a second to take a gold medal there. These British and American victories, however, were exceptional. The same German oarsmen who had appeared to be heavy and sluggish in all previous international competitions were now trimmed down like greyhounds. The Germans set record times that were the consequence of diligent physical conditioning and equipment that was so strong and so light in weight as to suggest the arrival of a new technology in rowing. Unexpectedly, German rowers took gold medals in the single sculls, the pair-oared shell without coxswain, the pair-oared shell with coxswain, the uncoxed fours, and the coxed fours. In 1936 the American sculls and shells weighed anywhere from 30 per cent to 70 per cent more than those of their German opponents. The weight differences were most apparent at the starts where the Germans usually dashed to impressive and disheartening leads. In 1936 the crews of the British, American, and Canadian clubs were astonished and outclassed.

Canoeing had been demonstrated at the Paris Olympics of 1924, but 1936 was the first appearance of a full program which consisted of nine events. Although the crafts used, rigid and folding kayaks and Canadian canoes, were of North American aboriginal invention, enthusiasm for the sport was confined almost entirely to Central Europeans.

An Austrian, Gregor Hradetzky, won gold medals in the one-seated, folding kayak over the distance of 10,000 meters and the one-seated rigid kayak for 1,000 meters. An Austrian pair won the 1,000 meters for two-seated, rigid kayak. Different teams of Czechs won the races for tandem Canadian canoes over the 1,000 and 10,000 meters. With a kind of token, poetic justice, a French-Canadian, Francis Amyot, was the victor in the one-man Canadian canoe. A Swedish team won in the two-seated folding kayak for the distance of 10,000 meters. Germans won the races for the two-seated, rigid kayak for 10,000 meters and the one-seated, rigid kayak for 10,000 meters. Germans, trained and equipped almost as well as the rowers, were prominent among the silver and bronze medal winners as well.

Yachting at Kiel

There were races for solo monotypes, two-man stars, five-man, six-meter sloops, and seven-man, eight-meter boats: four classes in all. Each competition consisted of seven races and victory was awarded on the basis of a point system. The special extension relay of the Olympic fire to Kiel arrived at its goal amidst stormy weather that continued and several times threatened the cancellation of the yachting program. There also was emotional storminess over disputed finishes. Germans and Italians were adamant protesters against Swedes and Norwegians for fouls that the judges did not see. The German navy supervised a huge field of entries that included yachts and sailors from Japan and several countries in South America.

The German Organizing Committee had supplied 25 twelve-foot or "monotype" class sailboats for the solo sailors who ran their course in the protected waters of Kiel harbor. The boats were new dinghies with stiff sails. The winner on the basis of his performance in his seven races was Daniel Kagchelland of Holland. A German was second; a Briton third.

The German pair won the star class competition. Swedes were second and a Dutch team was third.

The two races for small boats were relatively free of controversy which, unfortunately, deeply poisoned the judging of the performances of six- and eight-meter yachts. In the six-meter class, Great Britain, Norway, and Switzerland finished in a near tie. The judges on the spot had to endure the humiliation of appeals of their decisions to higher juries—which supported them. The final ranking was Britain first, Norway second. The Swiss team (and this is the Pandora's box of Olympic competition) was disqualified since the helmsman was found to be not eligible according to certain strict regulations concerning amateurism. So the Swedes took third place in the end.

There were howling disputes upon the announcement of the

ranking in the eight-meter class. Finally on the basis of movies taken from a balloon, Italy's team of seven got a gold medal. But a tacked-on sail-off was necessary to determine that the subsequent ranking should be Norway second and Germany third.

Wrestling and Boxing

These contests were held in two rings in Deutschland Hall. This side-by-side arrangement was objected to by the team coaches because of the disturbing comings and goings of two sets of spectators who shifted their seats to watch the most lively combat. For both wrestling and boxing there are divisions for bantam-, feather-, light-, welter-, middle-, light-heavy- and heavyweights. Boxing adds yet another division, flyweight, for the smallest men. In Olympic competition in wrestling and boxing there are meticulously detailed rules (consisting mostly of descriptions of what *cannot* be done) and a point system that reflects the concern of amateur boxing's international bureaucrats that there be no serious injuries to mar what, in origin at least, are the most deadly of sports.

The oldest style of wrestling practiced in Europe is the Graeco-Roman variety which severely limits the use of the legs, permitting holds only above the waist. Less restrictive are the catch-as-catch-can rules that had an evolutionary connection with the impromptu bouts in the provinces of the United States in the late nineteenth century. No North Americans participated in the Graeco-Roman contests in Berlin; almost all the medal winners were from a wide band of central Europe stretching from Sweden and Estonia and going through Germany, Hungary, and Czechoslovakia to Turkey whose Yasar Erkan was victor in the featherweight division.

The large American wrestling team, almost all of whom, curiously, were from Oklahoma, chafed at the delicate prohibitions of the so-called catch-as-catch-can wrestling. Worse yet, most of their severally concurrent rules disputes were complicated by linguistic difficulties. The debated problem was usually stated, "Did or did not both shoulders of a certain grappler touch the mat on his roll?" Only one of the Oklahomans, the welterweight, Frank Lewis, took a gold medal in his particular division, though several of his countrymen won silver or bronze medals in theirs. If there had been a team award (and there was not) the Oklahoma Yankees would have taken it. The other winners were from the same swath of territory in Europe that produced the best Graeco-Roman wrestlers.

Amateur wrestling attracts a limited and a not very vociferous public. The grimly engrossed fans usually express their absorption in unconscious agonies of sympathetic body English and in explosive and instantly regretted expletives of the nature of "Throw him!" or even "Break his neck!" Boxing's more numerous fans are continuously in an unrestrained tumult.

That the large American boxing team did poorly in Berlin very likely contributed to their complaints while there and later. A disagreeable jolt for the coaches upon their arrival was the requirement that the boxers weigh in each day. In contests where bulk is so important, this forced many Yankee lads to appear at the scales half starved and dried out in order to stay in a lower weight division. The judges were chauvinistic gentlemen who stemmed from the same areas of central Europe that had contributed so many of the winning wrestlers and, as it subsequently turned out, so many winning boxers. An American sports reporter wrote:

If there was ever a complete job of jobbing it was the one of the judges at Berlin. Before the competition had progressed four days, first the United States and then Great Britain threatened to withdraw. Neither did and both lived to regret the decision.[5]

The international field of 248 boxers in all eight divisions came from 31 nations. It was by far the largest competition in boxing until that time. The eliminations sometimes lasted until three o'clock in the morning. There were no team titles, but (unofficially) the Germans were ahead in medals won. The French and Argentinian boxers were close behind. An American, Louis Lauria, who placed third in the flyweight class, was awarded a separate trophy (outside the Olympic awards system) for being the "cleverest" boxer. Another Yank, Jack Wilson, who was six feet-two and weighed a mere 117 pounds, won a silver medal in the bantamweight class. Two other good American boxers, Joe Church and Howell King, were eagerly queried by reporters when they returned to New York early—even before the boxing began in Berlin. The official explanation was that they suddenly became "homesick." Rumors, never satisfactorily disposed of, had it that the pair had been caught rifling other athletes' lockers and stealing cameras in the Olympic Village. The American Olympic Committee in Berlin had been given two hours to remove these boys forthwith from the scene and the Olympic Games.

Weight Lifting

The divisions here were for feather-, light-, middle-, light-heavy-, and heavyweights. Each competitor was given three attempts at (a) a two-hands military press, (b) a two-hands snatch, and (c) a two-hands clean-and-jerk. The victors were determined by combining the weights of their best efforts in each of the three different lifts. The competitions took place on floodlit stages in Deutschland Hall.

Performances in this part of the Olympic competitions were outstanding. The performance of Khadr El Touni, an Egyptian with a huge jaw, was the most sensational of all. This middle-weight, as he grunted through the lifts for his totals, broke world records twice in the military press and once equaled the record for the snatch. His total for his three best heists was 387.5 kilograms (754½ lbs.) which was 35 kilos more than that lifted by his nearest competitor, Rudolf Ismayr, who, we remember, had grasped the Nazi flag as he took the Olympic oath for all the competing athletes at the opening ceremonies. But El Touni also did far better than any light-heavyweight and exceeded the totals of all but the five best of the world's heavyweights. Another Egyptian, Ahmed Mesbah, broke records and took a gold medal in the lightweight division. Josef Manger, a German, was victor in the prestigious heavyweight division and Germans were second to the Egyptians in the (unofficial) team competition. An American, Anthony Terlazzo, was the best featherweight. A Frenchman, Louis Hostin, was the best in the light-heavyweight class. Hostin, incidentally, competed in the only division where the world's weightlifting records existing prior to August 1936 still stood as the Games ended.

Cycling

The best wheelman have always come from those areas where they are most likely to be accorded the status of heroes. Those countries were all in Western Europe. Still, in 1936 there were entries for the various races from 29 nations. The short races took place on a new, banked, wooden track near the Witzleben broadcasting tower. The 100-kilometer (62.14 miles) road race started along much of the same route the marathon runners had taken and added a sprawling loop through the Olympic Village and around the almost level countryside to the west of Berlin.

The only race that was decided on the basis of a time trial was the 1,000 meters from a standing start. The victor was Arie Gerrit van Vliet of Holland with a new Olympic record of 1:12.0. A cyclist from France was second; a German third.

Another 1,000-meter event was decided on the basis of scratch races between pairs. There were several rounds to narrow the finalists to four. In the final of this event, all who saw the race were appalled to see a German, Toni Merkens, foul van Vliet who was coming around him for a sure win. Naturally the Hollander protested. His disgust was compounded when German judges at once fined Merkens 100 marks and yet declared the German the victor. Van Vliet's second Olympic medal was therefore silver. Another race had determined that a French cyclist would take the bronze medal.

An analogous series of scratch races (without major incidents) decided the 2,000-meter tandem bicycle races in this order: Ernst Ihbe and Charly Lorenz of Germany first, a Dutch team second, a French pair third.

The relay race of international cycling competition is the 4,000-meter team pursuit. Here, too, the four best quartets were determined in several rounds of races between two teams. In the final bout to decide first and second places, a French team of Robert Charpentier, Jean Goujon, Guy Lapébie, and Roger Le Nizérhy took the gold medal from an Italian team. In an unusual appearance at the top levels of international cycling, the British quartet won their final to take third place from four Germans.

The XIth Olympiad was the first occasion on which the 100-kilometer road race was begun with all (in this case 128) competitors starting together. This innovation was disputed not only because races against the clock were supposed to bring out the real ability of a rider, but because the course was narrow and therefore dangerous if crowded. And to the mixed satisfaction of the warning critics, there was serious trouble in the way of fouls—unintended and otherwise. A Peruvian who was inexperienced with the new three-speed gears (one of the first major innovations in bike design in decades) caused a gruesome spill which, due to the dense packing, took down twenty of the world's best cyclists. Robert Charpentier and Guy Lapébie, victors in the team pursuit, astonished the spectators near the finish by putting on a long, desperate sprint that took Charpentier across the finish with a time of 2:33.05. Lapébie was just two tenths of a second behind. Six tenths of a second later a Swiss cyclist took third. Frenchmen won a team award given on the basis of the three best times in the road race. In the team awards Switzerland was second, Belgium third. These rankings were a badly received upset for the Italians who, for the first time since team awards were instituted in 1920, failed to win the gold medal.

Shooting

Not many people give warm attention to these contests either at the Olympics or in the reports of the Olympics. Yet for the marksmen, the tests of composure and accuracy are the ultimate trials of a superior human being. The competitions in 1936 were held at a special pavilion at Wannsee. There were three sections of the competition: automatic pistols (six-shooters) at 25 meters at six moving silhouettes; target pistols at 50 meters; and miniature (.22 caliber) rifles at 50 meters. Cornelius van Oyen of Germany was victor in automatic pistols, another German was second, Torsten Ullman of Sweden was third. The same Torsten Ullman was first in target pistol shooting; a German was second, a Frenchman was third.

Long before the Games opened the (American) National Rifle Association had tried to stir things up in Berlin by demanding a "reasonable" rifle shooting competition. Yankee sentiment was that "twenty-twos" were so unlethal as to be beneath the consideration of real he-men. Americans also accused several of the foreign notables of not being true amateurs. The Americans sent no team and their carping was ignored. The victor in the rifle shooting was a Norwegian, Willy Rogeberg, who established with his thirty shots new world and Olympic records with a perfect score—the first ever witnessed—of 300 points. A Hungarian was second; a Pole third.

Team Sports

SOCCER. Americans are not noted for favoring this game either as spectators or as contestants. Still, a good American team showed up in Berlin, though most of them had Yugoslavian names. It was the unfortunate fate of this fine team to draw the aggressive Italians for their first match. The German referee frequently had to warn the Italians for their roughness which, in the end, resulted in serious injuries to two Americans; one because of an overt kick in the stomach; the other due to knee ligaments ripped after a deliberate shove.

The Italians were furious possibly because they had been able to score but a single goal. In the second half, the referee ordered Achille Piccini to leave the game three times. His teammates declared to all who cared to listen that the German was so incompetent as to be beneath any consideration and Piccini just refused to stop playing. Eventually the Italians surrounded the shouting referee, pinned his arms to his sides, and clapped their dirty hands over his mouth. After this scandalous show, the Americans protested, but the final score, 1–0, stood.

The German team had confidently expected a gold medal in soccer and was bitter when it lost its second game to the little-respected Norwegian team. Some Berliners attributed this failure to the absence of Hitler at the game.

At the final soccer match on August 15 before 100,000 at the main stadium, Austria struggled against Italy in a bitter contest that went into a tense overtime period. When the Italians scored the tie-breaking goal that left the score at 2–1, they all went into paroxysm wherein the winning players and many of their joy-maddened fellow patriots quite literally rolled around, kicking on the turf and screaming themselves hoarse and feeble with happiness.

Intense patriotic emotions were not a monopoly of those nations that were playing for the highest ideological stakes in the Olympic casino. In fact, a dramatic eruption by Peruvians at the Olympic Games of 1936 led to the biggest political muddle of all. The only serious, concrete "incident" of the XIth Olympiad developed out of the soccer game between the Austrian and the Peruvian teams on Saturday, August 8, in the second round of eliminations. A cohesive and loyal, though not large, group of South Americans was on hand, thrilled, buoyant with hope, and set for victory. At the half Austria led 2–0. Then in the last minutes of the game the Peruvian eleven tied the score, forcing that horror of all referees, overtime. The first 15-minute overtime period, to the agony of all 14,000 spectators, produced no goal. The emotions of the Peruvian fans were near the breaking point as the second overtime began and then, near the end of this period in which neither Austrian nor Peruvian appeared capable of scoring, the Peruvian fans found themselves against their good sense a howling phalanx rushing the field and lending assistance to their darling warriors. In the ensuing tumult the Peruvians quickly scored two goals. The Austrians protested the final score of 4–2. A committee of the International Football Federation dutifully declared the game void and scheduled a replay for Monday, August 10, at 5:00 P.M.

An imposed condition of this second game was that all spectators were to be barred—a condition that was duly enforced by barricades and cordons of Berlin policemen. The Austrian team appeared the appointed afternoon at the eerily empty playing field where they awaited their scheduled opponents—who never showed. The Austrian eleven then returned to the Olympic Village with clean uniforms. They had been declared winners on the basis of a default whereupon they went on to defeat Poland and then to lose to Italy, thus winning a silver medal in the Olympic Games.

In the meantime, versions of these contests were being cabled to South America. On August 9 Sunday idlers in Peru were on hand by the thousands in the public squares of Lima, the capital, and at Port Callao on the seacoast. The soccer *contretemps* was the subject of the hour. Local Olympic Officials were called to meet with President Oscar Benavides who told them to withdraw the Peruvian team from the Olympics. Mobs of students began surging through the streets to the presidential palace where they sang the national anthem and chanted for a public declaration from Benavides. The president appeared at a balcony, spoke of the atrocity, and declared that he had in his hand telegrams vowing solidarity from Argentina, Chile, Uruguay, and Mexico. The crowds grew, were addressed by various impromptu soap-box orators, and moved on to tear down the Olympic flag being flown by the German consul in Lima. In Port Callao stevedores vowed not to unload a German ship and (for reasons that are unclear) a Norwegian ship at the docks. Back in Berlin the whole team of Peruvian athletes (who had succeeded only in getting the even smaller Colombian team to join them) all received a vociferous sendoff at the railway station as they left in pique for Paris. Their forfeit being irrevocable, they had indignantly rebuffed all attempts to stage a "friendship" game with the Austrians.

Naturally the German Olympic officials, as well as German diplomats, rained expressions of regret upon Peru. They declared that the unfortunate decision against the gallant South Americans was attributable to a rigid international body over which the sympathetic Germans had absolutely no control. These communications evidently had some effect in Lima, for President Benavides a few days later publicly expressed his view that unruly protests in Lima had been instigated by opportunistic Communists.[6]

FIELD HOCKEY. This game has been played for millennia in various parts of the world under various systems of rules. The rules for the game as now played internationally were codified in the middle of the nineteenth century in England, whence colonialists carried the game to India. Indigenous Indian teams evolved a short-toed stick and a technique of ball control that seemed to be inimitable. The Indians had won the Olympic competitions of 1928 and 1932. Astonishing no one, the eleven-man team from India won the final from the German team with a score of 8–1.

FIELD HANDBALL. This game, sometimes called just "handball," bears no relation to court handball as played in the United

States. It is closer to rugby football, but is played only in central Europe. The year 1936 saw its sole appearance on the Olympic program. The eleven-man team from Germany won the gold medal. Austria was second; Switzerland third.

WATER POLO. This may be the world's roughest sport. In Olympic competition, as elsewhere, what takes place beneath the surface is scarcely considered the judges' proper province. The battlers wore tight rubber caps both for identification and to prevent their ears from being torn off. In water polo it is hell to have a reputation as an outstanding player because opponents will attempt to "weaken" the star from the start. Games develop into grudge fights and the members of the seven-man teams often involuntarily spew blood as well as ingest involuntary gulps of chlorinated water.

In the competition in 1936 the tough-looking Austrians made a warm impression on the Berliners because they "Heiled" Hitler *as* they jumped into the pool. No matter. The rugged Hungarians won their final game and kept the gold medal they had won at Los Angeles four years earlier. Germany's team was second; Belgium's third.

POLO. To the west of the main stadium Werner March, the chief architect of the sporting complex, had provided a great grassy area surrounded by low bleachers. This enormous field, called the *Maifeld* or Field of May, was used as assembly grounds for parades and for the special gymnastics exhibitions that involved tens of thousands. The *Maifeld* was also a magnificent polo field.

The Argentinians boasted that they had been the first to accept the invitations of the International Polo Federation to compete in Berlin in August of 1936. Early in the spring of 1936 the Argentinians had sent 56 of their ponies to Germany to become accustomed to their new surroundings. In order to maintain their fitness on their way over to Europe, the large Argentinian team stopped off in the United States for some practice games. Then they swept easily through their preliminary matches in Berlin. The score of the final match on August 7 between Argentina and Great Britain was 11–0. That is how good the Argentinian polo team was.

BASKETBALL. Americans had succeeded in placing basketball on the programs of the 1904, 1924, and 1928 Olympic programs as an exhibition sport. The Yanks were worried as the International Olympic Committee debated the acceptance of the "Y.M.C.A. game" as it was often called. Within the International Basketball Federation, Americans had struggled to establish and preserve rules as much as possible like the existing rules in American intercollegiate play. The efforts of the Americans were never wholly successful. Even as the teams were going through the eliminations in Berlin in August 1936, the International Federation, inappropriately dominated by continental Europeans, declared a height limit of just under 6′ 3″ which would have forthwith disqualified the three tallest players on the American team then irrevocably on the scene. After indignant remonstrances, the rule was rescinded.

One embarrassment to the American team was that they had to improvise uniforms for their last two games, since their lockers were burglarized the night before their game with the Philippines. Another embarrassment for the players was due to the deliberate snubbing by American and international officials of Dr. James A. Naismith who, because he codified some rules in 1891, was known as the "inventor" of the game. When Naismith turned up in Berlin, he was nettled upon learning that there was no reception planned for him, nor was he given a pass to the scheduled basketball games. Finally the American team members got the old gentleman some free tickets and a little parade was slapped together that involved a lot of singing of many national anthems before some 200 spectators.[7]

For the basketball spectators the German organizers had provided stands seating 2,000 at some old clay tennis courts. The spectators came and went. In the finals, played slowly in rain and mud, Mexico beat out Poland for third place with a score of 26–12. The score deciding the gold and silver medals was even odder. The Americans beat Canada 19–8.

Demonstration Sports

GLIDING. This exhibition was undertaken at the urging of the Germans and, because of the nature of the sport, could attract but few spectators. The demonstrations were held above the Staaken airport which was between the Olympic Village and the sporting complex. Seven nations, all from central Europe, sent gliders and men. Unfortunately, the impact of the exhibition was marred by the death of Ignaz Stiefson, leader of the Austrian squadron, who plummeted to the earth after a wing broke. The Luftwaffe provided a squadron of planes to escort his body back to his homeland.

BASEBALL. Thanks to the diligent advertising in Berlin, the record for attendance at a single performance of this most American amusement was set on foreign soil at the Olympic stadium at a night game on August 12, 1936. A capacity audience of 100,000 was on hand as two American teams, the "World Champions" and the "Olympics" warmed up and then began to play under glaring lights which unfortunately prevented the inexperienced onlookers from easily tracing the trajectories of the tiny white ball.

Leaflets handed out in advance and printed in three languages explained what was going on—to little effect. In German, third base came across as "third location," center field as "middle-outside," and the pitcher as "thrower-in." Somehow the notion took hold among the naïve onlookers that the object of the contest was to hit the ball—at least one could *hear* this— and thousands dutifully cheered when the pellet was resoundingly smacked.[8] Many in the thronged stadium (it was not thronged for long) grumbled that there were too few players in motion at any time for this to be called a real game.

In any case the final score was 6–5, giving victory to one or another of the two teams.

The preceding narrative has been too bald, too logical, but then, even Homer had to include a catalogue of ships. We must now restore to the sequence of athletic events of the XIth Olympiad their proper sequential and patriotic tension. As has always been the case in the modern Olympic Games, the track and field events in the main stadium were the most keenly observed and most prestigious parts of the whole festival. The track and field program began on Sunday, August 2, 1936, and was finished by Monday, August 10. Since weightlifting was classed as a track and field sport in 1936, these events were also finished early. In fact, by the time of the closing ceremonies in Berlin on August 16, almost all of the American track and field stars had left for various exhibition meets and personal appearance tours in Europe.

The middle days of the two week period were taken up with such sports as shooting, canoeing, cycling, yachting, and gymnastics. The number of fencing entries was so large that some contenders were kept busy the entire two weeks. Most of the selection of the winners of the teams sports, swimming, and the equestrian competitions took place during the last days of the Games. The 1936 Olympic chronology has been summarized here for more than idle reasons. The sequence had a lot to do with the particular emotional-patriotic impact of the Olympic Games in August 1936 and for long afterward.

It should be stated here, once again, that long before the summer Games had begun, the National Socialist propaganda apparatus had led the German people to believe that they were destined to be the victors in the coming athletic struggles of national strength and will. These propaganda decrees were issued despite the fact that German athletic teams had never, as a whole, made outstanding showings at a previous Olympiad. But the keen pride that the Germans were taking in their economic and spiritual recovery and the grand role of Germany in recent international dramas (see Chapter 3) had led them to believe that oracular statements from Nazism's pulpit were likely to become true—for had not so many scoffers, enemies of the new Germany, been proven wrong in the past?

The German fans were already terrifically stimulated by the inspiring opening ceremonies of August 1. The next day they were presented with the first hero to be declared at the XIth Olympiad, Hans Wöllke, the victor and setter of a new Olympic record in the shot put—an event heretofore assumed by all but the Germans to be an exclusively American event. On the same day Tilly Fleischer broke Mildred ("Babe") Didrikson's 1932 Olympic record for the javelin throw and was, incidentally, the first German woman ever to win a gold medal in any Olympiad. Germany's cup of joy was filled to overflowing! What might the next two weeks bring? The course of this international festival promised to be yet more satisfying to the Germans than anyone might soberly have hoped.

Inevitably, the performances of Wöllke and Fleischer were cast as parts of a dramatic battle between Germany and her critics and, by extension, between dictatorship and democracy. The peaceful Olympics were a metaphorical though important contest between those who rallied around Adolf Hitler (and all that he signified) and the distant, benignly noncommittal (as far as sports were concerned, in any case) American President (and all that he signified).

It is proper here to explain the "scoring systems" used to determine national rankings in the Olympic contests. Baron Pierre de Coubertin insisted that the world should not seek *national* victors in an Olympic contest. Coubertin's lofty view in his old age did, in fact, represent an evolution of his thinking since the 1890's. What had happened was that the young French *revanchard* had become a cosmopolitan at the very time that the sports journalists of the world (Americans particularly) were seeking a system of scoring that would permit their readers to keep track of how the home-grown boys were doing. American chauvinistic interest in the Olympic Games dates from immediately after the Olympic Games of 1896 which, we remember, were dominated by Yanks. News from subsequent quadrennial festivals reinforced Americans' confidence in American power and excellence and, conversely, their intuition of the flaccid decadence of the old world. The process of settling on a scoring system took place in the 1920's and scorecards were kept up-to-the-minute in the sports sections of all the American newspapers for every Olympiad. Despite the prohibitions of the International Olympic Committee, a final, ranking scorecard was even published in the official report of the American Olympic Committee.[9] More elaborate than other systems, the American system in 1936 worked as follows: Ten points were awarded for a first place and five, four, three, two, and one points for the next five places respectively.

In wrestling, weight-lifting, canoeing, equestrian, cycling (except in road race) and gymnastics (except in the women's all-around competition), first three places only are scored. In fencing, six places are scored in individual events and three in team events. In basketball, field hockey, handball, soccer, and boxing, only four places were determined. In polo, only five countries competed. Water polo is counted in with men's swimming.[10]

Scoring systems used in Europe merely kept a running account of the medals taken by each national team. The official Nazi party newspaper, the *Völkischer Beobachter*, eventually settled on a tallying system that gave three points for a gold medal, two for a silver, and one for a bronze. We should note that until 1936 it had scarcely ever been necessary to make allowances for any victorious nations aside from the Americans. However, in Berlin in August of that year, so set on victory were the National Socialists that they prepared to tally the winners yet more eagerly than the American journalists.

The German sports bureaucrats and their patriotically expectant tribe of compatriots became euphoric after the announcement of the first track and field victors. But these high spirits gradually dissipated as the Americans began to assert their customary dominance of the most prominent part of the whole Olympic program. The Nazi journalists were mortified and chagrined—for it was their assigned task to justify to the German *Volk* the evident failure of the German athletes to deliver the announced-in-advance victory. Some stacking was attempted in the first few days. The victors in the art competitions were included in the tallies of medals—for these winners, most of them Germans, had been determined before the sporting events began. One zealot, a reporter for *Der Angriff*, hastily devised an expressly Aryan scoring system that airily ignored the medals won by Negroes and presented the medals of the blacks to the first Germans that followed them. The claim was that the Negroes were not Americans (nor even humans!) at all, but were the "black auxiliaries" of the Yankee team.[11] The customary domination of the Americans, white and black, continued for a week —or until the track and field events were almost finished.

Though most Germans were proud of their own accomplishments in the nationalist revival, few could objectively have been convinced that National Socialist ideology could accomplish athletic miracles. The fact that German athletes were not sweeping the track events did not entirely dull the pleasure the Germans—or the foreigners for that matter—took in the festival as a whole. But athletic supremacy would have whetted German pride. As a vehicle for the expression of *völkisch* joy in sport and a hopeful spur to athletic excellence, the revelry directors of the Third Reich sought to devise a national yell. The *Reichs Sportblatt* printed proposals for three,

Deutschland! Deutschland! Heil! Heil! Heil!
All for Germany's Honor!
German Eagle, Fly to Victory!

plus a suggestion that the massed Germans cheer with Siegfried's smith song, "Heiao, Heiao!" from Richard Wagner's *Ring of the Nibelungen*. But in the end the *Sportblatt* was obliged to confess that no German had as yet come up with a yell spontaneously

bursting from the inner consciousness at the moment when popular enthusiasm reaches its highest pitch.[12]

After the happy delirium of the first day, when it appeared that the German athletes were indeed going to overwhelm those of all other nations including the formidable Americans, the widely read *Völkischer Beobachter* kept its own score with systems that varied from a simple recording of medals won to a ranked list based on weighted medals won. The Nazis used whatever scheme made the Germans look best. Then, as the results of the pentathlon, canoeing, shooting, and gymnastics began to be recorded, the German sports reporters foresaw that the Germans were truly going to "win" the Olympics no matter what scoring system might be used.

It was at this time, about August 9 and 10, or a little more than halfway through the program as a whole, that the Berliners and their German visitors became frantic to be admitted even to those competitions with which Germans were almost totally unacquainted and which rarely attracted vociferous spectators in any case. Germans crowded the swimming events apparently in hope that the effect of massed spectator will could move the mediocre favorites to supremacy over the superbly coached Americans and Japanese. The initially joyous mobs who flocked to the night baseball game on August 12 may have been there to see if, despite the fact that the two exhibition teams were American, they might conceivably cheer something German anyway.

Still, if there were to be constructed an enthusiasm rating on the basis of heat shown by the assembled national groups of athletes, officials, journalists, and spectators, the Germans had clear rivals. The uproarious and sometimes brutal enthusiasm of the Italians has already been remarked upon. The Japanese, conventionally viewed as being reserved, were very likely the most emotional. Teammates of the Japanese track and field athletes wailed and shrieked both in victory and defeat. Their journalists wept openly and out of control when they wrote their dispatches. And we should note that in keeping with the level of their enthusiasm, Germans, Italians, and Japanese—all from intensely militaristic nations—were all doing far better at the XIth modern Olympic Games than they had at any previous Olympiad. The correlation of enthusiasm and winners' points did not go unnoticed in the late summer of 1936.

The same days that witnessed the results of the effectively focused energies of the conspicuous totalitarians were days of carping on the part of the democrats. The Americans and the British gasped when the finals of the fencing and weightlifting seemed to produce kissing bees among huge, perspiring men. The Bulgarians seemed especially addicted to kissing. High passions revolted the traditional sportsmen. Some British athletes and coaches commented that anyone who altered his existence so monstrously as to be fit to break the records then in existence thereby made a fool of himself. A reporter for the Canadian women's track and field events noted, "We did not enter the field events, these being left to our heavier and more masculine type of opponents."[13] The man-woman problem was raised often and several officials (including some Germans who were obviously unaware of the Dora Ratjen hoax) expressed demands that women track and field athletes submit to physical examinations before registering for competition. French Olympic officials were the hottest seekers of infractions of rules or misjudgments among the coaches and judges. Americans—athletes, officials, and tourists—in the light of their decline from traditional supremacy—were rather cool. The nineteenth-century ideal of the "good loser" still had currency among them. Besides, the Americans could claim that their loss of all-around supremacy was a temporary lapse or, alternatively, that they had won the track and field events, in spite of the deconditioning trip over. Then, too, if the Americans finished in second place, no one was even close to them or to Germany.

It may be unnecessary to remind the reader that the mid-thirties was an epoch when almost all social and intellectual issues were politicized, ideologized, and polarized. A lesson drawn from the results of the 1936 Olympics was that the totalitarian politics could indeed produce wonders in fields of endeavor that were traditionally believed to be out of bounds for political ideologues. Inspired fascists could defeat decadent democrats in areas where the liberals and democrats had traditionally been supreme. We have in the discussion so far been distracted by the struggle between the two titans, Germany and the United States. In 1936 this was indeed a crucial confrontation—with its own symbolic lessons to be learned. But, it should be remembered, there were other allegorical struggles between old political ideologies and new ones. In the light of their performances in the 1936 Olympics the British who were the inventors of both modern sport and of constitutionalism and the French who were the originators of the modern Olympics and of the ideas of justice and democracy were far inferior to the Italians, Hungarians, and Japanese. The practice of modern sport came very late to those last named, all of whom skipped several stages of political evolution in arriving at their then regnant political forms.

If one looks at the final (unofficial) scoring tables as he keeps in mind the emotionally politicized atmosphere of the time, it should be clear that certain portents had to be gleaned from the "results" of the 1936 Olympics. The first table is taken from the American Olympic Committee's official report[14]; the second is from the *Völkischer Beobachter*.[15] It is worth noting here that, no doubt due to the sentimental attachment of Dr. Carl Diem to the stated ideals of Coubertin, the German official report refrained from printing a scorecard of the nations.

AMERICAN POINT TABULATION OF THE 1936 OLYMPICS

Nation	Track & Field		Swimming		Wrestling		Wgt. Lift.	Canoe-ing	Shoot-ing	Mod. Pent.	Polo	Fenc-ing	Cy-cling	Yacht-ing	Gym-n'tics.	Eques-trian	Soc-cer	Row-ing	Hand-ball	Bskt-ball.	Field Hcky.	Box-ing	Total
	Men	Women	Men	Women	Free	Gr.-R.																	
Germany	69¾	51½	25	25½	13	14	28	43	20	11	2	19	27	20	87	65	..	59	10	..	5	34	628¾
United States	203	22⅓	83	55	25	..	10	4	1	5	..	..	..	2	1	5	..	16	..	10	..	9	451⅓
Italy	20 13/22	16	..	..	..	..	..	..	1	4	..	68	5	12	..	..	10	13	..	..	..	15	164 13/22
Hungary	1 2/11	10	24	2½	20	14	..	..	5	2	3	37	..	..	4	4	..	7	3	..	..	16	152 15/22
Japan	51 13/22	7	77	16	..	..	..	..	..	..	..	..	..	..	..	..	..	..	..	..	..	..	151 13/22
Sweden	18 1/11	1	..	..	19	44	..	14	16	3	..	8	..	12	..	4	..	..	..	..	..	7	146 1/11
Finland	80¼	..	..	..	18	19	..	..	2	..	..	..	..	2	14	..	..	..	..	..	..	10	145¼
France	..	2½	7	..	10	..	10	5	5	..	..	14	39	..	..	5	..	11	..	..	3	23	134½
Netherlands	12	4⅓	2	52½	..	..	..	12	..	..	..	..	20	14	..	5	..	3	..	..	4	..	128⅚
Great Britain	43 1/11	10	2	3	..	..	..	..	..	..	5	..	6	17	..	4	..	18	..	..	..	..	108 1/11
Austria	2/11	3	1	..	..	..	5	49	..	..	..	4	..	..	..	4	5	7	5	..	..	..	83 2/11
Switzerland	9	..	..	..	..	..	..	..	..	..	..	..	4	..	46	..	..	16	4	..	..	..	79
Canada	22 1/11	8	..	2½	4	..	..	19	..	..	..	..	..	..	..	..	..	3	..	5	..	..	63 13/22
Czechoslovakia	3 1/11	..	..	..	5	5	5	25	..	..	..	..	..	..	15	..	..	..	..	..	..	..	58 1/11
Argentina	4	..	..	5	..	..	..	..	..	..	10	..	..	3	..	..	..	5	..	..	..	26	53
Poland	5 1/11	14	..	..	..	..	..	..	4	..	..	..	..	..	2	5	3	5	..	3	..	3	44 1/11
Estonia	..	..	..	..	15	18	4	..	..	..	..	..	..	..	..	..	..	..	..	..	..	5	42
Norway	5	..	..	..	..	..	..	..	10	..	..	..	..	10	..	..	4	..	..	..	..	9	38
Denmark	..	..	..	11	..	..	..	..	..	..	..	2	..	..	..	4	..	10	..	..	..	7	34
Egypt	..	..	..	..	..	..	33	..	..	..	..	..	..	..	..	..	..	..	..	..	..	..	33
India	..	..	..	..	..	4	..	..	..	..	..	..	..	..	..	..	..	..	..	..	10	..	14
Turkey	..	..	..	..	4	10	..	..	..	..	..	..	..	..	..	..	..	..	..	..	..	..	14
Mexico	..	..	..	..	..	..	..	..	..	..	4	..	..	..	..	..	..	..	..	4	..	4	12
New Zealand	10	..	..	..	..	..	..	..	..	..	..	..	..	..	..	..	..	..	..	..	..	..	10
Latvia	4	..	..	..	..	5	..	..	..	..	..	..	..	..	..	..	..	..	..	..	..	..	9
South Africa	1	..	..	..	..	..	..	..	..	..	..	..	..	..	..	..	..	..	..	..	..	8	9
Yugoslavia	..	..	..	..	..	..	..	..	..	..	..	..	..	..	8	..	..	1	..	..	..	..	9
Belgium	..	..	4	..	..	..	..	..	..	..	..	4	..	..	..	..	..	..	..	..	..	..	8
Philippines	4	..	..	..	..	..	..	..	3	..	..	..	..	..	..	..	..	..	..	..	..	..	7
Brazil	2	..	..	2	..	..	..	..	2	..	..	..	..	..	..	..	..	..	..	..	..	..	6
Australia	4	⅓	..	..	..	..	..	..	..	..	..	..	..	..	..	..	..	1	..	..	..	..	5⅓
Greece	2	..	..	..	..	..	..	..	3	..	..	..	..	..	..	..	..	..	..	..	..	..	5
Portugal	..	..	..	..	..	..	..	..	..	..	..	1	..	..	..	4	..	..	..	..	..	..	5
Rumania	..	..	..	..	..	..	..	..	..	..	..	..	..	..	..	5	..	..	..	..	..	..	5
Chile	..	..	..	..	..	..	..	..	..	..	..	..	..	3	..	..	..	..	..	..	..	..	3

GERMAN POINT TABULATION OF THE
1936 OLYMPICS

SUMMER OLYMPICS

Nation	Gold	Silver	Bronze	Points
Germany	33	26	30	181
United States	24	20	12	124
Italy	8	9	5	47
Finland	7	6	6	39
France	7	6	6	39
Hungary	10	1	5	37
Sweden	6	5	9	37
Japan	6	4	8	34
Netherlands	6	4	7	33
Great Britain	4	7	3	29
Austria	4	6	3	27
Switzerland	1	9	3	26
Czechoslovakia . . .	3	5	—	19
Canada	1	3	5	14
Argentina	2	2	3	13
Estonia	2	2	3	13
Norway	1	3	2	11
Egypt	2	1	2	10
Poland	—	3	3	9
Denmark	—	2	3	7
Turkey	1	—	1	4
India	1	—	—	3
New Zealand	1	—	—	3
Latvia	—	1	1	3
Mexico	—	—	3	3
Yugoslavia	—	1	—	2
Rumania	—	1	—	2
South Africa	—	1	—	2
Belgium	—	—	2	2
Australia	—	—	1	1
Philippines	—	—	1	1
Portugal	—	—	1	1

OLYMPIC ART COMPETITORS

Nation	Gold	Silver	Bronze	Points
Germany	5	5	2	27
Italy	1	4	—	11
Austria	1	1	2	7
Poland	—	1	2	4
Finland	1	—	—	3
Switzerland	1	—	—	3
United States	—	1	—	2
Japan	—	—	2	2
Belgium	—	—	1	1
Czechoslovakia	—	—	1	1
Sweden	—	—	1	1

WINTER OLYMPICS

Nation	Gold	Silver	Bronze	Points
Norway	7	5	3	34
Germany	3	3	—	15
Sweden	2	2	3	13
Finland	1	2	3	10
Switzerland	1	2	—	7
Austria	1	1	2	7
Great Britain	1	1	1	6
United States	1	—	3	6
Canada	—	1	—	2
France	—	—	1	1
Hungary	—	—	1	1

7
Heroes

Everyone knows that Jesse Owens was the hero of heroes of the 1936 Olympics. He deserves our detailed discussion and shall duly receive it in the later parts and the bulk of this chapter. Jesse Owens probably had no rivals as the greatest achiever of the entire group of 5,000 athletes who performed in Berlin in 1936, but there were hundreds of others whose stories are worth telling. Unfortunately for the object of narrative completeness (and perhaps even fairness) it is impossible to focus on more than a few.

That the three outstanding heroes of this chapter competed in the track and field program is not entirely arbitrary, but is an acknowledgment that the most prestigious part of the Olympic program took place on or near the red cinder oval in the main stadium. This writer was tempted to pursue the candidacy for heroic stature of such figures as Robert Charpentier, the French cyclist; Hendrika Mastenbroek, the versatile Dutch swimmer; Khadr El Touni, the remarkable weightlifter; and Willy Rogeberg, the first man to shoot a perfect score with a miniature rifle. To do so, however, would have exaggerated their stature in 1936 and have erected myths that were not in formation either soon after or long after the Games ended.

I might be queried as to why I have not chosen as heroes some of the Germans who were, as a group, the unexpected and therefore most dramatic victors of the Olympic Games. The explanation is that I felt that sport is (or should be) an activity in which one best pursues individual excellence. The German athletes were part of an emotionally and artificially aroused political collectivity. None of the German athletes stood out as sympathetic individuals or eccentrics before the Games and few did afterward. Can anyone, for example, think of a German Olympian of 1936 who captured the public imagination like the professional boxer, Max Schmeling? My choice for a German heroine would have been Helene Mayer who came so close to retaking her Olympic title in fencing despite the most difficult of personal and political circumstances. But the enthusiasm with which this non-Aryan embraced her persecutors suggests ironies so complex and even sinister, that they are outside the rubric of even a broadly conceived sports story. Other German candidates for hero were the stunningly beautiful discus thrower, Gisela Mauermayer, and the pentathlon victor, burly Lieutenant Gotthardt Handrick. But splendid as they looked and spectacularly as they performed, these two were too modest of their individual accomplishments. Before the Games they were merely characters in the newsreels who wore hooked crosses on their jerseys. After the Games they became swallowed in the German masses' self-effacing preparations for war.

The three heroes of this chapter were all representatives of rather new currents in the evolution of international athletics in the 1930's. All were members of minorities who had to gather extra courage in order even to be considered as competitors at the world championships. The careers of all three are useful paradigms for certain themes in society and politics in the middle 1930's. They all performed marvelously well in their events and then went on to have interesting careers (or fates) after the Olympic Games of 1936 were over.

Helen Stephens

Women were barred as competitors and as spectators from the ancient Olympics. One of the principles of Pierre de Coubertin was that if the international sporting congresses he envisioned were to be truly modern, they would have to be sensitive to changing popular tastes in sport. Consequently, the Olympic program has steadily grown larger, adopting such things as team games, winter sports, and the growing participation of female athletes.

The socially sanctioned participation of women in organized, competitive athletics has been closely paralleled and indeed dependent upon the growth of the women's suffrage movement, which, like the modern taste for sport, had origins in the nineteenth century. The first women athletes, in fact, were likely to be suffragettes.

In 1908 women made their first appearance in Olympic competitions as halves of figure skating pairs and also as solo figure skaters. In 1912 at Stockholm there were three aquatic events for ladies. Fencing with foils was added in 1924. In 1928 there was a five-event program in women's track and field to which were added the javelin and 80-yard hurdles in 1932.

It is worth noting here that the pressure to include women's events in the Olympics typically came from European educationalists and intellectuals. American sports bureaucrats have been the conservative resistors of competitive athletics for ladies. In both amateur and professional sports the contrasts in opportunities for men and for women are greatest in the new world. Consequently, it has required great courage for an American girl to seek excellence and personal satisfaction in manifestations of her athletic prowess.

The few years on either side of the Berlin Olympics could be considered the period in which the female athlete became good copy for the sportswriters and therefore an object of hero worship analogous to that of her male counterparts. The way to athletic glory for women had been partially paved in the 1920's by Sonja Henie, the fabled Norwegian figure skater, and by the heroic Gertrude Ederle who swam the English Channel in 1926. By the next decade there was a *Fédération sportive féminine internationale* which had meets and scientific congresses every four years. The outstanding star of the 1932 Olympics was probably Mildred "Babe" Didrikson who was a good wisecracker in her interviews with reporters and who won gold medals in the javelin throw and the hurdles. She also set a new world record in preliminaries of the high jump in Los Angeles, but was disqualified in her jump-off in the final and settled for a silver medal in that event.

One envious admirer of "Babe" Didrikson was a tall, slender girl who lived on a 115-acre farm in Callaway County in Missouri. Helen Stephens loved to run. As a child she was able to beat all the boys she knew in mile-long races home from the schoolhouse. For a while she used to trot along the side of her cousin who rode a horse. "There were a couple of ditches on the way to school and the horse and I would take them together," she later boasted.[1] As a child who lived in the open spaces, she also had been taught to use a rifle and to use it well, but she gleaned more satisfaction in rabbit hunting by running the beasts down.

Helen Stephens was "discovered" as a fifteen-year-old high-school freshman by the athletic director of the high school in Fulton, Missouri. In the process of sending entering students through the 50-yard dash, Coach Burton W. Moore clocked her at 5.8 seconds which was then the record for that distance held by Elizabeth Robinson. When Coach Moore had his watch checked by a jeweler downtown, it was pronounced sound. Burt Moore did not know what to do with this guileless, rather somber-faced prodigy who was not quite fully grown. Once in a physical education class she equaled the women's record for the standing broad jump. Helen Stephens really liked running best and Moore decided to prepare her for international competition in the sprints. He coached her in the technique of starting in the dashes so that she came out of the hunkered crouch gradually and then leaned forward more, using her powerful arms as pistons.

Helen made her first major public appearance in the summer of 1935 at a national A.A.U. meet in St. Louis. Most of the 4,000 spectators at the meet were on hand for an exhibition by "the fastest woman in the world" who then was a Polish girl dubbed "Stella Walsh" by the American sportswriters who were frightened by the orthographic treacheries of her baptized name, Stanislawa Walasiewiczowna. At the 1932 Olympics the "Polish Flyer," as she was also called, had broken Elizabeth Robinson's 1928 record for the 100 meters and had afterward set new records for almost every other running event in the women's track program, as then conceived. In St. Louis Helen Stephens was matched with the Polish girl in the final of the 50-meter dash and the American streaked to the front to tie the existing record for the event. While being congratulated for having beaten Stella Walsh, Helen looked puzzled and asked, "Who is Stella Walsh?" Though her remark was really a joke, the tale of such rustic naïveté swept through the track fans present at the meet. In the course of the meet the 17-year-old farm girl then went on to establish a new world's record of 24.4 in the 200 meters, a new world's record in the standing broad jump, and also won the ladies' shot put. Now dubbed the "Fulton Flash" or the "Missouri Express" the girl was obviously Olympic material. To the delight of the reporters, when the meet was over Stella Walsh called Helen "that greenie from the sticks." Their many races thereafter could be portrayed as grudge matches.

A rule prevented women from entering more than three events in the Olympics. Helen's two specialties in the field events, the standing broad jump and the shot put, were not on the Olympic program, so she qualified for the discus, the 100 meters, and a leg in the 400-meter relay. Alas, once in Berlin, her form with the discus was faulty (she had never been well coached for this maneuver) and she succeeded in reaching a maximum of only 112′ 7½″ which was far from her best of 133′ 6½″ and very distant from the record of 156′ 3³⁄₁₆″ established by Gisela Mauermayer. Helen finished tenth in the event.

She was more successful as a runner. The stadium eagerly awaited the appearance of this already famous sprinter. The crowds saw her first as she warmed up for her qualifying heat in the 100 meters. She was almost six feet tall, flat chested, long necked, and appeared rather rangily relaxed as she crouched for the start. Then she gave the stadium a treat by finishing ten meters ahead of her field, setting a time of 11.4 which was fully half a second better than Stella Walsh's best in 1932. To Helen's sorrow, like that of Jesse Owens who had clocked a 10.2 in one of his preliminary heats, her mark was disallowed because of a following wind. Still, Helen's time in the final was 11.5, good enough to set a new world's record (which held until broken by Wilma Rudolf in 1960). In this race Helen coaxed along the hotly pursuing Stella Walsh who set *her* best time ever of 11.7.

There are lots of "if-y" problems in sports history. As narrated in Chapter 6, Helen Stephens anchored the victorious American quartet of Harriet Bland, Annette Rogers, Elizabeth Robinson, and herself in the 400-meter relay. Going into the final exchange of that relay, Helen was trailing Ilse Dörffeldt by about ten meters when that unfortunate dropped the baton at the pass. The Americans' time in the final was 46.9; the German girls had earlier set a record of 46.4. However, the first three Germans had not done their best in their final and Helen Stephens was a very much faster runner, especially under pressure, than Dörffeldt. Would the "Missouri Express" have won her second gold medal *if* the last German girl had hung on to her baton? We can never know.

Helen's career as an amateur lasted just two years. Once back in the United States, she was bored by a lack of good competition and decided to cash in on her fame before the Tokyo Olympiad. Because there has been no professional track circuit since the nineteenth century, she toured for a while with the House of David basketball team giving half-time exhibitions of running and heaving the shot. Sometimes she was hooted at and when roused to anger, while idly tossing the iron ball from hand to hand, would take the public address system to challenge any male present to put the shot with her. Since there were few takers and the few always lost, that silenced the catcalls. A natural athlete (like her idol, the great "Babe") she subsequently became a star basketball and softball player and for a while was captain of her own touring teams. Helen was also a good fencer, swimmer, and bowler. She served as a Marine in the war and since then has remained in Missouri. For some time Miss Stephens has worked as a librarian near the farm that was the first arena for a tall rangy girl who became and remained for so long "the world's fastest woman."[2]

Kitei Son (Sohn Kee Chung)

What determines who shall have the stature of an athletic hero at a certain moment? The ideological-political tensions of the 1930's were reflected in the propaganda themes of the time. Supreme athletic skill became spiritualized into a portentous virtue nurtured and praised as never before in modern times—and nowhere more so than in Nazi Germany. That is what made the outcome of the 1936 Olympics so significant. The weight of ideological significance was not distributed evenly over all the events on the Olympic program. The gymnasts, platform divers, and pole vaulters are required to have great strength and to have elegance and intricately managed restraint as well—but these last-named qualities were not given prestigious priority in the 1930's. Efforts requiring brutal, continuous strength and will were more keenly applauded—probably more so in 1936 than before or after. Since 1896, against Coubertin's desires and very likely against certain culturally ingrained feelings about *hubris* and good taste, the marathon had gathered hoary prestige. The Germans even referred to the 42.195-kilometer (26 mile-385 yard) run as *der klassische Lauf,* though no self-respecting classical Greek athlete would consider running one tenth that distance.

Therefore it was a peculiarly expectant, capacity crowd of 100,000 that waited in the Olympic stadium for the start of the marathon on the afternoon of August 9, 1936, in Berlin. The number of spectators in the stadium was augmented by an estimated 1,300 officials and 1,000,000 spectators outside who lined the route which wandered west along the Havel River, cut across the Grunewald, and veered northeast to a halfway point at the end of the long Avus racetrack. The runners were then to reverse their course. The final few hundred meters went through a tunnel below the stands of the stadium and then ran for a stretch along the track to the finish line before all those spectators. The appointed day for the race was hot and sunny. Most of the route was treeless and much of it was on unyielding, concrete surfaces.

There was a cosmopolitan field of 56 starters. A friend of the Germans was handsome Carlos Zabala, the tiny Argentinian who held the existing Olympic record of 2:31:36.0 which he had set in Los Angeles in 1932. For months Zabala had been training in Berlin. He was a familiar sight to the picnickers and hikers as he practiced pacing in the Grunewald. Three young Finns, Tamila, Muinonen, and Tarkianen, were also notorious. The Nordics were big and crafty. The word most often mentioned in connection with them was "tactics"—for the pupils of Paavo Nurmi were known for the passing of arcane confidences among themselves during distance races and for practicing an alternate-lead technique that extended their capabilities and incidentally demoralized their non-Finnish opponents. There were also some fabled distance runners from South Africa and Sweden and one from Portugal. The oldest of the starters was Ernest

Harper, an Englishman whose contorted, worried face while running made him look both ancient and awful.

In April of 1935 some rumors had come all the way from Tokyo that someone there had broken the formidable barrier of two and a half hours for the marathon distance. Then in November there was a report of a race in which a certain Kitei Son had been clocked at 2:26:42. Son was actually a Korean (his Korean name was Sohn Kee Chung) and had been a fierce nationalist even when a child.[3] He claimed to have trained as a distance runner by carrying sand in his baggy pants and by running with rocks strapped to his back. His country had been conquered and annexed by the Japanese in 1910 and the only way for Son to compete internationally was with the hated, red, rising sun on his jersey. He traveled with the rest of the Japanese Olympic team as they crossed Asia on the trans-Siberian railway. It was a twelve-day trip from Tokyo to Berlin. One of Son's teammates was Shoryu Nan (Nam Sung Yong), another Korean who in 1936 had beaten Son in several long-distance races held on the streets of Tokyo. They were friends and contenders. Unlike the Japanese who in 1936 were wildly emotional, the Koreans gave the impression of being very stern and quiet. They ran methodically, with passive faces, and looked straight ahead. Like most distance runners, Son was small and sparely built. He weighed just 120 pounds and had very stringy, bowed legs. He wore peculiar running shoes with a split between the great and little toes, like Oriental sandals. All the while he was in Berlin, Son signed his Korean name in his national script on official registers and drew beside it a little map of Korea as well. When offered the usual opening gambit of a question as to where he was from, Son replied that he was from Korea. None of his gestures was given attention at the time.[4]

The paradoxically both reluctant and fiercely determined members of the Japanese marathon team were forgotten soon after the start of the big race. The curly-haired, grinning Zabala, wearing a white hat as he did in 1932, was clearly bidding early for a new record in the event. His "splits" at the five and ten kilometer marks were astonishing the judges and coaches and at 12 kilometers he was 1½ minutes ahead of the plucky Portuguese who most closely followed his lead. Far, far behind and clearly of the opinion that they were entirely in control of the race were the gruffly talking and easily loping Finns. Ahead of the Finns was a second group of talkers, the odd pair of the brush-cut Son and the blond Harper, who despite his apparent agony in effort and his competitive zeal, was cautioning the Oriental with whom he was running parallel and in cadence, not to panic at Zabala's hurrying figure, far ahead and small in the distance.

At the U-turn marking the halfway point, the Englishman fell back two paces to let Son go around first and then drew up again for more rhythmic treads. Son's face was expressionless, but he nodded curtly as he took advice.[5] The dangerous Finns were meanwhile narrowing the gap between them and Zabala, the leader. The little Argentinian still had a lead of almost a minute over Son and his incongruous partner.

During the long straightaway back on the Avus racetrack, Son accomplished the awful task of stepping up the tempo of his strides. He was in keen pain. As he later remarked, "The human body can do so much. Then the heart and spirit must take over."[6] Harper also adopted the change in pace. The decisive and grimmest part of the contest had begun. At the 28th kilometer, Son and Harper reached the astonished Zabala. The heartbroken little champion then knew for certain that he had squandered his strength. Zabala was able to join Son and Harper to form a trio of leaders for just 100 meters. Then he fell back in what was an emotional as well as a physical collapse. At 31 kilometers, the Argentinian, devastated, gave up. Earlier, at that same mark, Son had left Harper to fly alone.

It was just a little more than halfway through the race when Zabala, Son, and Harper passed them *going the other way* that the Finns realized that they had perhaps over-plotted. They were far behind, too far behind. Subsequently they picked up their speed, narrowing their distance from the leaders and pulling with them some other runners who had not understood Finnish chat, but had faith in its wisdom. At 33 kilometers the Finns were third, fourth, and sixth. Fifth was the other Korean, Nan, who had adhered to the Finnish strategy in the first half of the race and who now perceived its error. Nan picked up his pace. Was he too late? The Finns began to try to erode Nan's will by alternately passing him and letting him pull up, briefly. The Korean's face revealed little distress and, of course, no humor. He ran as gracefully as ever. The Finns then became frightened. In the meantime other competitors, perhaps unnerved by the sight of spectators bathing their feet in the Havel or quaffing tankards in beer gardens along the way, were ending their race by staggering into the arms of tender officials who wrapped them warmly and offered them cool drinks.

For the toughest, those who managed to stay with the leaders, the goal was not far off. At the stadium groups of trumpeters on the battlements on either side of the Marathon Gate announced with fanfares that the victor approached. Then into the expectant stadium from the dark tunnel far below the cauldron holding the Olympic fire, there emerged the small figure of Kitei Son. His appearance caused the crowd to split the air with cheers and Son graciously called forth from his reservoirs of will and power a puff of agony and exuberance which manifested itself in a graceful sprint to the finish tape, which he parted with a lunge and a grunt. Son's time of 2:29:19.2 established a new world record and the hero of the hour was thus the first to break the hard barrier of two and a half hours for a marathon. Somberly, Son sat on the grass, removed his fork-toed shoes, and leaving the tumult of the stadium behind, jogged off to the showers. The marathon victor, then, was not present when Harper threw himself at the goal two minutes and forty seconds later. The Englishman had injured his foot some time before and, desperately exhausted, just fell into the blankets of waiting attendants. Less than nine seconds behind Harper with a third place time of 2:31:42.0 was Nan! Unseen by spectators, the two had been dueling in the tunnel beneath the stands!

The too-cunning Finns had parted company at about the thirty-third kilometer and thereafter it was *sauve qui peut*. They had indeed started too slowly, but Tamila finished fourth after Nan. Muinonen was fifth a minute later still. After these finishers there was a gruesome looking trail of brave, perhaps foolish, men who crossed the finish line and collapsed into the caressing, warm robes of empathic German helpers.

It should be noted that almost all the starters and almost all the finishers of the marathon were members of nations who were not then playing for great stakes on the world's political stage. Exceptions were Harper and his English teammate, Donald Robertson, who finished seventh. The first runner to finish for France was twelfth and was, in fact, an Algerian. The only American to finish was eighteenth. The sole German was twenty-ninth and crossed the line, looking horrid, a half hour after Son did. No Italian finished. Among the thirty-six who completed the distance were a Greek (eleventh), Manoel Dias, the Portuguese who chased Zabala at the beginning of the race, two Peruvians, three South Africans, and a Bulgarian (who was last with a time of 3:08:53.8).

It was (and has remained) the expectation that the truly great marathon runner will appear out of the boondocks and that his extra oomph may be due to specialized, patriotic inspiration. Significantly, at their award ceremonies in August 1936, Kitei Son and Shoryu Nan attempted to get across to the reporters that they were Koreans and not Japanese. Son later succeeded in being a leader in the struggle for Korean independence after the war and became a coach of specifically Korean track teams. However, in 1936 the patriotic messages of tough individuals from little countries was simply passed over. So, against his wishes, Kitei Son, as a great Olympic hero, was elevated above politics where, perhaps, it is most salubrious for athletics to stay.

Jesse Owens

The most dramatic performances by minorities at the 1936 Olympics were by American Negroes. Blacks first began appearing in competitive American sports, rather tentatively, to be sure, in the 1890's. Since the overwhelming American sentiment was still against permitting them to participate fully in any aspect of life in the United States, the usual route to enter competition with whites was to join the athletic teams of those ancient citadels of tolerance, the best northeastern universities. Yet even at the Ivy League colleges, these select forerunners, these cheeky youths, often had to put up with judges who felt their probity not damaged when they cheated against a black man. Negro athletes who were winning sometimes had to defend themselves against interference on the part of resentful spectators.[7]

In view of the hostility against the Negro in general and the Negro athlete in particular, it is quite extraordinary that any of them made it to the top at all.[8] White fear and detestation had succeeded in instituting a "save the white race" period in the prizefighting industry after the heavyweight championship (1908–1915) of Jack Johnson. Much later, the skill, imperturbability, and earned riches of Joe Louis inspired many Negroes to seek personal excellence (and fame and fortune) in the fight game, as it is called. The period of preparations in the United States for the 1936 Olympics might be viewed as a sort of seed period of opportunity for the superior Negro athlete. However, if the outlook for the Negro athlete had improved, the atmosphere he competed in was still humiliating.

Even the great Joe Louis, who was assiduously quiet and publicly unobtrusive, had to fight his bouts to the accompaniment of choruses such as, "Kill the eightball! Hit him in the body! Downstairs! Downstairs! He'll quit!" Despite the rottenness of his industry's promoters, the Negro boxer had to be a "good nigger" knowing "his place." The chief demonstrable evidence that one "knew his place" consisted of "self-obliteration and a cheerful willingness to accept the white man's ban as inevitable."[9] When the Negro amateur boxer traveled with his team, local mores in the United States usually required that he eat apart from his mates and, if he was allowed to use the same hotel as they, to use the back entrance established for cleaning women and garbage men. There were, of course, no Negroes on any major league baseball team. There were no Negro swimmers and it was claimed as it still is (and as it was for distance running until the 1968 Olympics) that the Negro could never be a good swimmer because of certain inherent physical primitivisms. Even in college sports, during the time of the XIth Olympiad the Negro football player had to be alert for efforts of an opposing team or perhaps even members of his own team to cripple him "accidentally."

The happy situation described above existed in the enlightened far North. Things were worse in the South. Incidentally, relative to the Negro question, the South consisted of some states in the Midwest which had fought slavery in the Civil War. In all of these states, there was no possibility for a Negro to compete in any sport unless he competed solely with his own kind. White, Southern football teams that ventured North were able to impose their prohibition against contact with black skin. The recalcitrant Negro football star or his coach who refused to bow to the demands of the lily-whites invited deliberate maiming and risked murder.[10] Few were so brave.

Still, however dismal things appeared for the Negro athlete in the 1930's, they were somewhat better than they had been in the long, bleak period on either side of the First World War. A few Negroes had performed spectacularly well in the Olympiads of the 1920's. DeHart Hubbard won a gold medal in the broad jump at the Paris Olympics of 1924. But we can note here (as in the discussion of sports for women) that much of the early support for the inclusion of Negro Olympians came from Europeans.

The first time more than just a couple of black athletes made their appearance in international competition was at the Los Angeles Olympics in 1932 when the relative ease (and cheapness) of transportation made it possible for many of them to show up. The performances of Eddie Tolan and Ralph Metcalf were inspiring to Negro leaders who praised athletics to their people as one of the few "open" activities in which a submerged people could manifest superiority. And, however dismal this period looks from our vantage point in time, the prospects for the Negro, in sport particularly, were brighter than they had been in decades.

College enrollments of Negroes were up from what they had been ten years earlier. Ohio State University, which had about ten Negro students in 1924, had about a hundred in 1934. Some of these individuals competed in the varied intercollegiate athletic program at Ohio State. A freshman member of the track team was James Cleveland (J.C., hence "Jesse") Owens.

Jesse had a reputation even before he was recruited for the team by Coach Lawrence N. Snyder. Born in Danville, Alabama, in 1913, he had picked cotton as a small child. His mother moved North in 1920 and it was at East Technical High School in Cleveland that Jesse first attracted attention as an unusual athlete. As an uncoached teenager he is supposed to have run 100 meters in 10.3 with the assistance of a wind. It was at the Interscholastic Championships in Chicago in June 1933 that Jesse first revealed his grace and speed to a large audience. At this big meet the high schooler long-jumped 7.56 meters (24′ 9⅗″) and in his races of 100 and 200 yards performed his feat of seemingly effortlessly leaving his competitors a pathetic distance behind. In Chicago in 1933, Jesse's time for the 200 yards was 20.7 and for the 100 yards 9.4, a record unequaled until 1954 and which at this writing remains for high-school competition.

In his first year at Ohio State Jesse was already twenty-one years old, married, and the father of a small daughter. He was distracted as most freshmen are and failed to do well in his classes or to rise to the expectations of his track coaches. Still, he ended his 1934 track season by taking second in the A.A.U. nationals in the 100 meters. The winner was Ralph Metcalf who had been second to Eddie Tolan in the 1932 Olympics.

It was during the track season of April to June 1935 that Jesse's great fame began. Besides his regular races of the 100 and the 200 which he ran in a closely packed series of heats, he also ran in the 400 relay and competed in the low hurdles and in the long jump. One authority has called Saturday, May 25, 1935, "the greatest single day in the history of man's athletic achievements."[11] In Ann Arbor at a Western Conference meet on that day Jesse Owens equaled the world record in the 100 yards and set new world records in the long jump (26′ 8¼″ or 8.13 meters), 220-yard low hurdles (22.6), and the straight course 220-yard dash (20.3). Then at the national A.A.U. Championships on July 4, 1935, a capacity crowd of 15,000 at the University of Nebraska's stadium watched the "Ebony Antelope" or "Buckeye Bullet," as he was dubbed by the reporters, take only a third in the 100 meters. In this race the winner was Eulace Peacock whose record-setting time of 10.2 was disallowed because of a following wind. Second to Peacock was Ralph Metcalf. All three were Negroes. At this same meet Peacock beat Owens in the broad jump and Metcalf beat Owens in the 200 meters. Jesse was not an even-tempered, consistent performer.

There were several notable characteristics of Jesse Owens aside from his fine, dark complexion and his speed. He seems to have arrived upon the scene as a fully-formed, nearly perfect, and inflexible athlete. It is significant that, despite the expert coaching he was exposed to at Ohio State, his performances never were remarkably better than they were when he was an independent high schooler. His relationship with his coach was warm and close. Larry Snyder and Jesse would have pre-competition, inspirational, preaching-type talks that were so intense that both would end their sessions with tears streaming down their faces. One of the few fits of pique that Snyder ever had from Owens was Jesse's refusal to bow to a training command when it seemed that the favorite was being slighted due to the demands of a lesser performer on the other side of the track.[12]

In 1936 there was an established method for a handsome, perfectly formed Negro to behave in order to be admired or (possibly) even loved by the masses, black and white, of the American people. Jesse accepted the world as he found it and was hotly appreciative of affection. So he smiled with big, perfect teeth, said little, and most of what he said to the reporters was rustically humble. He avoided any trace of a cake-walking, flashy style in his deportment. He submitted, glowing with gratitude, to the grabbing demands of autograph hounds and souvenir seizers. Graciously, appreciatively, Jesse always congratulated his opponents, those fortuitously proximate individuals whose inferiority permitted him the opportunity to gather more evidence of his own lovability. As a superior individual who was a self-effacing gentleman, Jesse Owens was both a paragon and a refutation and therefore was considered "a credit to his race."

During the spring track season in 1936, Jesse was not faster, but he was more consistent. At the final Olympic tryouts early in July, he qualified in every event he tried for. The performances of his near rivals were less impressive. Ralph Metcalf would go to Berlin, but poor Eulace Peacock suffered injuries that kept him from making the team.

The American Olympic Committee allowed individual coaches of outstanding athletes to go to Berlin at their own expense, so Larry Snyder tagged along on the S.S. *Manhattan* when it sailed from New York on July 15, 1936. The trip was pleasant for Jesse. There was little opportunity for truly serious workouts on the decks of the rolling ship. He was a focus of attention and responded with glamorous modesty. His ship- and teammates, in an election smacking of the high school yearbooks, voted him second "most popular" (first was Glenn Cunningham, a fine middle-distance runner). In the meantime,

Snyder was faced with the task of obtaining more kangaroo-hide track shoes in London for his protégé. For of the three pairs that the runners were required to furnish at their own expense, two pairs had been stolen from Jesse by souvenir hunters.[13]

Long before Jesse Owens appeared in Berlin he had been a prominent subject of the German illustrateds. Snyder felt that his charge performed best in his many events when he was kept reasonably secluded before and during a meet and was given frequent rub-downs. Yet because of a democratic regularity imposed upon all the athletes at the Olympics it was difficult for Snyder to find a table at the sporting complex to administer these rub-downs. Also the rigid scheduling of the buses from and to the Olympic Village required that Jesse be cramped in small quarters and that, en route, he endure the compliments, back slapping, and roistering of fellow athletes as he was supposed to be gathering physical and psychic power for the climaxes of his life.

Once at the stadium, the mere appearance of Jesse Owens' neatly molded head from some pit below the stands would cause sections of the crowd to break out in chants of "Yes-sa Ov-enss! Yes-sa Ov-enss!" (which was the effect on the Germans of his name's orthography). "The autograph maniacs grabbed him and twisted him around and people poked the snouts of cameras into his face."[14] Some mornings at the Olympic Village the athletic hero of the hour was awakened by amateur photographers who flocked outside his bedroom window to click at the athlete before he could gather poise for one of his many appearances before the mobs in Berlin.

Jesse was determined to do what was expected of him. His training and conditioning in Berlin were far from ideal, yet it seems likely that his extraordinary yearning to please was so intensified that this last factor more than compensated for the lack of physical amenities. In the finals of his four events he either equaled (in the 100-meter dash) or set new Olympic records (in the broad jump, 200-meter dash, and 400-meter relay). In spite of all his twelve appearances in the 1936 Olympics, Jesse

Owens' supremacy was seriously threatened only once—by Lutz Long in the broad jump. His customary finishes gave much the same impression as when he was in high school. He was way ahead of his field.

Still, it was claimed at the time by several observers that Jesse Owens gave little evidence of having absorbed the lessons available from his coaches. His performances had not, in fact, been improving for some time. A British observer attributed his supremacy in the long jump solely to his speed at take-off. He could have done even better if he had had Long's kick and/or Naoto Tajima's lift.[15] And his style as a runner, upon critical, scientific observation, was less than perfect.

Actually what was most stunning about Jesse Owens in motion was that he gave the *impression* that he was not one jot or tittle away from perfection. His triumphs seemed to be "derived less from a study of the mathematics of athletics than from his possession of an exquisite body."[16] His proportions were so harmonious that he did not look outstandingly powerful. When Jesse Owens ran he never seemed to be desperately pressed. He merely focused on the finish tape and unswervingly, seemingly effortlessly, approached it faster than any competitor did. In movement he was breathtaking to watch and whether on the course or off of it, Jesse seemed incapable of an unrhythmic or graceless gesture.

Aside from the reward of four Olympic gold medals in 1936, Jesse Owens was the recipient of more adulation than any modern athlete had yet received. The hero of heroes of the 1936 Olympics was understandably euphoric and was generous enough to extend the universe of his lovers to the person who was the high priest of the racial theories that Jesse Owens was temporarily laying low. For Owens claimed that at the stadium once, while in transit, he caught sight of Adolf Hitler nearby and, "When I passed the Chancellor he arose, waved his hand at me, and I waved back at him. I think the writers showed bad taste in criticizing the man of the hour in Germany."[17]

This leads us to the tale, much better known than Jesse's Hitler story, that Germany's man of the hour pointedly snubbed the athletic hero of the Berlin Games by not congratulating the Negro for his triumphs. What gave rise to this story was the following string of events: Hitler was in his loge on August 2, the first day of competition, when Hans Wöllke broke the Olympic record for the shot put and, incidentally, became the first German to win a track or field championship in an Olympiad. Wöllke and the third place winner, also a German, Gerhard Stöck, were, at Hitler's request, led to his box for a personal congratulation. Soon afterward Hitler personally and ostentatiously congratulated the three Finns who took a "grand slam" in the 10,000-meter run. Then he greeted the Germans, Tilly Fleischer and Luise Krüger, first and second place winners in the women's javelin throw. In the meantime, Owens, Metcalf, and other Americans were running in their semifinal heats of the 100-meter dash. The only other final scheduled for that day was in the high jump which was running late. When all the German high jumpers were eliminated, Hitler left in the darkness and threatening rain and was not on hand to clasp the hands of first place Cornelius Johnson, second place David Albritton, and third place Delos Thurber—all Yanks, the first two of whom were blacks. A legitimate question to ask here is, "Was Cornelius Johnson snubbed?"

In any case, Count Baillet-Latour, president of the International Olympic Committee, sent word to Hitler that he was merely a guest of honor at the Games. He should congratulate all or none.[18] Hitler chose to congratulate none—in public at least. (Thereafter, he did warmly felicitate German victors in private, however.) So when Jesse Owens won the final of the 100 meters the next day, August 3, he was not publicly greeted by Hitler—nor was any other winner on that or any of the following days. What the "man of the hour in Germany" would have done, if ceremony required that he handle the paw of a being he considered a sub-human, is conjectural. Perhaps he would have begged off on his own; perhaps he would have beamed on all and stroked the Negro medal winners, for he had found it wise to appear hotly gracious to those whom he loathed when his ambitions demanded that he do so. But still there was enough substance here for the establishment of a persistent myth. One of the common tales which is still perpetuated in popular accounts is that in Berlin in 1936 Hitler snubbed Jesse Owens by refusing to shake his hand.[19]

Hitler and Owens were rivals for popularity in Berlin during the track and field competitions of August 2 through August 9. But Jesse Owens' reign in Berlin ended on that last day for he and other American track and field athletes were swept off on a barnstorming tour arranged long in advance by the American Olympic Committee in order to recoup some of the expenses of bringing the American amateurs to Berlin. Jesse's first stop was an exhibition meet in Cologne on August 10.[20] An incident there illustrates the fact that his kindness could, on occasion, be stronger than his keenness for victory.[21] Owens and Metcalf, the man who had been second in the 100 meters for two Olympiads in a row, were matched for this race. Twenty meters from the tape, Jesse was leading by two meters. A whim led him to slow down in favor of Ralph, a pal as well as a rival. Metcalf's time was 10.3 and Jesse (who was clocked at 10.4) was forced to realize that the chance of a lifetime, the establishment of a record of 10.2, had just escaped him![22]

Officials in Cologne gave a banquet for the American athletes which lasted until midnight. Jesse had to catch a plane for Prague the next morning at 8:30. During the trip he discovered he had no money at all and was treated to a sandwich and a glass of milk by a fellow passenger. He arrived in Prague at 4:30 in the afternoon, ran at 6:00, and then returned to Germany to run in Bochum the next day. The day after that he was in London and was informed that a high official in the A.A.U. had acted as agent for the American athletes and had signed a contract for a series of six exhibition track meets in Sweden and Norway. After being separated (for added exposure and revenue Snyder had been leading a separate group of Yanks on a different tour) Jesse and his coach were reunited in London where they confessed that they felt like "trained seals."[23] In the meantime both were being teased with offers from American promoters lusting after Jesse and any fast bucks that might be harvested due to the runner's great fame. The most sensational rumor had it that the radio comedian Eddie Cantor was offering Jesse $40,000 for just ten weeks of his time.[24] Snyder hinted to the reporters that they had better offers and that Jesse was indeed waiting for the best opportunity to snatch the financial security that was otherwise wholly unobtainable for a colored boy who had only grace, speed, and likeability to his credit.

In the face of such siren songs, the command to appear in Scandinavia was too much to bear. Jesse and Snyder refused to fly north. Claiming breach of contract, the A.A.U. suspended Jesse Owens from amateur competition. Snyder's job as manager of his particular section of the American team was taken by Glenn Cunningham who was just ahead of Jesse in the popularity poll taken on the S.S. *Manhattan* during the trip over. Larry and Jesse left immediately on the *Queen Mary* for New York and Jesse had his own Broadway ticker tape parade as he sat smiling and waving on the folded tonneau of an old Lincoln touring car. The rest of the American Olympic team came home later.

Once in New York, Jesse and his coach waited in a hotel room for the bonanza. A friend who advised them to sit tight during these days was Bill "Bojangles" Robinson, the great tapdancer, who was skeptical about all the "offers." As it turned out, none of the big deals materialized. Eddie Cantor and many others had succeeded in getting their names connected with a wholesome American hero and it had cost them nothing.

Jesse was still exquisitely graceful, supremely fast, likeable, and poor. The next spring he began his series of stunts and job changes. Before eagerly curious crowds he raced horses (and won) in New York and in Chicago.

He ran against cars, trucks, dogs, and baseball players with a head start. He ran against anything and anybody, anywhere, and when there were no contestants, he just ran to please the customers.[25]

Then when he was no longer fast, but only famous and like-able, he hung up his shoes and took a series of public relations jobs and got in trouble with the American Internal Revenue Service—but that is way beyond our story.

The great Jesse Owens made a deep impression at the Berlin Olympics and his charisma still endures, but he was, of course, not the only Negro on the scene. In fact, a favorite of some French observers was Ralph Metcalf who appeared to them to have more elegance and dignity. Second place to Jesse in the 200 meters was Matthew Robinson, a black. Archie Williams and James Lu Valle, first and third in the 400-meter run, were Negroes from California. John Woodruff, the gangling winner of the 800-meter run, was a deep brown color. Cornelius Johnson and David Albritton, the gold and silver medal winners in the high jump, have already been mentioned. The third place winner in the high hurdles was Frederick Pollard, also a black.

Negro members of the American team who failed to win med-als were the following: John Brooks, a high jumper; John Terry, a featherweight weightlifter (read it again); Jackie Wilson, James Clark, and Arthur Wilson, all boxers. Two black women on the track team took part well but failed to have their names immortalized in the record books. They were Louise Stokes and Tidye Pickett.

An outstanding member of the Canadian team, the physician, Dr. Phil Edwards, was third in the 800-meter run in 1936. It was Edwards' third Olympiad. A second Canadian Negro, Sam Richardson, competed in the hop-step-and-jump. Several mem-bers of Brazil's Olympic team were blacks as was Haiti's sole athletic emissary to the Berlin Olympics.[26]

All of these individuals, but Jesse Owens particularly, made two contributions to the world in 1936. They made the general, abstract one of gnawing away at the frontiers of human accomplishment. The Olympics and sporting competitions exist partly for this purpose. Another contribution was that they all lifted their race a little from imposed obscurity and degradation. Now it might be objected that these youths with their "impeccable manners and unimpeachable demeanor"[27] were only saying "yes" to a system of exploitation that was too rotten to serve in any form. But the scene here described was the middle 1930's in the United States. There had been 18 lynchings in 1935 and 8 in 1936—all of Negroes. If there were those, white or black, who castigated the black Olympic athletes for their excessive modesty at the time, I have been unable to locate them.

Significantly, a Briton who was dismayed at the relatively undistinguished showing by his own team, observed that, "As citizens of the Empire containing most of the Negroes in the world, we may well be delighted with their [the black athletes'] successes."[28] Those American sports fans who had some stake, psychological or otherwise, in white supremacy, were expressing fears that in order to maintain American preponderance at future Olympiads it might be necessary to send an "all-sepia" squad. Paul Gallico reassured them:

Athletes go in cycles, and our next Olympic team may by natural processes have only one or two Negro stars. But if natural processes won't work, I have great faith in the white man's ability to keep the scales balanced in his favor. He always has in the past.[29]

8
Villains, Victims

The chief hero and villain of the age and "man of the hour," as he was called, was also one of the heroes and villains of the Berlin Olympics of 1936. Without examining all the ingredients that went into the making of the triumph that was the Olympiad of 1936, we can say that its enormous success was ultimately due to sponsorship by the most powerful individual of the epoch. Shortly after his seizure of power in 1933, Adolf Hitler had promised financial and moral support for the Berlin Games. And, very likely, he was the main beneficiary of the favorable impressions the new Germany left upon the world at the great international festival of August 1936.

While writing *Mein Kampf* in prison in 1924, Hitler had included some theoretical statements about the value of purposeful, physical activity. The views on physical training, however, do not bulk large in the book and are only adjuncts of his reforming schemes for all of German education. Characteristically, Hitler viewed the failures of Germany in the past as attributable to a pedagogical regime that was too intellectual, too "un-natural."

In a race-Nationalist [*völkischen*] state the school itself must set aside infinitely more time for physical conditioning. Not a day should pass in which the young person's body is not schooled at least an hour every morning and evening, and this in every sort of sport and gymnastics.[1]

Education must seek to instill self-confidence in the young Aryan:

Through his bodily power and agility he must fortify his faith in the invincibility of his whole race and nation. For what once led the German army to victory was the sum total of the faith which each individual felt in himself, and the faith all together placed in their leadership.[2]

The only specific sport about which Hitler had strong views was boxing which those whom he reviled as "populists" regarded as "rough and unworthy." Consequently, it was natural that one of Hitler's German culture heroes was Max Schmeling. Hitler also scorned "the cultivated" who favored fencing over boxing:

No other sport is its equal in building up aggressiveness, in demanding lightning-like decision, and in toughening the body in steely agility. Naturally in the eyes of our intellectuals this is regarded as wild. But it is not the duty of a race-Nationalist state to breed colonies of peaceful aesthetes and physical degenerates.[3]

In his early theoretical treatise Hitler also proposed a reform of fashion and asked for a healthier mode of dress which would uncover the bodies of the best of Aryan youth so that

The maid should know her knight. If beautiful bodies were not completely placed in the background by our foppish modes, the seduction of hundreds of thousands of girls by bowlegged, disgusting Jew bastards would be quite impossible.[4]

Like the patriotic educational programs of "Vater" Friedrich Jahn, Hitler patriotically elevated the aggressively physical over the pensively intellectual. In fact, Jahn's muscular, anti-intellectual, reforming zeal very likely was the distant source from which Hitler gleaned his ideas about physical education. If the new German nationalist was not directly indebted to Jahn, then he restated strong motifs in German patriotism that were first forcefully stated by Jahn and persisted in the thoughts of generations of disciples. Consequently the exposure of the body and bodily prowess came to be integral themes in National Socialist educational and social policy. Still, in contrast with Benito Mussolini who was himself a sportsman, the German dictator was sedentary and extremely mistrustful of his own body which he kept covered. He was a vegetarian and a worried health crank. "To Hitler's inner nature, sport was entirely foreign."[5]

If Hitler's paradoxically, ideologically posed favoring of the body over the mind was one of his intellectual principles, another one was his detestation of cosmopolitanism. In fact, as the National Socialists moved toward complete power in Germany, it seemed at first unavoidable to Dr. Theodor Lewald, Dr. Carl Diem, and the organizers of the XIth Olympiad that the xenophobic new leader would surely wreck their project. His new *Reichssportführer*, Hans von Tschammer und Osten, and Joseph Goebbels, the Minister of Propaganda, soon convinced Germany's new boss that he should support the festival because of the benefits it might produce at home and abroad. That the presentation of the XIth Olympiad was so lavish owes much to Hitler's viewing of the festival as a grand opportunity to raise gigantic monuments and to stage civically beneficial pomp and ceremony. During the years of preparation (1933–36), Hitler did little to show that he was a sports fan other than to express his joy in the symbolically rich boxing victory of Max Schmeling over Joe Louis. His few contacts with Tschammer und Osten were ceremonials staged for the photographers. His contacts with Werner March, the architect for the *Reichssportfeld*, were more frequent and more stimulating occasions for the leader. He was pleased to be cast as the inspirer of such grandeur. Still, we recall that the Führer's usual comment on viewing the construction at the vast site was that "all was too small."

Once the meticulously synchronized, generous festival was underway, the man who was pointed to as the Maecenas of the epoch was obligingly on hand for ceremonial appearances. He delighted the crowds as he cruised slowly in a long touring car from the Chancellery to the various sporting sites and back again. He was probably convinced, as many of the journalists and athletes of the time were, that his presence and projected psychic force at a difficult contest provided the extra spiritual inspiration that pushed so many German warriors in sport on to their victories.

Hitler, then, played the role of statesman, host, and hero. Like almost all his people, Hitler was eager to please. His rejoicing in specifically German victories was intense. Upon receiving news of a German win he would grin, slap his thigh, and stomp happily. At a loss he would be crestfallen and attempt to hide it. When Ilse Dörffeldt dropped the baton, Hitler was already standing for the triggering of a grand display of jubilation. Then his face fell and he turned toward Hermann Göring as though he wished to leave. He sat down and stared at the ground. By the time the attention of the crowd returned to Hitler he had regained his composure. To Baldur von Schirach, Hitler expressed his view:

The Americans ought to be ashamed of themselves for letting their medals be won by Negroes. I myself would never even shake hands with one of them.

When Schirach suggested that the impression of amiability that was the theme of the hour might be strengthened if Hitler were to be photographed with his rival in popularity, Jesse Owens, the Führer blew up and screamed at what he thought was the grossest insult.[6] However, these reactions were viewed by few and were suppressed. Compared to the public demonstrations of the Japanese and the Italians at the 1936 Olympics, Hitler appeared restrained indeed.

If anything, the master of Germany was probably a moderating influence on political tempers in August 1936. We have already observed that he consented to the pulling down of almost all the filthy, Jew-baiting signs in order not to upset international Olympic officials. Early objections from Olympic officials that he was playing too large a role as benefactor and that he ought to be more subdued, particularly in his role of congratulator, produced compliant self-effacement. He feted German victors in private thereafter. During the preparatory stages of the Games there were discussions in the Chancellery that the new stadium be called *"Adolf Hitler Kampfbahn,"* but these proposals were never sanctioned by Hitler himself.[7] Hitler probably only dimly or casually perceived what was going on athletically at the international festival for which he was cast as host. Schemes for new adventures against the Jews and in Austria and Czechoslovakia were occupying his imagination. The triumphant leader of the new Germany was no dunce as an administrator. He correctly perceived that there was little for him to do at the Olympic Games. The preparations and then the festivities went about as well as they possibly could, since they were in the control of brilliant, inspired underlings.

The critical figure upon whom Hitler could depend was Dr. Carl Diem (1882–1962), the secretary-general of the German Olympic Committee. Since the turn of the century Diem had been an energetic leader in the cosmopolitanizing of German sport and had been campaigning for decades for a German Olympiad. He had been greatly saddened by the aborting of his and Pierre de Coubertin's plans for an Olympiad in Berlin in 1916 and was relieved when the National Socialists declared their support for Diem's international festival.

If Carl Diem was disturbed by the harsher aspects of the National Socialist regime, he stifled his internal torments. When his old friend, internationally respected, though racially tainted Dr. Lewald, was hustled from his post as president of the German Olympic Committee and was assigned to perform only window dressing functions for foreign observers, Diem took full command of preparations in Berlin. The Weimar Republic had required that the German Olympic Committee get its financing independently of the government treasury. Diem, undaunted by the seriousness of the German depression, had already gathered a large sum when the Nazis seized power in 1933. Then, suddenly, the secretary-general of the German Organizing Committee was released from money grubbing when the Nazis gave him a blank check for an athletic festival as lavish and as complex as this formidable Teutonic organizer could envisage. In return, Diem had to accept as titular President of the German Olympic Committee the *Reichssportführer*, Hans von Tschammer und Osten, the "old battler" whose actual duties were to impose the *Gleichschaltung* on German sport, to produce a victorious Olympic team, and in other ways to assure that the Olympic Games of 1936 impressed the Germans and the world at large in ways that would produce benefits for the National Socialist regime.

Scholarly, cosmopolitan, jovial Dr. Carl Diem had to tolerate a certain amount of vulgarity imposed from above. However, he objected only in private when Adolf Hitler was installed as "patron" of the Olympic Games—an intrusive innovation since heads of state were supposed to be barred from what was, in theory at least, entirely an international function. Tschammer und Osten's brutal anti-Semitic campaign aroused no public objections from the doctor, though it must be admitted that Diem's compromises never went to the point of acknowledging the strident racism of such sporting pedagogues as Bruno Malitz. The Nazis' euphoria extended to their sporting literature and Diem wrote introductions to rotogravure pamphlets and books with whole series of photos of exercising, rapturous, thin-nosed troops, their hairless, oiled bodies encumbered only by posing straps. For the low-angled Leicas of the Ministry of Propaganda these big, ideal paragons of the super race dashed happily in bright sunlight along the shores of the North Sea, put the shot, tossed the javelin, or heaved medicine balls in unison and in stirring proximity. *"Die Bewegung"* or "the Movement" as the Nazis called their cultural renaissance forced sport on the Germans as a technique for fitness and discipline, as a means of promoting the mindless joy that was to be a salient feature of the inspired *Herrenvolk.* Looking grim, barrel-chested Dr. Diem, pale, mustached, and in his fifties, even allowed himself to be photographed with other sporting bureaucrats in white shorts and running shoes as they jogged about, keeping fit on a track near the offices of the German Olympic Committee. Goebbels distributed the photo. Absent from the running group was Tschammer und Osten, a party hack with but marginal interest in sport as such.

Doctor Professor Carl Diem, scholar, sportsman, statesman, and bureaucrat was not a Nazi. In fact, besides being thrilled with his opportunities, he was also frightened and repelled by the *Gleichschaltung* in general and its effect upon sport in particular. Is it possible that this maintained balance of ambition and danger was the particular emotional mélange that made possible creative prodigies on the part of Diem and others like him? Some of the administrative smoothness of the Olympic festival in Berlin was due to the fact that the large staffing requirements provided a resting place for uprooted and talented non-Aryans. In Diem's staffs many Jews who had been fired from the German civil service found a (temporary) haven due to the loose scrutiny given to experienced personnel that Diem needed as subordinates. His wife, Liselott, herself a noted educationalist and scholar, was racially tainted by a Jewish ancestor and the couple were occasionally reminded of their peril.[8] Often their plans to journey outside of Germany were mysteriously canceled by an unknown government official. A rebellious principle of Dr. Diem's that he had to conceal until after the war was that he made a game of avoiding Hitler in the course of all his preparations for the Games of 1936. His score was nearly perfect. Dr. Theodor Lewald, who was humiliated by the Nazis, was often seen with his principal persecutor, but there is just one extant photo of the cosmopolitan scholar and the Führer to-gether.[9] Diem was, then, for a long time one of those in the silent opposition, but, terrible irony, his greatest organizational tri-umph was also one of Hitler's greatest triumphs. Both men were keenly eager to use the German athletic festival to advance the prestige of Germany. Both the super-sportsman and the super-politician, though they had totally different ideas about sport, were nationalists. One favored the old Germany; the other the new Germany.

One of the most curious results of festivity is that its organizers are the most unhinged by festivity's distortions upon intellect and judgment. As he worked for the success of the Olympics Carl Diem very likely felt that the cooperation he was receiving from the National Socialists was conclusive evidence that those whom so many foreigners considered the outlaws of Europe were taking a turn toward the historical tradition of the "classi-cal," "good" Germany of spiritual culture. Diem had long been proposing a pedagogical center and capital for German physical education with himself as head. A dividend (a bribe perhaps?) for Diem was the *Haus des deutschen Sports* which was the big-gest and best-equipped facility the world had yet seen for re-search and education in physical education and recreation. This lavish academy, equipped with swimming pools, many gym-nasiums and classrooms for the furtherance of Diem's plans for educational reform within Germany, was located at the north-eastern part of the *Reichssportfeld*. More evidence for Diem of the fact that those whom so many of the world considered barbarians were in fact not entirely so, was the willingness of the Nazis to support another of Diem's great dreams, the recom-mencing of the excavations, abandoned by the Germans in 1882, at ancient Olympia. If one blurred his vision a bit the Nazis then could be compared with the royal patrons of Johann Joachim Winckelmann and Ernst Curtius. The investigations at Olympia were also the occasions for many side trips on Diem's way to and from Greece. He journeyed through Eastern Europe and perceived everywhere an enthusiasm for the cultural revival to which he had decided to lend his energies.[10]

Despite his duties as a creator and executor of festivity and a heavily burdened educational administrator, the pace of Diem's scholarly work actually quickened. Aside from his enormous and admirably objective two-volume official report on the 1936 summer Games, he was assembling a lavish preview of the 1940 winter Olympics he hoped would be held at Garmisch-Partenkirchen. He published several other books and the flow of his articles in journals and newspapers increased from 10 in 1937 to 27 in 1938, 45 in 1939, and 73 in 1940.[11] By this time he had become an enthusiast for both the old and the new Germanies and he felt that as he served one, he served the other. Greater things were to come.

Upon Baron Pierre de Coubertin's death in September 1937, Diem succeeded in appropriating Coubertin's *Revue olympique* which became the richly produced, scholarly aloof *Olympische Rundschau* (1938–44) published in Berlin. He posed as Coubertin's successor. However, his attempts to shift the library and the headquarters of the International Olympic Committee to Berlin were thwarted by some of Coubertin's Swiss disciples in Lausanne.[12] During the time of the heady first military successes of the Nazis, the scholar was quite intoxicated with the apparently unopposed triumphs of the new Germany. His euphoria manifested itself in greater prodigies of production. In 1941 he published 66 articles; in 1942, 158.[13] In 1942 Diem also published two books on ancient horsemanship, three volumes of his collected essays, *Die olympische Flamme*, and his attempt at prophesy, *Der olympische Gedanke in neuen Europa*, which, despite the inappropriateness of the time and topic, were also published in Berlin in a French and in an English translation.[14]

This last long essay is the work of a man who was at once more European than German and who had been metamorphosed and made giddy. What had unhinged the aging scholar was an almost nonstop series of Nazi victories over so many of the traditional sites (and principles) of old European culture. Whereas Diem had earlier attempted to sell the peaceful, tranquilizing effects of Coubertin's inspiration, now he pictured Coubertin and, by extension, himself as swashbuckling geniuses whose grand schemes for sport in the universe would, despite blood spilled along the way, lead to Olympiads so culturally rich and inspiring that they would both mark the chronology and influence the evolving of a splendid new culture.

He had become an unwitting contributor to the myth of Nazi invincibility and then one of the millions of enchanted good Germans who believed that Germany was creating as she ruthlessly destroyed.

When the tides of war began to turn against the National Socialists, Diem's scholarship came increasingly to dwell on sport in the age of Hellenism, always a refuge for "good" Germans. He attempted to be aloof from the struggles of his nation and then dropped entirely out of playing any role in the Nazi state. His scholarship ceased for a while as he struggled to house and feed his family in 1945 and 1946. It is an indication of the man's extraordinary will and flexibility that his efforts in the postwar years to become again a good German, a sports administrator, and a scholar were in the end successful. But until his death in 1962 at the age of eighty he had time to reflect on how his judgment had been skewed in the fantasy-inducing excitement of the *Nazizeit.*[15]

The career of Dr. Carl Diem is a good illustration of the fact that the great orderer of the universe does not allocate talent and energy democratically. Two other individuals (of many) who illustrate this lack of fairness in the distribution of talent also played interesting roles in the 1936 Olympics. Avery Brundage and Eleanor Holm were remarkably similar in that they had been exceptional athletes and were immersed as well in the larger world where ambition can be financially focused and can yield, for the clever and lucky, large rewards.

The prettiest member of the American Olympic team on the

S.S. *Manhattan* as it sailed across the Atlantic in late July in 1936 was Eleanor Holm Jarrett, the world's record holder in the backstroke and the expected victor in her event in Berlin. Eleanor had been practicing diligently for four years. Despite some distractions along the way she maintained her form and stamina. No one doubted that she would, in August 1936, maintain her possession of the Olympic record she established in 1932.

And what distractions Eleanor had enjoyed! She had been born in 1914 in Brooklyn and as a teenager had discovered several things about herself. She was sought after because of her vivacity and her quite exceptional, healthy good looks and she was exceptionally swift in the water. When only sixteen she had been offered a job as a Ziegfeld Follies girl. In 1932 when she was nineteen she finished the 100-meter backstroke with a time of 1:19.4 at the 1932 Olympics and thereby took almost three seconds off the record set in 1928. During the next three years Eleanor captured new world records for all the distances competitively swum by women in the backstroke.

After the Los Angeles Olympics Eleanor Holm had stayed behind in Hollywood and signed a movie contract that paid her $500 a week. She posed at all the usual sites but more often at swimming pool edges for publicity stills. Her drama coach was Josephine Dillon, Clark Gable's first wife. She loved Hollywood: the parties, the masculine attention, the celebrity accruing as a result of her appearances in the gossip columns, and her money. Alas, an inevitable conflict in filmland was the plan of the producers at Warner Brothers to get her to swim for the silver screen. Eleanor's refusals were adamant, for to lie on her back in the water and smile for celluloid would prove to officials of the Amateur Athletic Union that she was not serious about maintaining her amateur status. She might wreck her plans to establish new records in her athletic specialty. There was a crisis when the studio offered to raise her salary to $750 a week if she would swim before the camera; nothing if she would not. Eleanor was already diligently training to defend her record in Berlin, so she quit. Late in 1933 she married Art Jarrett, a crooner, and toured around the United States singing at night in her husband's and other crooners' bands and working out in the afternoons in any swimming pool that happened to be nearby.

Eleanor Jarrett's voice was feeble, though confident, and those who saw her in her screen tests avowed that she would have benefited from a few years more exposure to the acting coaches of Hollywood. But the swimmer-entertainer, as stunningly beautiful as she ever had been, was a delight to interview. She radiated joyous vitality as she laughed in the night clubs. A quip for the reporters who asked if she was still in condition was, "I train on champagne and cigarettes."

An innovation for the American Olympic team in 1936, of which Eleanor was a member, was a *Handbook* issued to all the athletes and their coaches and their trainers. The *Handbook* unequivocally outlined the respective responsibilities of the American Olympic Committee and those of the individual athletes. In addition to precise prohibitions intended to preserve each athlete's amateur status, the A.O.C. declared itself responsible for all financial arrangements, medical care, insurance, and, in addition, "Provision for moral and social welfare, through adequate chaperonage." In order to forestall the expression of amorous high spirits, the male and female athletes were quartered in widely separate sections of the S.S. *Manhattan* as it steamed across the Atlantic. The *Handbook* gave schedules for transportation and the many athletic events, emphasized the athletes' necessary submission to the judgment of coaches and trainers, told them to carry suitcases and not trunks, and commanded them to preserve their white uniforms until the opening ceremonies. The *Handbook* specifically warned:

It is understood of course that all members of the American Olympic Team refrain from smoking and the use of intoxicating drinks and other forms of dissipation while in training.[16]

The views in this statement of principle were those of Avery Brundage, the president of the American Olympic Committee and the man who, "almost alone, engineered the United States into the 1936 Olympics held in Nazi Berlin."[17] During the trip across the Atlantic, Mr. Brundage was not the object of much attention on the part of the reporters. He had succeeded in gathering finances or prospects for finances for the large American team. He was, as he always had been and would remain, convinced that the Olympics were a festivity crucial for the furthering of world peace and (perhaps conversely) a force for the strengthening of American pride and patriotism. There had been, for some time after the Nazi revolution of 1933, serious and nearly successful attempts on the part of many American pacifists and anti-Nazis to lead a boycott of the Nazi Olympics. But the protesters against American participation in the Games in Berlin had been overwhelmed first by the skillful political tactics of Avery Brundage and his supporters and then by indications that the Nazis were reversing some of their repugnant racial policies. During the voyage over Mr. Brundage was proud of his athletes. His young charges, he claimed, were "following the pattern of the Boston Tea Party, the Minute Men of Concord, and the troops of George Washington at Valley Forge."[18] On the whole his team of battlers for both peace and American prestige were cheerful in third class on the S.S. *Manhattan.*

Eleanor Holm Jarrett was not happy in third class where her companions in a tiny stateroom were two very young swimmers. She did not like Avery Brundage. He had tried two years earlier to have her amateur status taken away and had just prevented her from securing first class passage on her own. But movement about the ship was rather easy. Eager for compensations, Eleanor found in the first class bar the company she preferred—that of newspaper reporters who shared both her dislike for the boss of the whole Yankee show and her fondness for strong drink. A fellow who became a sort of chum was the journalist and playwright, Charles MacArthur, who was fresh from an alienation of affections suit brought by his first wife against his recently acquired bride, the actress, Helen Hayes. On the *Manhattan,* Mr. MacArthur was without either wife and, perhaps lulled by the gentle motion of the huge liner and the conviviality that only the passengers of a great ship know, on the first night out he and Mrs. Jarrett and a few others got riotously plastered on champagne. News of their antics got to some members of the American Olympic Committee who met and deputized one of their number to remind the championship backstroker of certain rules in the *Handbook.*

More toots brought further warnings. Then on the night before the *Manhattan* was to dock in Bremerhaven, at a sort of farewell party, Eleanor outdid herself and, on the way back to her simple quarters which contained two sleeping young girls, lurched into Mrs. Ada T. Sackett, chaperone of the women's swimming team. Alarmed at the backstroker's condition, Mrs. Sackett (a) sent for a nurse and, subsequently, both the team's doctor and the ship's physician and (b) called an emergency meeting of the American Olympic Committee. Before settling in, Eleanor had enunciated some vivid pronouncements about what she thought of the rules and officials of the American team, but once down, she could not be roused by the team of doctors sent to examine her.[19] After an emergency, two-hour Committee meeting, Eleanor, as a second-offender roisterer, was suspended from the American Olympic team. The next day it fell to Avery Brundage to make the general announcement to the reporters, "This is no joyride!," and the specific one that relative to Eleanor's behavior, his committee had "considered all the possible grounds for leniency and found none."[20]

Thus the already nettlesome president of the A.O.C. precipitated a fracas. Eleanor was popular among her teammates and was immediately the subject of petitions signed by 220 of those who urged her reinstatement. The poor girl, in a characteristic mood of post-boozing *tristesse* wailed, "I'll never touch another drop again if I'm given another chance."[21] Some of the journalists had devilishly led the champion down a path that they knew in advance was perilous. They might have felt that they were defending their own actions when they radioed stories back to the United States that pictured Brundage as an ogre and Mrs. Jarrett as a misused innocent. Back home, one reporter sought out Art Jarrett who admitted,

It may have been necessary for the morale of the team. Eleanor isn't a ten-year-old. Those fellows have a job on their hands taking care of that Olympic crowd. I don't know whether they were right or wrong.[22]

So that the lovely girl might have something to do to keep her busy (and to capitalize on her notoriety) the International News Service quickly appointed Eleanor Holm Jarrett a reporter at the Games in Berlin. She appeared at the press gallery at the Olympic stadium for the opening ceremonies and was apparently her usual cheerful self in a rose-colored dress and picture hat. But then after a tough internal struggle, she collapsed sobbing in a corner when her joyfully expectant team, led by the stars and stripes, passed by. She was a spectator at the swimming races and watched a Dutch girl take the gold medal in Eleanor's event at a timed mark that the patriotic American felt she could have surpassed. Naturally her journalism and her remarks to the many who sought her out were unkind to Avery Brundage. That man who combined within himself the offices of the president of the American Olympic Committee and president of the Amateur Athletic Union bore well the accusations that he was kicking a girl while she was down as he banned her not only from Olympic competition, but subsequently from any amateur competition in Europe and then from further amateur competition in the United States. Mrs. Jarrett threatened law suits. A reconciliation between the two was clearly out of the question.

Was time unkind to this swimming beauty? Did the embroilment with the powerful Avery Brundage damage the prospects of Eleanor Holm Jarrett? Certainly not! More than ever a source of good news copy, she announced in October 1936 that she was currently earning $2,500 a week touring in a vaudeville company and that her annuities were paid up until 1940. She was planning to regain her amateur status so that she could swim for her country at the Tokyo Olympics of 1940.

I'll wait until Brundage is out of the A.A.U. and then try to get it back. To this day I don't see why they have me under any ban.[23]

In Cleveland in the summer of 1937, Eleanor was the main swimmer in an "Aquacade," which was a sort of big girlie revue that took place in or near the water. To reporters she simultaneously revealed that she was seeking a divorce from the crooner, Art Jarrett, and denied that there was strong affection between her and the "Aquacade's" producer, Billy Rose, then the husband of Fanny Brice, who, in turn, had earlier been married to "Nicky" Arnstein.

Billy Rose's "Aquacade" was a leading entertainment and financial success at the New York World's Fair of 1939–40 and Eleanor Holm Jarrett Rose was, in turn, a star of that show. In 1940 *Life* sent a photographer-reporter to call on Mr. and the new Mrs. Rose at their $200,000 apartment on Sutton Place in Manhattan. The glamorous swimmer, now a New York celebrity, declared that her second husband was the most fascinating man she had ever met and showed the journalist (and through him the millions of readers of *Life*) her wardrobe closet which held 100 dresses and 350 bathing suits, the most precious of which cost $250 and was encrusted with rhinestones.

In 1940 Mr. Brundage had not been dislodged as a powerful administrator and ideologue of American amateur sport, but he was rather out of the news, since there was not an Olympiad in that year. However, in 1944 Avery Brundage caused a characteristic flurry when he declared to a nation devoted to ending a difficult war that he favored the admission of the Germans and Japanese to postwar Olympiads.[24] And Mr. Brundage has been a source of lively news copy ever since.

9
The Olympics Preserved

Dressed in white robes and aloofly posed at a throne across from the crowds of spectators at the stadium at Olympia, the priestess of Demeter was the only woman allowed at the ancient Games. The precise role of this exceptional woman was frozen in hallowed customary usage. She was mysterious and somehow considered powerful because as a representative of Demeter, of an ancestry so ancient as to be pre-Olympian, she connected the Games as the classical Greeks knew them with much older, cult origins.

White too were the costumes that Leni Riefenstahl wore as she forced the importance of her presence upon all the spectators and participants at the Olympic Games in Berlin. As a twentieth-century priestess of beauty, Leni Riefenstahl, who was very much a modern woman, stayed at no throne, but rather drew the curiosity of millions because of her already fabled past and her aura of importance.

When night came and the exposure meters could no longer register, she appeared in white gowns at the parties in Berlin, often as a companion of Adolf Hitler. When she and Dr. Joseph Goebbels were present at the same party there could be a falsely jovial scene where she and the Minister of Propaganda, also dressed in white, would flash public, deep, movie star smiles at each other from their well-tanned faces. Though strong and large breasted, in 1936 Leni was not conventionally pretty. Her eyes were small, her mouth was a straight, long line, and her strong nose was distinctively arched forward along the top, leading edge, giving her an elegantly Semitic appearance.[1] She was not addicted to the heavy cosmetics that were the hallmarks of café society women. Leni moved grandly and gracefully with an air that was suspiciously dewy-eyed and disingenuous and chatted only with men who were powerful or becoming so. Much of her renown was due to her healthy though ethereal good looks and her notoriously exercised animal magnetism. But adding to her *cachet* was her reputation as one of the most respected artists of Germany's cultural renaissance.

During the day, Leni wore a brimmed *cloche* hat and a white, waterproof greatcoat with large pockets. Light meters on black cords hung from her neck. Notes and schedules bulged from her pockets and handbags. She barked orders to the platoon leaders of her forty-five cameramen. She sped in a chauffeur-driven car with high priority clearances from one athletic complex to another. Always Leni was surrounded by big, burly men—who wore *dark* raincoats also bulging with memoranda. Her serious work at the Olympics would not, however, prevent her from breaking loose from a group of sycophants to congratulate the new winner of a gold medal for the Reich—which congratulations were, of course, preserved on her own movie footage.

For in August of 1936 Leni Riefenstahl was wholly devoted to the production of *the* Olympic film. Her cinematic record of the Nazi Olympics would bring the splendor of this unique festival to the whole German race and to the whole world. Greatly strengthening her in the difficult organizational tasks that went along with her work was the fact that Leni was known to have the protection of the highest ranking government officials including and most especially the Führer himself. Even Goebbels feared her. Among her underlings, who were some of the best technicians of the German movie industry, she was a tyrant with her unequivocal demands. She was set upon pulling as much beauty as could be taken from the Olympic festival. Who was this woman?

She was born on August 22, 1907, in Berlin.[2] Her father was a plumber. At some sacrifice, her family gave her dance training when she was very young and she became a sort of ballet prodigy in Berlin in the early 1920's. She was engaged by the great stage producer and impresario, Max Reinhardt, as a star when she was seventeen. Then, before she was twenty years old, she was "discovered" by Dr. Arnold Frank, a maker of movies about passions in the Alps. Frank needed an athletic female to play opposite his male mountain climbers. The roles of Frank's heroes required that they scramble, grunting and laden with Alpine hardware, across exposed granite faces as they were filmed against shifting cloud masses. Eventually the leads in the movies would relax at some cumulus-framed summit where the male would light a pipe and he and his consort would muse with contempt about the doings of the "valley pigs."[3] Leni became and remained a skilled and joyful mountain climber. She became an aesthetic devotee of the contemplation of the masses of still rock and moving clouds that she with her movie lovers viewed with such supremacy and anti-intellectual contempt for others of human flesh. With characteristic wholeheartedness Leni customarily entered into a passionate relationship with the men she worked with. The liaisons usually began as love and ended in hate, or more often, an exciting combination of the two. In these years in the late twenties she was closest to Frank who directed her in six films and who became a sort of Svengali to her Trilby. The films had titles like *Die weisse Hölle Vom Pitz Palu* or *Der heilige Berg*. These tales of adolescent detestation of the *Spiessebürger* and of beautiful outsiders in settings of mystical nature were all widely distributed and made money for their comfortably wealthy distributors in Berlin. In the thirties several of Leni's silent films were dubbed with spare conversation and a lot of Bach and Beethoven largos in minor keys.

Characteristic of the dialectical momentum of her ambition, Leni had clearly decided to use Arnold Frank in order to master the technique of the cinema herself. Their last project together was a film made on location about a shipwreck in Greenland. In 1933 she published a book, *Kampf in Schnee und Eis*, on her adventures in Greenland and in it remarked, *"meine Leidenschaft—die Kamera."*[4] Her discovery of the films and specifically of the innovating camera angles and abrupt editing of Sergei Eisenstein gave her the courage to shed the influence and the person of Dr. Arnold Frank. She took a big apartment in Berlin, was invited out a lot, and produced *Das blaue Licht* in which she herself starred. This movie was filmed in the Italian Dolomites and was largely composed of Eisenstein-like brief sequences from unconventional camera angles. There are also deliberately off-focused, back-lit figures in fogs and at dusk. All of this gave *Das blaue Licht* a confusing but enchantingly mystical power and it was conceded to be an artistic though not a commercial success. Still very young, she was strikingly lovely and now had a reputation as an established artist. She had her own studio and well-placed friends in Berlin, two of whom were Joseph Goebbels and Ernst ("Putzi") Hanfstängl, who, in turn, were very close friends of Adolf Hitler.

It seems likely that Goebbels, a compulsive and tireless womanizer, had never had an affair with Leni.[5] However, one of the devoted henchman's campaigns to add to the happiness of his demigod was to inveigle Hitler into a sensual relationship with some woman or other. A skilled bed partner would, presumably, calm him, perhaps even more than the piano playing of "Putzi" Hanfstängl, which Hitler needed when depressed. An earlier attempt to mate Hitler with Gretl Slezak had failed. One night Leni and Adolf were at the Goebbels's for dinner. Afterward "Putzi," who was also present and who had been instructed to move unobtrusively, played soft music. Joseph and

Magda Goebbels chatted inconsequentially in the background, but were alert to the evening's drama. Hitler, almost in a panic, examined the spines of books and each time he looked around or straightened up, Leni was invitingly dancing at his elbow, "a real summer sale of feminine advance." Hanfstängl caught the Goebbels's eyes to communicate the message, "If Riefenstahl can't manage this, no one can."[6] The others left and the projected pair were left alone. A few days later, encountering Leni, "Putzi" lifted his eyebrows in a wordless, obvious query. Leni shrugged her shoulders in a wordless, crestfallen answer.[7]

However, Hitler recognized genius, vitality, and loyalty when he encountered them and came to value Leni Riefenstahl for more serious matters. She was a decorative escort who gave rise to flattering tales of his virility. More important, he, like Goebbels, was singularly aware of the possibilities for extending festivity that were inherent in the cinema. Leni was a connection with artists in Berlin and was already one of the best film-makers in the business. She was suitably enchanted by Hitler's charisma and was suitably both opportunistic and ideologically empty headed. It is still not clear what her official connections were in the National Socialist hierarchy. There are organization charts showing her projects to be a responsibility of Goebbels's Ministry of Propaganda, but in this instance, as in many others of the supposedly rigid prescriptions of the *Gleichschaltung*, there were severe faults in the working structure. Declaring the supremacy of art, she seems, for most of the time we are here considering, to have answered directly to Hitler who gave her unqualified *laissez-passer* and *cartes blanches*. She and Goebbels feuded though never endangered each other. Though rumored to be enemies, both seem to have been gratified each time Hitler ordered a patching up. Early in 1936, upon receiving an award on a stage at a Berlin theater from Goebbels, Leni fainted with joy (no novice at acting, she!).[8] Sometimes the pair would parade arm in arm at large public occasions such as film festivals which customarily recognized the excellence of her work.

Leni's first film for the Nazis was *Sieg des Glaubens*, a hastily made record of the 1933 party rally. After its premiere in Berlin in December 1933, Hitler publicly gave her a bouquet. She had more time to prepare the filming of *Triumph des Willens*. Indeed, the party rally of 1934 was, to some extent, staged for a script written in advance. Unexpectedly, the film took almost two years to edit and was released early in 1936. As was noted in Chapter 3, the purpose of this film was to communicate the rally's festive affirmation of loyalty to the millions unable to be present. The critical literature on *Triumph des Willens* is large and the praise it has received as art is doubtless deserved.[9] Still we feel a profound uneasiness while watching it, since we know that its myth-making was a conscious tread on the road to the Nazi holocaust.

There are some more things worth noting here about that extraordinary film. Like the films she made with her Svengali, Dr. Frank, *Triumph des Willens* was an intended antidote to the defeatist agonies and paralyzing introspections of the German filmmakers of Expressionism. The purpose and tone were to be optimistic and to communicate a relentless power. Another debt to Frank's work was Leni's use of massed formations of clouds and other inorganic matter. However, in the film of the 1934 party rally, paradoxically impersonal, perfect masses of people replaced the masses of Alpine granite. The impact of the film is also heightened by her use of montage, or dramatic editing. By "editing" I mean the use of many short bits of film and of using the emotional residue of one sequence to apply it to another. It is also clear that the film's maker was an enchanted admirer of Adolf Hitler.[10] Her cinematic footage devoted to this individual is unabashedly worshipful. Such a slick job of myth-shrouding and adoration could have only been attempted by someone totally in Hitler's spell. Was he Leni's second Svengali? For us who now watch *Triumph des Willens*, those views of Hitler reviewing troops, accepting adulation, or playing the focal speck for a parade formation numbering hundreds of thousands—all this now strikes us as too sudden, too huge, too grossly distorting. One almost feels a visceral revulsion that the beautification of something so awful should be so successful.

A curious sequel to her film of the 1934 rally was a movie Leni made for the Wehrmacht whose generals had objected to the small role the army played in the so-called "documentary" of the Nuremberg festival. So in 1935 Leni made what at the time was hailed as

an experimental short, using a montage technique both pictorially and aurally to create what must be a dazzling as well as a deafening impression of military force.[11]

In the meantime the first years of the Nazis in power were years of glory for Leni Riefenstahl. She herself was a heroine and a molder of a new, terrifically optimistic society that was itself enthusiastic for the kind of optimistic art that she was creating. Critics of the cinema, both in Germany and abroad, greeted her work. She remained an admirer of the Russian, Eisenstein, and was gratified to know that her work was praised in the Soviet Union. She was even invited to make films in Moscow, but would not go. As she later said,

I did not feel really capable of expressing myself except in my own country. I didn't imagine working anywhere else. I had to live in my country. That's all.[12]

She had, since leaving Frank, shed the elfin, smooth looks that had masked her self-confidence and ambition when she was a girl. She now wore severe, conservatively cut white clothes and was tough in her business dealings. She succeeded in imposing her will on large production staffs. Sometimes she won others to her views by means of all-night discussions at the end of which her collaborators, all near collapse, assented to her judgment.

Evenings, in clinging gowns, she would make sorties in the company of Nazis of high rank—sometimes with the very highest ranking of all. When it was prudent for her to do so, she could laugh richly, swoop about at large parties like the glamorous star she still was, and pose, pensive or smiling, for the flashbulbs of the tabloids and movie magazines. As always her name was amorously linked with many men, but she had long had a special arrangement with the World War I ace and stunt pilot, Ernst Udet, whom she had appeared with in three films. Leni Riefenstahl was stunningly handsome, internationally famous, rich, and in late 1934 had embarked on one of the most novel undertakings ever conceived of. This young woman was going to force an artistic marriage of sport and the cinema.

It may be wise to pause here and review the state in 1936 of the cinematic art—or at least those aspects of that art or technique that were relevant to that task that Leni Riefenstahl set herself. Upon viewing Eisenstein's *Potemkin* (1925) we cannot now gauge the impact of his novel angles of shooting (from below, through grillwork, back-lit closeups, etc.) and his rapid shifts of angle or scene to produce a rounded impression (a distorted impression, the one *desired* by the editor, it should be noted) of the drama portrayed. Riefenstahl had mastered and possibly advanced this technique of combining temporally disparate and spatially various views of a crucial instant or drama to produce a cinematic scene that was far more temporally compressed and visually dramatic than reality could ever be. By means of editing out the intervals of preparation she was able to distill exciting instants into the imposed flowing of images that is the essence of the art of the film. In his (or her) selection, the film editor is thus able to violate actuality and time and assemble near abstractions of motion and light. In Riefenstahl's time, no one with her foresight, her equipment, or her sense of the artistic-dramatic had either the ambition or the extent or variety of footage that would permit the making of sports films of intensely concentrated images. We might also note that in 1936 there was not much range in the light sensitivity of the film available—which limited the depth of field of the long focal length lenses that were used by her cameramen who might be poised on towers of scaffolding or on cranes. She later recalled that the fire-fighting equipment used in Nuremberg in 1934 had to be abandoned. One of her specialists with the most advanced telephoto lenses worked sometimes with a depth of field of less than twelve inches. The oscillations at the extended top of a fireman's ladder wrecked his narrow focusing. We should note too that the sound film was only about seven years old in 1936.

To say that sports cinematography was in its infancy before August 1936 is metaphorically as well as factually inaccurate, since self-conscious sports cinematography was introduced to the world by Leni Riefenstahl. The newsreels of the sporting events of the 1930's, particularly those of large athletic meets, were merely the result of some button-pusher holding a whirring camera. Filming at slow motion was timidly done. There were no sporting close-ups, and no attempts to heighten effect by lighting or low angles. One saw athletic events as though he were an astigmatic, myopic, palsied spectator in the stands. For a great artist to produce such films would be contemptible. As an artist Leni Riefenstahl knew that her work had not only to surpass previous technique, but to transcend in beauty even the events that were to be the subject matter of her film. She later claimed:

I had the whole thing in my head. I treated the whole thing like a vision. I was like an architect building a house.[13]

In the German *Official Report* of the Berlin Olympics, Riefenstahl says that Reich Minister Goebbels gave her permission to form an official Olympic Film Company which would have exclusive rights to film the athletic events of the 1936 summer Olympics.[14] She also obtained exclusive filming rights from the International Amateur Athletic Federation. However, this later permission cited the boundaries on the playing fields that the cameramen would not overstep and warned that she was not to distract the athletes in the smallest way. There were specific prohibitions. For example, Item 4 on their list warned that

in the throwing contests, the broad jump, and the hop, skip and jump, only the first attempt (in the qualifying test, preliminary and final) may be photographed. In the men's high jump, photographs may be taken of the qualifying test only up to a height of 1.80 metres, of the final up to a height of 1.85 metres . . . in the pole vault to a height of 3.60 metres in the qualifying test and up to 3.80 metres in the final.[15]

Probably only Dr. Carl Diem was more familiar with the program of events of the sixteen days of the Olympic festival. Using his schedules, Leni wrote a film script. She assembled and partially trained a crew of 80 cameramen and assistants. She later recalled that six months of training with special lenses were necessary before the shooting of the diving sequences. She was able to requisition a building for technical and administrative purposes at the Geyer Works near the sporting complex. Haus Ruhwals had dormitories and daily served 160 people in its cafeterias.[16] Long before the Games began the crews lived together even on Saturdays and Sundays. They planned and argued late into the night.

Physical preparations for the filming were underway many months before opening day and were unlike preparations for any other film. The stadium itself contained sunken passageways for the technicians to get to the pits that held the cameras to record the perfect musculature of Jesse Owens and of lesser figures at the starts of the dashes and in the course of the broad and high jumps. The muffled clacking of automatic cameras that slid along hidden rails followed rowers and runners and distracted neither athletes nor spectators. During parts of the marathon race a camera, hidden in a basket and towed along a camouflaged rail, recorded the tortured faces of Kitei Son and

Ernest Harper on the straightaway at the Avus racetrack. Leni's engineers devised a camera whose scarcely perceptible whirring could not distract the athlete who was the object of close-ups. Leni's crew wished to synchronize the motion of the tripping, flicking shutter with the motion of a horse. A special new camera was designed for a saddle. This camera rested on a rubber bag filled with feathers. For high panoramic shots besides the film taken from the "Graf Zeppelin" there were automatic cameras in small baskets suspended from balloons. Ads in the newspapers told the Berliners how to return the apparatus to the film studios. When the Organizing Committee vetoed her experimental balloon over the finish line of the scull races at Grünau, Leni wept.[17]

Like the gunnery crews of a dreadnought, Leni's cameramen had had many hours of practice at wheeling around the long lenses. Difficult weather was the occasion for special expeditions to the empty sporting sites to shoot and learn from the unexpected conditions in order to be prepared for the unusual and, possibly, uniquely dramatic. The challenges at the swimming and diving competitions inspired inventors and offered the greatest room for improvisatory coups. They obtained permission to attach a camera to the prow of a little rubber boat and to insert the contraption into the water during the practice laps of some championship swimmers. The camera was at the athlete's face and was pulled backward as the swimmer labored at full speed. These shots were later added to films taken during competition and gave the spectator in the movie house an immediacy of kinesthetic perception that was not available to the spectator at the spot. There were underwater shots and some footage taken with the lens half submerged. For some of the sequences of the 10-meter diving competitions, the camera followed the athlete from his take-off, down the 33 feet to the water to trace his bubbling change of trajectory beneath the surface, and finally emerged with him from the pool. This trial for camera and technician required several abrupt changes of lens opening and even a rapid changing of lenses under water.[18] Naturally the final filming in August was preceded by a great deal of rehearsal work before the athletes gathered for their actual event. Some athletes even graciously repeated their performances for Leni after the Games were over.

For everyone working on the project, these were exciting days. Leni recalled:

The abundance of impressions surpassed any expectations, so that every day was a new ordeal for all concerned. These camera-men, not being mere robots, but artistic and sensitive human beings, found themselves placed in a paradise for any camera-man. They had not only to define their own personal impressions in a way never experienced before, they had also to work with lightning speed in order to lose no valuable second. Dripping with perspiration they rushed to and fro untiringly with their heavy cameras.[19]

The raw material that was the product of all these efforts was some 400,000 meters (approximately 1,300,000 feet) of film sent to the developing firm. During the next two and a half months Leni and a small crew worked ten-hour days examining it all in a small projection room. The proportion of adequately aimed, focused, and exposed footage varied. For some of the swimming sequences, only 5 per cent of what was exposed was useable. But still, what remained was enough to make a dozen or more standardly conceived films of the Olympic Games of 1936.

During the winter, Leni Riefenstahl dispersed her crews and began what she envisioned as her special contribution. She wore a technician's white lab coat and worked as a solitary. Her place of work was a quiet, white painted laboratory with many back-lighted opaque screens for the examination of individual frames with a magnifying glass. She entered into a close association with that precious footage, eliminating, repeating, compressing, combining, and dubbing in order to compose and orchestrate the film that was to be the artistic distillate of a modern sporting festival. The use of the words "compose" and

"orchestrate," of course, suggest that what was on Leni Riefenstahl's mind was not at all a "documentary" (as has been
claimed—by Riefenstahl, among others), but a sort of difficult
creation most analogous to the writing of symphonic music. Indeed, in her recollections of her editing, she unaffectedly uses
the terms "melody," "harmony," "tones," "scales," and, most particularly, "rhythm."

For *Olympia* I spent, I lived in the editing room for a year and a
half, never getting home before five o'clock in the morning. My life
was tied to the material and the film. In my editing rooms, I had glass
partitions built, on each side of which I hung filmstrips that went
down to the floor. I suspended them one to the other, in order to look
at them, compare them, so as to verify their harmony in the scale of
frames and tones. Thus in the long run, as a composer composes, I
made everything work together in the rhythm.[20]

Versions of the film with varying languages of narration were released in two parts of nearly three hours each in the late summer of 1938.[21]

The opening of Part One, called *Fest der Völker (Festival
of the Nations)* opens with a sort of visual metaphor of creation.
To grand orchestral music, clouds, rock masses, and then off-
focused architectural masses gradually sharpen. The buildings
are those on the Acropolis at Athens and then the fallen column
drums of the temple of Zeus at Olympia. This part of the film
most clearly reveals Leni's debt to the mountain movies. Her
Triumph des Willens also fades from nature's masses to blocks
of massed humanity. However, in *Olympia* the blocks of humanity are the harmonious forms of humanity's surpassingly beautiful individuals. Figures are often hazily back lighted and they
are sometimes nude. We have some lyrical, slow-motion scenes
of running males and some slender females—all presumably
evocations of the Greek athletic spirit—who appear to be offering their beauty to the sun.[22] The scenes fade to a solitary runner who carries a torch. This figure is Riefenstahl's transition

from ancient Greece to modern Germany. He becomes part of a relay. A final runner in the series gradually approaches a vast public square, packed with people who are clearly National Socialists (they wear swastikas) in Berlin. Then we see Schilgen, the last blond runner, climb the steps at the Olympic stadium to light the sacred fire (whose flames, incidentally, are back lighted by the sun). The cinematic narrative then takes us rapidly throughout the opening ceremonies, with some rather noncommittal dwelling on Hitler and rather more attention to the parade of athletes. There are long clips of the packed stadium, clearly shot from the cruising Zeppelin.

The rest of Part One is an earnest peering into the kinesthetic (as well as interpreted aesthetic) essence of certain athletic events, particularly those of the track and field program. So as not to depart from classical Greece too quickly, we ponder slow-motion spins of the discus thrower. The girl winner of the gold medal is the lovely German, Gisela Mauermayer, and there are inserted shots of happiness in the spectators suggesting the effect of beauty upon those not having it. The film settles for some time on Jesse Owens. What is most surprising about movies of this fabulous individual is that as we examine his physical perfection we divine the intensity of his psychic effort. The deeply cut lines separating the muscles of his thigh, the pulsing arteries at his temples, the slight pout of his lips—all reveal inner gathering for the abstract pursuit of supremacy. We suffer the noble forbearance of Jesse Owens when this Olympian must glide out to loosen after some other runner's shameful, false start. As Jesse breaks the records the camera leads us to ponder the deep power of his perfect grace, not the crass evidence of the stopwatches. In Riefenstahl's films, as at the Games themselves, Jesse Owens receives more lavish attention than any other individual.

Films of the rest of the track and field program are edited to show the pith of each event in spirit and motion. The heroes are less heroic than the last torch runner and Owens. We have incisively intimate views of the shot putters at the penultimate instant, gathering their wills as well as their big bodies. The spinning of the hammer throwers is best understood by rapidly succeeding clips of their accelerating shadows. In the 800- and 1,500-meter races, quite exceptionally we watch the battle for leadership from afar. We suspect, however, that Leni's choice of these inclusive shots was due to the fact that the gigantic John Woodruff, victor in the 800 meters, was no beauty and that the significantly photogenic fact about Jack Lovelock, winner of the 1,500 meters, was his solitary black costume as it wended its way to the front. The shifting pack of leaders in the 10,000-meter run is shown in short clips. In these races we glimpse the terror of a leader as he looks back, losing time as he does so, yet we see that his fearful glance of terror is an inescapable human compulsion. The liberty of the film editor permitted Leni Riefenstahl to offer us the extracted substance of what was at once the most beautiful athletic event and the most difficult to see, the javelin throw. There is a section of Part One which consists of stacked, slow-motion clips of javelin throwers at the lunging instant of release and more stacked clips of the quivering shafts jabbing the turf. Riefenstahl was especially proud that her cameras, normal speed as well as slow-motion, caught the dropping of the baton by Ilse Dörffeldt. The directress also includes many scenes of athletes brooding, blanket-wrapped against chill, awaiting their events. We also rejoice with the victors as they take embraces and fanny slaps from teammates and coaches. The crowds, when they appear, are the contrary, disembodied presence, clothed in woolens and, though excited, devoid of physical appeal. They are a relief from the kinesthetic intensity of the athletes.

The closing sections of *Olympia* Part One are an effort to communicate the doggedness of the pole vaulters in Berlin as their struggle was unexpectedly prolonged into the evening. Creased with fatigue, the athletes repeatedly mass their strength and will for what is surely one of the complex maneuvers a man can perform at full strength. Night falls and the scene at the Olympic stadium takes on the same mysterious aura as the closing moments of the rallies at Nuremberg. All the youths but one dislodge the high bar. We then have montages and dissolves of the empty stadium, the ring of flags around its high edge, the great bell calling the youth of the world, and the tossing flame of the cauldron atop its classically inspired tripod.

As a tight artistic unity, Part One of *Olympia* is more impressive than Part Two, *Fest der Schönheit* (*Festival of Beauty*). Though it contains long sections of the highest art, Part Two fails as an artistic unity because it attempts too ambitiously to show all of the sports festival outside of the track and field program. Inevitably, since the rest of the schedule is so various, the results are disjointed (though far less than one might fear!) and of inconsistent quality. Riefenstahl also tried to show something of the humor (German humor is inevitably puzzling west of the Rhine) and some of the tragic ugliness of a big sporting competition. In the prelude, a pastoral metaphor of dawn, consisting of closeups of dewy grass and chirping insects, gradually broadens to a survey of the Olympic Village. Youths jog with long strides along a lakeside path lighted with shafts of sunlight filtered through mist and foliage. Some sweaty, shimmering Finns, naked, genitals revealed, luxuriate in their sauna. For the first time the music (specially composed by Herbert Windt) becomes painfully obvious as it stretches for jokes. The grotesquely ebullient Italians kick soccerballs to Sorrento tunes. The Japanese limber up to what a German felt was Noh music. A Filipino shadowboxes to something vaguely Oriental. American Negroes laugh and caper to jazz. Everyone fraternizes. The Olympic Village is a success.

Then there follows one of the most spectacular sections of movie footage ever assembled. First from the ground we watch three Nordic, leotard-clad, full-breasted girls swinging exercise clubs in unison. They are splendid! Accompanied by rhythmically sympathetic music, the narrative fades in, fades out successively to 6, to 20, to 100, and then to perhaps 10,000 perfect women in faultless patterns in perfect unison. As the camera angle rises the viewer is transported with aesthetic emotion. The scene is clearly derivative of analogous masses in *Triumph des Willens*, but now the political ideology has been poured off. We swoon with the instinctive grasp of the pure power of these massed *völkisch* gymnasts as the camera immortalizes their actions, ever more drained of fleshly beauty—for the artist in control has shown massed human motion abstracted, epitomized.

Curiously, these thousands of females and the nudes in the prologue of Part One are the most beautiful women in all of *Olympia*. The next section, on individual and team gymnastics, shows (or does the editor reveal her views?) that the peaks of male effort are more suitable for cinematic abstraction than female athletics. Our views of the girl gymnasts focus on the shiny, sweaty fabric which bunches like deformities at their heavy thighs. Ridges of folded skin roll up at their necks. The men— many of whom are also filmed in furrowed concentration—are shown in agony but briefly, and, we suspect, the camera's focus was softened. Leni used sound synchronization most effectively in these gymnastics sequences where she times the whirling whoosh of the hero on the high bar to occur as his pointed toes fly past the photographer's lens.

The scene shifts to the aquatic events. As may be well known, one may watch a swimming race, but it is difficult to have kinesthetic empathy with those swimming. Also, the exhortatory screams of the audience are inaudible to the swimmers and for the audience the sleek bodies and even the tortured faces of the competitors are nearly invisible. In *Olympia* we have a few closeups of swimmers racing in the water (filmed, we now know, long before) and some perfunctory attention to the faces of victors and losers at the finishes. The divers, however, were more amenable to artistic assemblage. In fact the editing of the last sections of the platform-diving sequence is so far in the direction of cinematography's more abstract reaches as to be only tenuously connected with the athletic or festive parts of the Olympic Games or, perhaps, with sport of any kind.

The famous platform-diving sequence begins conventionally enough. A series of harmoniously built male and female athletes climb to their perches, run for their takeoffs, maneuver in swans, pikes, or twists, and then plunge faultlessly to hit the water where they then perform an arc below the surface and rise with dignity to the pool edge. But gradually the preparations and exits are truncated in ever shorter sequences. Then we feel ourselves being hypnotized by the slowed motion of splendid males cleaving the air in twists and birdlike postures that are apparently without arduous preparation or dangerous consequences. Their motions are accompanied or rather followed by a full orchestra that leaps and spins in joyous sycophancy. Then the divers, even the splendid Dick Degener, lose all their features as the athletes are deliberately underexposed to reveal only their silhouettes that are soon maneuvering without takeoffs or entries at all. We see closely following, muscleless, faceless forms against looming, cloudy skies. All then is in slow motion in order to help us savor the exquisite pain of the impossibly lovely motion in grace-imposing, thickened air. Then, when the scenes are almost unbearable in their splendor, the gently turning, jack-knifing, plunging figures are sped up, not by changing the slowed motion, but by shortening the individual sequences, by having two or more in the air at once, or superimposing images. Sport as a human effort is transcended. The athletes have been stripped of the limitations of space and time and then of their humanity itself. We have been carried to an artistic realm of the ineffably beautiful and the undeniably false. We want it all to stop and it does. The cameras move to the North Sea where Leni, reluctant to leave Berlin and unsympathetic to the elements of choppy water and gusty wind, is perfunctory with the yacht races at Kiel.

Considering Riefenstahl's preconceived musical analogies, it is no surprise that she dwells on the rowers at Grünau. Her cameras lead us to become enchanted with the contrast between the requirements of steady pulses of the oars and the inexorable need of the body to slow after long efforts at full power. Still the coxswains push the teams on to the finish where (inspiring sight!) an exhausted German crew is still able to "Heil Hitler!" as victory wreaths are placed over their bent shoulders.

We have some scenes of the bicycling races blurred with speed and cranking machinery. No chance to dwell on flesh. Then the agony of the equestrian steeplechase where with cruel persistence and perhaps a viciously sardonic curiosity, the camera (or really the editor's eye) refuses to leave the notorious No. 4 jump, which leads from a grassy bank to a muddy pond that almost always is a calamity to the mounts and their aristocratic riders. Pratfalls for neurotic thoroughbreds and dilettante dukes. Horses and men thrash, flounder, churn up mud, and leave appallingly begrimed and chagrined beyond measure or are unable to rise at all. The more sport is contrived, the more it is degrading. Can this be Riefenstahl's message?

The later sections of Part Two return to the adored athletes of the track and field. We rapidly review the process that selects "the greatest athlete in the world," i.e., the winner of the decathlon. It is Glenn Morris, but this Olympic victor's cinematic immortalization consists largely of studies of the effect of sunlight off the flat planes of his squarish, serious head. From the movie alone, we would learn nothing of this conglomerate of events.

Then the marathon. Kitei Son plods on and on. Almost as guilty voyeurs we watch those intimate moments when Ernest Harper, his English rival, talks to him—presumably about strategy. The camera settles on Son's feet, on the piston-like arms, and then on the face that barely reveals a tortured, irrepressible will. Windt's music itself tries to suggest the conflict of will and human flesh. The music changes tempo and, as runner and beat are out of step, illustrates the reluctance of flesh to surpass the limits of fatigue. The athlete and the music, signifying will, are out of synchronization. We see here some parable of the body's opposition in the face of soaring spirit. Is this what sport is all about? Son, his face torn with anguish, does, in the end, speed up. He enters the stadium first, upright, and is greeted as a hero. His followers, weaker men, fall into the thick warming blankets of disappointed, tender coaches. The long movie ends rather quickly with some superimposed views of flags and the symbolic bell summoning the youth of the world. So much for the content of the two parts of *Olympia*.

It is worth noting again that *Olympia*, as a movie about athletes, was a radical departure from previously existing sports photography. Before 1936 the sports moviemaker merely recorded. Leni Riefenstahl's selective use of humans in motion is heavily indebted to Arnold Frank's editing of nature's more dramatic forms in the high Alps. Similarly, in the cutting rooms in 1935 Leni played with cordoned masses of loyal party members and the visually useable qualities of the Führer. During the year and the half when Riefenstahl combined the strips to make *Olympia*, it was Jesse Owens' body that fascinated her. It was its very darkness and its communicable potential for speed that she wished to turn into a fresh production of her own making. Thus her conceptions were all aesthetically nonideological in the sense that abstract art is privately ideological only within the conventionally circumscribed technical limits of the particular art being practiced. By my statement about abstract art in general, among other things, I mean that, though a brilliant film, *Olympia* is juvenile philosophically and, of course, non- or even anti-political.

Given the political obsessions of the age and the particular political ambitions of the hosts of the Olympiad of 1936, it may be nearly miraculous that the movie is so politically neuter. There are swastika banners and insignias. We do see Hitler. He is present, speaks and slaps his knee at news of victory—though it is not clear in the film that his rejoicing is in *German* victory. The Führer is generous, amiable. "*Il s'amuse.*"[23] The very fact that so much of the love (I beg to use this word) of the film is devoted to Jesse Owens and to Kitei Son, both non-Aryans, should indicate that Riefenstahl was at least offhand about the racial proscriptions of the Nazi hierarchy. On the other hand there are no evident efforts to mask the peculiarities of German patriotism at the time. The film shows that the German competitors enjoy a keener togetherness. They are less happy and less privately individuals than they are battlers for their nation's fame. They are inspired.

When Leni's great work was ready, it was offered to critics who had hardened considerably to the National Socialists. In 1936 the world had been eager to believe that the Nazis were reforming. The splendid production of the Berlin Olympics helped to give that impression. In the autumn of 1938, after the horrors of the *Kristallnacht* which signaled the vigorous re-imposition of the racial persecutions and after Hitler's brutal cynicism was revealed in the long Czech crisis, it was impossible for many outside Germany to be convinced that the Nazis were respectable and were merely correcting just grievances. Still, many film critics acknowledged the magnificence of *Olympia*. It won a gold medal at the film festival in Venice in 1938. The sportswriters who saw the film acknowledged that athletics had never been better recorded. One correspondent for the United Press called *Olympia* "the finest motion picture I have ever seen" and said that at times "it was all I could do to keep from rising from my seat and yelling."[24] A French critic stated that the film was one of the "summits of the cinema."[25] However, during Riefenstahl's communion with the rivers of celluloid, the world's fear of the creator's nation of origin made it impossible to ignore the strategic friendships she had formed.

There were many boycotts of German goods either being considered or imposed at the time. Many American film distributors were Jewish and were understandably revolted by tales of the stepped-up Nazi persecutions. In 1938 Leni herself journeyed to Hollywood to give a private showing of *Olympia*. As ever, the film was praised by those who saw it. However, Leni was socially boycotted and the only person of importance who would receive her was another creator of artistic childishness, Walt Disney. The bowdlerized American version, consequently, was scarcely shown at all. When the war broke out in 1939, prints of *Olympia* were seized at the German embassy in London and the film, or rather parts of it, saw service as training or instructional shorts for conditioning courses for British army recruits. In Germany, however, the film performed its festive purpose. Like Leni's film of the 1934 party rally, it took the Berlin Olympics to all the German people.[26]

Perhaps her travels outside of Germany altered Leni's views of the National Socialist regime. As a favor to Hitler, in 1938 she quickly assembled a crew for an excursion to Berchtesgaden to shoot footage which she edited into a fifty-minute lyric to the rugged scenery around Hitler's new mountain retreat.[27] She became enchanted by Heinrich von Kleist's tragedy, *Penthesilea*, and began a film of this story of the blonde Amazons and their queen. Production was interrupted by the war. She was, in fact, taking part in the invasion of Poland in September 1939 as a uniformed war correspondent when she witnessed a massacre of twenty-eight Jews by German troops. She abruptly quit her film unit, protested to General Walter von Reichenau and eventually to Hitler, but to no avail. Her influence waned and she devoted the war years to planning a romantic idyll about Spain, an adaptation of Eugène d'Albert's operetta, to be called *Tiefland*. Adequate financing was impossible to obtain and she gradually had to discharge her employees. She dropped from the scene and married Major Peter Jacob, a winner of the *Ritterkreuz*, in 1944.

In May of 1945 the American army entered Kitzbühel in Austria and seized Leni's lakeside villa for use as a rest center for the Forty-second Division. To her captors she wept that she had never, never been a Nazi and that some of her best friends were Jews.[28] A major calamity was her encounter with the writer, Budd Schulberg, early in 1946. Schulberg had been an arranger of the

Hollywood boycott when Leni came to America in 1938. Using the ploy that he was seeking films for the National Archives in Washington, Schulberg interviewed Leni and obtained from her some childishly stated disclaimers of complicity which were very likely true in her case, but which rang jarringly in those days when every German blamed the whole debacle on Hitler and Goebbels—who were dead. Unfortunately and possibly characteristically, when Schulberg left her Leni naïvely begged him for some gasoline. "These French take everything," she complained. The hatchet job was published in the *Saturday Evening Post*.[29] Later she spent time in a French detention camp.

Between 1948 and 1952 she appeared several times before de-Nazification courts and the verdict was always the same: "No political activity in the Nazi regime which would warrant punishment." Concurrently she began a campaign to clear her name. In the spring of 1950 she sued a journalist who claimed that Leni, for authenticity in *Tiefland*, had gone to a death camp to select a group of Gypsies to be extras. There was not much doubt that these same Gypsies were afterward taken to the gas chambers—for Gypsies, like Jews, were poisonous *Untermenschen* to the Nazis. Who did the choosing for art and who for death? The defiant journalist could produce no proof that Leni was a killer and was fined 600 marks.[30]

Her films were blacklisted or censored by the new democratic Germans. When she submitted *Olympia* to the German Commission for Voluntary Self-Control (*Film Selbstkontrolle*) to obtain permission to show it again, she had to cut 86.5 meters from the first part and 1.5 meters from the second part. The censored footage showed the German victory medals, Hans von Tschammer und Osten, Hitler, and various Nazis who were members of the then current government of Germany.[31] She worked with Jean Cocteau on a film about Voltaire and Frederick the Great which was aborted when Cocteau died. Her husband died. She had a nervous breakdown. She traveled in Africa as a still photographer and later submitted a script for a documentary, *Black*

Cargo, to the Anti-Slavery Society in London. Her Land Rover overturned, she fractured her skull, and recovered slowly in a hospital in Nairobi. The money dried up.

In the past few years Leni Riefenstahl's artistry has been receiving respectful scrutiny due to the widespread interest in the route by which the cinema, the salient new art of our century, approached vigor and maturity. *Triumph des Willens* and the parts of *Olympia* are classics of the film festival repertory. Occasionally these films are shown commercially in the "art" cinema houses. Available for nothing, *Olympia* has been shown on educational television shows where its splendor cannot be communicated on the little, flickering screen. Her earlier films—in total length far surpassing the two that are the basis of her present fame—are either lost or otherwise impossible to view. They are legends.

For the historian-moralist the story of Leni Riefenstahl poses some problems. On some occasions she has claimed that she was just a "young girl" in the early thirties and cites the admiration of Winston Churchill, who was far older, for Hitler. She sometimes calls her films for the Nazis "purely historical" and uses the terms "documentary" and "*film vérité.*" She reminds her interviewers that before the war and the death camps, English, French, Russian, and American critics, many of them Jewish, praised her genius.

Still, of all the personages who moved at the apex of that exhilarated society in Berlin during the *Nazizeit,* Leni is almost the only one who after 1945 was permitted to run about the world free—is one of the few, in fact, who was given the chance to pursue any kind of normal life at all. Though her career was truncated by events she could not control, she had indeed played a role in launching that string of events and still she confronts us as a piece of human goods soiled, though very long ago, by close contact with diabolical politicians. Her tragedy can be compared with the tragedy of the Olympic festival of 1936 which, like her film of the Games, masked the ambitions of those whose apparent openhandedness made the Games so splendid.

It seems inevitable that Leni Riefenstahl's reputation as an artist will someday be secure. Germany is respectable now. In 1966 we were confident enough to accept a reconstructed Nazi as Germany's prime minister. Someday all the art historians will acclaim the white-clad goddess whose spirit and energy produced great art in the movies. As in 1936 the goddess will be Leni Riefenstahl, but by the time all the hatred is gone, she will be dead.

10
Farewells, Conclusions

The last day of the Olympic festival in Berlin in 1936 was a Sunday, August 16. The augmented numbers of Germans in Berlin had met the demands made upon them for self-discipline during the fifteen-day Olympic festival. Officials no doubt felt that it would be possible to relax some rules toward the end. Consequently, on August 16 in the Olympic stadium the spectators were packed in to a number totaling more than 20,000 over its measured 100,000 seating capacity. It was a warm, summer day, just slightly overcast. The last athletic events were the precision riding competitions, really a sort of formalized, military steeplechase, called the *prix des nations*. The infield had been transformed into the "pasture of a fine country estate" with freshly laid green turf, dark green hedges, low white fences, and smooth pools for the water jumps. Here, happily for the overwhelmingly German audience, the three members of the German team were the clear winners on the basis of their lowest number of faults. Because of the military overtones of this equestrian event (as well as the others), the excellence of the riders and mounts entered was high. The judging was done slowly and thoughtfully and was based on exquisite distinctions that were left unexplained and which, in any case, would not have been of interest to the vast numbers present.

There were too many teams and the judging process dragged on. It all became tedious. Then, when it appeared that the stately unfolding of this final event was past, the disembodied voice over the loudspeaker casually announced that there had been a tie for some place of less than medal-earning rank and that the teams of Belgium, Rumania, the United States, and Hungary had to go through a runoff. This accomplished by the stately figures on the turf, there were drawn-out victory ceremonies with more than the usual playings of national anthems. All this official paraphernalia pushed the ending of the last Olympic sporting event into the dusk. And it turned out that this timing was the reason for the stretching out of the afternoon's events—for the planned coda of the Olympics was based on long National Socialist experience as to what made closing ceremonies most dramatic. The sun had to be in the right place. An essential theme for an *Abschied* or farewell was waning daylight.

The spectators had already been alerted that they were to watch the sun as it passed in farewell in the west behind the five Olympic rings that were suspended by cables strung between two squat towers in back of and on either side of the Marathon Gate. The reddening sun then slipped farther and passed in back of the tossing Olympic flame. With its solar brilliance it briefly dimmed that holy fire, and then fell farther, so that the flame seemed greatly restrengthened in the gathering darkness.

A distant clap of a cannon signaled the beginning of the formal leave-taking. The distinctively deep gong of the colossal bell began a steady tolling at the top of the slim tower at the other end of the *Maifeld*. The vast theater of participants and spectators in the stadium was moved to breathless anticipation as the darkness deepened. From below the patiently waiting, white-clad choir in the stadium, a large group of trumpeters began a slow fanfare. At the moment the horns first sounded powerful searchlights in a ring outside the stadium simultaneously shot tall beams into the sky. At first the columns of light were straight up, but then the infinitely distant tops of the shafts gradually converged to enclose the darkened stadium in a temple composed entirely of glowing spirit.

As the fanfare drew to an end, the flagbearers of the national teams marched on the field in an order that was the reverse of that used at the opening ceremonies and which, coincidentally, brought forth first the winning swastika and then the second place stars and stripes. Then came Uruguay and the rest of the flags of the participants, with Greece last. Lit by floodlights, the flagbearers assembled to stand in a long row before the Tribune of Honor. In back of the flag carriers, Count Henri Baillet-Latour, the president of the International Olympic Committee, mounted a rostrum facing the most honored guests and recited a tribute, electrically amplified, to the German people and their Führer, Adolf Hitler (who was present) for being such generous hosts on so solemn and splendid an international occasion. His speech was short and Baillet-Latour ended it by announcing a recent decision of the body of which he was president:

we proclaim the closing of the eleventh Olympic Games and in accordance with tradition we call upon the youth of every country to assemble in four years at Tokyo, there to celebrate with us the twelfth Olympic Games.

As the Belgian nobleman left the rostrum, the augmented Berlin Philharmonic orchestra and chorus began playing Ludwig van Beethoven's hymn, "The Flame Dies." The tense seriousness of the mood was emphasized by regular, pulsed cannon shots, muffled by the far distance. For some time in the stadium, only the flagbearers of the nations were illuminated and then, quite suddenly, out of the darkness fifty-one tall girls appeared. They were dressed in white and carried small laurel wreaths. They marched by two's and soon each girl paused before one of the athletes carrying the flags of the nations. The long row of banners was lowered (including the stars and stripes which, we remember, had not dipped in the opening ceremonies) and at the tip of the standards the stern girls fastened the laurel.

Then the orchestra began a new choral work, "Farewell to the Flag," by Paul Höffer. The girls filed off and spotlights fell to the base of a flagpole at the west end of the infield. There six sailors slowly brought down the huge, five-ringed Olympic flag. As this banner came near the turf, it was gathered by five white-uniformed members of the German Olympic team. Simultaneously the orchestra trailed off to silence and the tossing, sacred flame over the Marathon Gate, given life more than two weeks before from a fire born of the sun at ancient Olympia, slowly fell, stretched languidly a bit, and sputtered out.

The five athletes carried the open flag, large as a boxing mat, to the loge containing Adolf Hitler and his guests of honor where the banner was rethreaded on a short staff. Then twelve white-uniformed German fencers, their sabers drawn, formed an honor guard, six to a side, which accompanied the Olympic emblem to the little rostrum on the field. The majestic group presented the flag to the Bürgermeister of Berlin who then expressed his honor at being requested to cherish this flag for four years until all should assemble once again in Tokyo. At once three other flags were raised above the big announcement board at the east end of the stadium: the first flag was the blue and white flag of Greece, originator of the Olympics; the second was the red, white, and black hooked cross of the new Germany, host of the Olympiad just ending; the third was the red and white rising sun of Japan, site of the next peaceful assembly of the world's best. A clear voice over the loudspeaker system—which until that time had been quiet—declared, "I call the youth of the world to Tokyo!"

Everyone in the stadium rose to their feet. The orchestra began a farewell hymn, "The Games Are Ended." In a spontaneous expression of *völkisch* affection, the enormous gathering of rev-

erently wet-eyed participants was to unite itself in the flesh. At
several places in the crowd people began crossing their arms in
front to grasp the hands on either side. Quickly the movement
spread and more than 100,000 people rocked in time with the
music of a last chorus. All were "schunkeling" to music and the
words,

> Friends farewell.
> Even if the sun should sink for us,
> Others will beckon.
> Friends farewell!

The great bowl of the stadium was in darkness and it was time
to leave. Some, in a reverent mood, began to move toward the
well-lighted exit routes, but at the same time a curious, un-
scripted thing began to happen. The Führer had been present
and, though not floodlit, had of course been the polestar of interest. Still, he had not spoken nor had he been permitted a
dramatic gesture. Vast numbers of those present apparently felt
a deeply agitating sensation of uneasiness, an unsettling lack of
closure, the intuited, unaesthetic omission of a climax or a final
chord. The intention had been that the dusk-lit, somber festivities would leave all its participators awesome and warmly
pensive. Then in the massed tens of thousands who were unable to leave, the restlessness began to be expressed subtly and
then openly. The sentiment was general: the Germans had
been cheated out of an essential ingredient of their festivity.
There were murmurs that swelled into shouts and then unexpectedly into cadenced screaming from which, eventually, one
could make out the unified expressions of isolated, large agglom-
erations, better disciplined than the rest, who shrieked in unison,

> Sieg Heil!
> Unser Führer Adolf Hitler!
> Sieg Heil!

These passionate yearnings were for a formal appearance by the leader acknowledged to be the inspiration for Germany's greatest triumph since the ending of the Second Reich. Nineteen-thirty-six had, in fact, been a year in which the new Germans demonstrated to themselves and to the world their rapid maturation and their capacity for heroism. The winter Olympics in Garmisch-Partenkirchen, while not especially victorious for individual German athletes, had demonstrated to the heretofore isolated Germans that they were not pariahs, that the world would participate in and enjoy a festive occasion for which the National Socialists were hosts. The Rhineland invasion had shown the Germans that their leader could right old wrongs without fear of international reprisals. Max Schmeling had in single combat symbolically proved the power of the inspired German race.

However, the scorecards of the summer Olympics meant more than all of the earlier victories. The tables of points kept by the sports reporters in Germany and abroad demonstrated that (1) Nazi Germany did better than the United States; (2) Italy outperformed France; (3) Japan did far better than Great Britain. Consequently the inescapable implication was that fascism and totalitarianism were more effective mobilizers of human energies. These novel, anti-historical, anti-egalitarian ideologies were obviously the waves of the future. The inspired totalitarians would inevitably overwhelm the soft, super-intellectualized democracies. The more thoroughly a nation turned away from liberalism and democracy, and the more enthusiastically its people embraced totalitarian notions of the state, the greater power it seemed able to evoke from its human and natural resources.[1] The Germans, particularly, were self-enchanted, for they had gathered still more evidence to crush internal and external criticism and to convince themselves that the frenzied experimentation of the previous four years had been vindicated. *Der Angriff* was unrestrained:

If one may be permitted to speak of intoxication from joy, then every German may be said to have reeled from happiness. It is an odd but familiar experience and once again we have discovered after sturdy struggles what reserves are contained within us.[2]

The risky submission of the Germans to their demanding leader and his dubious ideology was more than proven to have been a correct decision. A German newspaper declared:

The preparations rested on the totality of the nationalist art of government and its fundamental idea of the community of the whole people. The world stands in honest admiration before this work because it has totalitarian character. Without unitary will, that which today has astonished the world would have been impossible. It is the supreme achievement of the totalitarian state.[3]

A domestic result of the Berlin Olympics, then, was a great increase in German self-confidence.

It is not easy to voice unrestrained patriotic emotion in the presence of large numbers of persons whose patriotism is different from one's own. Also, nationalistic self-flagellation (what the French Olympic Committee called "the mania for self-disparagement which is, alas, one of the most specific characteristics of the Frenchman"[4]) usually occurred in small, rather secure groups whose alarmed sobriety was expressed out of the hearing range of what were generally supposed to be Olympic and therefore internationally pacifistic circles. The tallies of the medal and point winners of the sporting contests of the 1936 Olympics evoked more than they stated, yet the ambiance in Berlin itself was self-consciously congenial. After all, almost everyone could convince himself that, in a world that seemed to be going to antagonistic pieces everywhere else, this Olympiad *had* been more harmonizing than not. And because of the euphoria communicated by the Germans, Berlin was an infectiously happy place to be as the Olympic Games drew to a close.

In 1936 the pessimists—those enemies of Germany who were

cynical about the various pronouncements made at the Olympic season in favor of international harmony—warned that a result of the Nazis' triumph would be the pressing of Germany's advantage in prestige and power in order to increase her might. On the other hand, we have already noted that an intention of the Olympic festival's directors had been to convince the critics of the National Socialists that the new Germans were working hard, playing hard, and were whole-heartedly devoted to peace. Visitors to Berlin during the festival could not escape the evidence that the Nazis were preparing to relent on the intense demands of the first four years of the new regime.

During the following months it turned out that the pessimists were wrong. For more than a year after the closing ceremonies at the Olympic stadium, Germany seemed devoted to consolidating the gains made in the course of her recent exertions. Hitler's sorties in foreign policy in the year 1937 were almost confined to the wooing of Benito Mussolini. The Italian Fascist eventually adhered to the anti-Comintern pact that Hitler signed with Japan in November 1936. A festive diversion for the Berliners was the spectacular show of parades and assemblies put on for them and for Mussolini when he visited the capital of the Reich in September of 1937. As measures of German discipline and determination, politicians and traders all over the world could ponder statistics demonstrating German full employment and rising German imports and exports—the latter rising somewhat faster than the former. For almost two years after the Olympics ended, the defenders of German good will could also show that, though there was no dramatic sign of the alleviation of the lot of the German Jews, there were no new repressive measures of dramatic importance to the Jews, either.

Hidden from the foreign observers were certain shifts in the role that sport was to play in the Nazi regime. Before 1936, German sport had been mobilized to produce a diplomatically useful international triumph. Within Germany after 1936, the role of the German athlete at the Olympic Games came to be posed by the propaganda apparatus in retrospect as a useful aberration, the fictions of which could now be abandoned. Sport became more unapologetically a paramilitary activity; the organizational and athletic lessons of the XIth Olympiad (themselves indebted to Nazi experience with the Nuremberg rallies) were applied to promoting more effective and more specifically Nazi festivities.

The man who was most responsible in 1936 for such pseudo-classical trappings such as the torch run and the shows of ancient Greek art was Dr. Carl Diem, the internationally renowned scholar and administrator. Though never a party member, he had nevertheless been sufficiently impressed with the Nazis' accomplishments (to which he contributed) to feel that as he worked for them, he was instilling in large numbers of Germans the appreciation of classical culture that had been a hallmark of "good" Germans for centuries. But Diem was especially proud because, before his work, German classicism had been more or less elitist. Now he felt it was a mass movement. He came to consider himself not only a representative of German culture who was the rival of Winckelmann and Goethe and an effective teacher of the Germans, but also the natural successor of the aging Coubertin as the leader of the international Olympic movement.

An incident in Switzerland assisted Diem in his ambitions for the evolution of international sport. On September 2, 1937, on a path in the Park Lagrange in Geneva a small, elderly gentleman stopped in the lively pace of his customary promenade, pressed his hand to his chest, and fell in a heap. Baron Pierre de Coubertin, the founder of the modern Olympic Games, in his youth a French patriot, now long since an internationalist and president of the International Olympic Committee, was dead. Shortly afterward, in accordance with the great man's wishes, his body was taken to remain in Lausanne and the heart that had failed him was torn from his body and buried in an urn in sacred Greek soil at ancient Olympia. In the eyes of the world, Coubertin's only rival as a philosopher and a saint of sport was Dr. Carl Diem.

Even before the 1936 Olympic Games opened, Diem had convinced the National Socialists that they should take on another project that would identify the new Germany with the inspirational sources of the old Germany. A sort of spiritual place of pilgrimage of many Germans had been the excavated ruins at ancient Olympia which the Bismarckian Reich had abandoned in 1881. The great scholar and humanist then was the moral force behind the Führer when Hitler issued a proclamation that said in part,

The philosophical foundations for presenting the revived Olympic Games to the world are of hallowed antiquity. These spiritual forces come out of a sacred city which for more than a thousand years was the site of festivals expressing the religious feelings and the basic convictions of the Greek *Volk*.

As an enduring monument to the celebration of the XIth Olympiad in Berlin, I have decided to recommence and to see to a conclusion the excavations at Olympia. That these projects will succeed is my and our sincerest wish.[5]

Diem sent an archaeological expedition to Olympia before the year 1936 was out. The new excavations concentrated on the large (and rather late, relative to Olympia's long history) stadium to the east of the sanctuaries. The great scholar and patriot acquired the backing of certain organizations of German classicists to support the work and also got some funds from the German sports federations, but so attached was Diem to the project that much of the financing came out of his personal fisc.[6] The reverent Germans pursued the work in Greece until late in 1941 and then (again at Diem's urging) started once again to dig, catalogue, and describe at the site in 1952.[7] As had been the case with German artists and philosophers since the Enlightenment, since the days of Winckelmann and Goethe, Diem would attempt to legitimize, glorify, and sanctify young Germany by establishing her kinship with a fairyland of long ago. This great scholar in Nazi Germany sought to further his own and his nation's ambitions by increasing the world's knowledge of Greek antiquity.

Thus far in this last chapter I have confined my conclusions on the impact of the Berlin Olympics mostly to Germans. The results of the 1936 Olympics had international implications. A large part of the narrative has been devoted to showing the importance of the Berlin Olympics as a stage in the de-individualizing and consequent politicizing of the German sport. This grim process was not confined to Germany. In fact, one could cast the Berlin Olympics as the beginning in earnest of the evolution (still underway) of the role of the athlete as society's sap. In 1936 as never before, the better an athlete was as an athlete, the less he was allowed individualism and the more he was cast as an allegorical, ideological battler. Whether participating in a team sport or as a solo performer, he or she was forced to be treated as the symbol of the organization whose jersey he wore. Many modern social critics have denigrated the big-time athlete, whether amateur or professional, as a mere "gladiator." Actually since the athletes' (both fascist and democrat, be it noted) cheerful pandering to the ideologues of the 1930's, the athlete has become a more complex figure who is far more than an entertainer. The superior athlete of our times has been overburdened with symbolic importance. He has become ever more of a patsy, an exploited fool, a whipped drayhorse hauling dangerous ideas. And the de-individualization of the athlete has not been confined to the great nations. During the Olympic tryouts in 1936 a little news item out of Poland announced that the shot putter, Zygmunt Heljasz, back-talked to a doctor who was examining him. He was forthwith dismissed from his team for "misconduct."[8] The deep thinkers about the nature of sport have seen its ultimate bases in the need of the physical organism for play, in relief, in joyful activity without object.[9] In the light of what has happened to organized sport in the middle decades of the twentieth century, these philosophical declarations of sport's purposelessness or the pleasure given to its participants become subjects for mocking, bitter laughter. Modern spectator sports have been purged of true play and have rapidly gathered encrustations of myth, iconography, ritual, and dogma that make the meets or "games" (as they are called) take on sacred significance. And paradoxically, it is the best "players" (as they are called) who must be most deadly in earnest in mastering tactics and in living up to the yearnings for patriotic supremacy that their society imposes upon them.

Take the performances of the American Negroes at the Olympic Games, for example. In 1936—and surely even more since then—their performances were viewed not as those of exceptionally gifted, handsome individuals, but as those of good Negroes and—better yet—good Americans. It is indicative of some of the racial-moral viciousness in American society that the blacks most praised for their superior performances at the Berlin Olympics were also those who were the least critical ones. They did not publicly question the ways in which their personal identities were subordinated to the objects of the American Olympic Committee, their race, and their nation—all of which were desperately eager for victory and who all wanted medals for different reasons. Perhaps we should not cavil over the claim that the Olympic Committee, the Negroes, and the nation were better off due to Jesse Owens' grace, speed, and amiability. Perhaps (and there is good substance for debate here) Jesse Owens himself was better off. But was sport better off? What did the greatest sports hero of the 1936 Olympics and his black teammates tell us about sport as an activity of the expression of exuberance or for the manifestation of *personal* excellence and power?

It was in 1936 or thereabouts that the assault on the sporting records became a fetish, a monstrously serious undertaking. The compiling of statistics is an obsession with the shallow sports historians. The record of ever "improving" (is this the right word?) performances causes the deeper sports historians to brood over the reasons for the steady chiseling away at the inscribed best mark for an athletic event at any particular moment. What has happened since the early 1930's is that, in addition to more scientific training of the athletes' bodies for physical trial, there has been a parallel investigation of training of their wills.[10] For body and spirit must be keenly and synchronistically trained, tuned, and then keenly roused in order successfully to assault the existing concepts of what are the ultimates in physical prowess. For most athletic activities, only the young have either the physical or the un-eroded spiritual capacity for total athletic efforts. And those who have snatched records since 1936 have done so by means of such intense focusing of their physical and psychic powers that in consequence they probably atrophy other youthful pursuits such as fantasy, pleasure, love, privacy, and wisdom. The regimentation of the athlete of world-competition class has made him (or her) the acolyte of a special kind of temple prostitution. That athletes' bodies are used by businessmen, ideologues, and patriots, who cheer and do not touch, does not lessen the fact that their individual destinies and their bodies are conceived of by the priests of school or local or national ideologues as tools to be used until they are spent husks. There is really little difference between the Soviet gymnast, the isolated and subsidized darling of his society, and the so-called American "amateur." Each is a victim of his society's view of the athlete as a precious national (or local) resource. His training schedule isolates him from other youths less "blessed" with outstanding physical skills.[11] The fact that the American "amateur" is barred from reaping substantial financial rewards for his submission only points up the fact that the better the athlete, the more he is indeed a sap and a plaything of perverted ideologues and ambitious politicians.

The unexpected triumphs of Nazi athletes at the 1936 Olympics (unexpected by all except Germans, that is) were the bases of several new views of the athlete. The only acceptable explanation for Germany's athletic victories at their Olympiad is that her athletes were in the grip of psychic forces and were submitting to urgent political demands that were not acting as strongly on the youths from other lands. Horrible though it may be, it appears that totalitarian inspiration seems capable of working wonders upon the will and, through the will, upon the body. We have learned since then that anywhere in the world a skilled, though uninspired soccer or basketball team is a push-over for a similarly skilled team urged on by frenzied fans and cheerleaders. Cheerleaders are holders of no political theory— indeed they have no ideas at all. But evidence of massed support works to squeeze latent superiority out of a potentially record-breaking athlete. He must feel that he is not alone; that he is part of a larger community as he competes and that his triumphs are also those of his club, school, region, or nation. He must be moved by totally absorbing emotions whether childish or mature, noble or diabolical. He may be trained and conditioned to perfection, but cynicism or skepticism, by eroding his unitary will, will exclude him from the ranks of the very best.

A trend that was strengthened by the results of the 1936 Olympics was to view athletes increasingly as national assets procurable like fighter planes, submarines, or synthetic-rubber factories. A territorial area encompassing people with a common heritage can be considered a nation when it has the certain prerequisites for national standing. A distinct language and literature, an army and a navy have long been without-which-nothings for national standing. After 1936 a stable of athletes also became necessary for national standing. Coubertin and his international group of aristocratic patriots, financiers, and political string-pullers graciously supplied quadrennial festivals where nations could compete through their athletes. The performers, inevitably, have come to be considered a fleshly national asset. Athletes have had to respond to alterations in budgets, changing national priorities, or shifts in foreign policy. Athletes are comparable to infantry privates, gun boats, rockets, and space satellites. And we ought not to pretend that the pitting of one ideologically burdened athlete against another is greatly more soothing (though less immediately dangerous) to abrasive patriotism than the pitting of border guards and the competition of propaganda ministries. Nor should we assume that the Olympic Games of 1936 were indeed so very pacifistic. The world was still girding, quietly to be sure, for war.

When the Berlin Olympics were over the preparations of many nations for war were paralleled by preparations in much of the world for the Olympic Games of 1940. The winter Games were scheduled for Sapporo on Hokkaido, the northernmost island in the Japanese archipelago. Athletes, coaches, and Olympic officials also followed news of grandiose constructions at the site of the summer Games of 1940 in Tokyo. But within Japan not everyone favored the international festival. The country had been falling increasingly under the control of a military clique that was avid for adventures in China. All along, these same chauvinistic officers had been sarcastic about the preparations for the 1940 Games, claiming that such pandering idealism (for modern Olympism does have an appealing pose as a force for peace) was contrary to the code of Bushido which traditionally governed the lives of the Japanese fighting aristocracy. By the middle of 1937 the militarists were dominating the government and were soon digging into the torpid and corrupt body of republican China. News of the Japanese campaigns in Asia consisted mostly of atrocity stories and petitions began circulating in Sweden, the United States, and Great Britain to move the Games to a nation more respectful of Olympic ideals. Opposing a shift, Avery Brundage, who was still president of the American Olympic Committee, declared that "sport transcends all political and racial situations," and "Whether our Committee or athletes like or dislike Japan's military policy is beside the point."[12] World-wide expressions of distaste for Japan's cynical aggressions mounted as did the sincere reassurances from Olympic officials in Tokyo that they would indeed play host to the world's best in 1940. Then, suddenly, on July 12, 1938, the Japanese cabinet announced that it was requiring the withdrawal of the invitations for an international Olympiad in Tokyo. There would be, instead, specifically Japanese "Olympic" Games in 1940 and Japanese athletes would be forbidden to travel to an international meet if a festival were to be held elsewhere. Despite a lack of time for preparations, there were many cities eager to play host to the now floating XIIth Olympiad. Some Americans proposed that the Olympics become a part of the New York World's Fair at which Eleanor Holm Jarrett was a starring "aquamaid." Soon Finland was designated as the new host nation, however.

In the meantime, the hiatus in German aggressiveness following the triumphs in the Olympics in 1936 had ended. Early in 1938 Germany absorbed first Austria and then the Sudetenland of Czechoslovakia. After the Munich crisis of September 1938 Hitler's gross ambitions could no longer be disguised and his possible victims began preparing more diligently for war. The savage imposition of the Nazi racial laws in Austria during the summer of 1938 was surpassed in horror by the atrocities in Germany of the *Kristallnacht* of November 9–10, 1938. Hitler had used the excuse of a murder of a Nazi functionary in Paris by a Jew, Herschel Grynszpan, to unleash the worst pogroms of modern times. The optimists about the National Socialists had been proven wrong.

A little setback to the arrogance of the Nazis was the result of the second Louis-Schmeling fight the evening of June 22, 1938, in New York. Scientific, unsmiling Joe Louis this time did not drop his guard and stalked his opponent with a keen concentration. Joe's pursuit lasted only 124 seconds. Max landed just two punches before being put down and out. This symbolic lesson never gathered in Germany the mythic importance of the first Schmeling-Louis fight. By the summer of 1938 the whole German nation seemed to have abandoned all traditional political restraints. The Germans were now backing a juggernaut that was lurching ponderously on a course directed at letting loose a universal war of ideas and power. The illusions offered to the Germans and to the world by the results of the 1936 Olympics were emboldening to the aggressors and were debilitating to the scheduled victims in that war. The confident loosing of the ambitions of the new Germans was the worst consequence of the onerous symbolic burdens that the Olympic Games and their athletic participants had taken on since the Games were revived in 1896.

Festivity as a modern political force has been an implicit subject of this book. But festivity is a peculiar political technique; its designers are often themselves those most enchanted and deceived by the festivities they have synthesized. We have seen how Dr. Carl Diem, a good German who had all the qualifications to be ranked as a spiritual hero of sport, became unbalanced by his own theatrical constructions. Since he became for a while a bad German or at least a cooperator with the worst Germans, he had to be considered part villain, part victim of the Nazi Olympics.

Also entranced by the Nazi Olympics was the world's "man of the hour." Adolf Hitler, who was entirely unathletic and was no classical scholar, became convinced that his athletes' triumphs were omens, portents whose significance was clear. The athletes, like other exceptional Germans, were to inspire the whole German *Volk*. The new master race would lead a cultural movement toward accomplishments whose glorious, though dimly divined, outlines suggested that the Germans of the future might surpass the greatest culture creators of all time. Inspired, hard-working, unerringly-led Germans would rival the classical Greeks as inventors of new beauty and joy-intoxicated styles of life.

The athletes were symbolically to embody German physical supremacy. After the German Olympiad they were cast by Hitler as "the forerunners of new types of Germans, . . . tough, well-formed men and graceful women."[13] Contestants in athletic meets were to be watched and admired not as sportsmen, but rather as political troops who treat the sporting contests only as their particular branch of the great struggle as a whole.[14]

It turned out that the Führer's relatively modest demeanor in August 1936 (interpreted at the time as a decisive turn toward sweet reasonableness) was but a useful pose. Hitler's consistent seeking of grandeur soon became apparent in his plans for German sport. The regime inaugurated National Socialist sporting meets (*National-sozialistische Kampfspiele*) which, like the original Olympiads of the classical Greeks, were to be racially exclusive. These new, racially proud athletic festivals were the occasion for greatly expanding the temple complex outside the holy city in southern Germany. Nuremberg was increasingly the focus of Hitler's architectural ambitions. We recall his displeasure with Werner March's Olympic stadium for 100,000 in Berlin. It was pretty, but "too small" and was too cheap because it was only faced with marble.

The favored architect was Albert Speer who had been instructed to prepare colossal settings for the "national" or "German" Olympics. The new and satisfactory stadium, itself but a part of the whole Nuremberg *Reichssportfeld*, would hold four times as many as the Berlin stadium and would be by far the largest facility for public spectacle ever built or even envisioned.

Speer, the Phidias of new German culture, has described Hitler's inspired fantasies in the spring of 1937 as that Pericles and Alexander of new German culture first pondered Speer's white, floodlit model of the "stadium of four-hundred-thousand." Hitler mused about the future of the international Olympic Games. Speer informed him that the vast structure would not meet the specifications of the International Olympic Committee or, for that matter, the requirements of conventionally conceived athletic events. It was just too big. Confident in his visions of the future Hitler brushed these international considerations aside:

No matter. In 1940 the Olympic Games will take place in Tokyo. But thereafter they will take place in Germany for all time to come, in this stadium. And then we will determine the measurements of the athletic field.[15]

The stadium was to be entirely finished in 1945.

Notes

CHAPTER 1

1. See: H. A. Harris, *Greek Athletes and Athletics* (London, Hutchinson, 1964); E. Norman Gardiner, *Athletics of the Ancient World* (Oxford, Clarendon, first ed. 1930); Rachel Sargent Robinson, *Sources for the History of Greek Athletics* (Cincinnati, the author, 1927).
2. Gardiner, p. 101.
3. *Ibid.*, 49 from *Corpus Inscriptionem Latinorum*, IV, 1177, 3883.
4. For a discussion of the documentary evidence, see Robinson, pp. 206–208.
5. See *The Oxford English Dictionary* (Oxford, Oxford University Press, revised edition, 1933), vol. 8, p. 107.
6. Lodewyk Bendikson, "Forgotten Olympics in King James' Reign," *Game and Gossip* (Los Angeles), X. No. 5 (1932), p. 7. This article discusses a rare quarto volume of poetry, *Annalia Dubrensia,* in the Huntington Library.
7. Quoted *ibid.*, pp. 8, 14.
8. See his letter quoted in J. J. Jusserand, *Les Sports et jeux d'exercice dans l'ancienne France* (Paris, Plon, 1901), p. 19.
9. Pierre de Coubertin, "A typical Englishman: Dr. W. P. Brooks of Wenlock in Shropshire," *Review of Reviews*, XV (January 1897), p. 62.
10. For a discussion of the impact abroad of German culture during this period, see Claude Digeon, *La Crise allemande de la pensée française (1870–1914)* (Paris, Presses universitaires de la France, 1959).
11. See *Die Ausgrabungen zu Olympia*, 5 vols. (Berlin, 1876–1881); *Olympia: die Ergebnisse der von Deutschen Reich veranstalteten Ausgrabung*, 5 vols. (Berlin, 1887–1897). More accessible is E. Norman Gardiner, *Olympia: Its History and Remains* (Oxford, Clarendon, 1925).
12. *Une Campagne de vingt-et-un ans* (Paris, Librairie de l'éducation physique, 1908), p. 1.

13. Marie-Thérèse Eyquem, *Pierre de Coubertin: L'Épopée Olympique* (Paris, Calmann-Lévy, 1966), p. 131.
14. See Théodore Reinach, "Une Page de musique grecque," *La Revue de Paris*, I, No. 10 (June 15, 1894), pp. 204–224.
15. Coubertin later claimed that he alone was responsible for the selection of Athens as the site. See Coubertin, *Une Campagne de vingt-et-un ans*, p. 98.
16. *Ibid.*, p. 115.
17. The European press took almost no notice of the 1896 Games. There were just one German, one English, and one French article (by Coubertin) in the journals of the time. There were, however, at least two lively American magazine articles: George Horton, "The Recent Olympian Games," *The Bostonian*, IV (July 1896), 215–229; Rufus B. Richardson, "The New Olympian Games," *Scribners Magazine*, XX, No. 3 (September 1896), 167–186. The Boston and New York newspapers fully reported the arrival of the American athletes back from their triumphs.
18. The following report is taken principally from *Les Jeux olympiques 776 av. J.-C.–1896*, 2 vols. bound in one (Athens, Beck, 1896). Printed in Greek and French, this is the official report. An English edition was also printed.
19. See: France. Ministère du commerce, de l'industrie, des postes et des télégraphes. Exposition universelle internationale de 1900. Direction générale de l'exploitation. *Règlements et programmes des concours nationaux et internationaux d'exercices physiques et des sports* (Paris, Imprimerie nationale, 1900).
20. See his "The Meeting of the Olympic Games," *North American Review*, CLXX, No. 523 (June 1900) 802–811.

CHAPTER 2

1. R. L. Quercetani, *A World History of Track and Field Athletics 1864–1964* (London, Oxford, 1964), p. 185.
2. *The New York Times*, March 19, 1915.
3. The consensus then as well as subsequently was that the fouls were deliberate. See the discussion in Donald E. Fuoss, "An Analysis of the Incidents in the Olympic Games from 1924 to 1948 with Reference to the Contribution of the Games to International Good Will and Understanding" (Unpublished Ed.D. thesis, Columbia University Teachers' College, 1951), 119–124.
4. "D. J. Ferris Predicts German Victory," *The New York Times*, June 15, 1930.
5. Kurt Doerry, "Ein Schlusswart über Los Angeles: eine Lehre der Olympischen Spiele für Deutschland," *Die Woche*, XXXIV (1936), p. 1107.

6. *The New York Times*, May 26, 1930.

7. *Olympic Games: Official Organ of the XI Olympiad*, No. 2, p. 14.

8. In the following discussion, the author is indebted to Hamilton Burden's *The Nuremberg Party Rallies: 1923–1939* (New York, Frederich A. Praeger, 1967).

9. *Ibid.*, 39.

10. H. R. Trevor-Roper, *Hitler's Secret Conversations* (New York, Macmillan, 1953), p. 362.

11. Burden, p. 61.

12. From the film *Triumph of the Will*.

13. *Ibid.*

14. Former member of Hitler Youth Choir interviewed by Burden, pp. 115–116.

15. *Ibid.*, p. 119.

16. She published an account of the film's production in her *Hinter den Kulissen des Reichsparteitagfilms* (Munich, Zentralverlag der NSDAP, 1935).

17. See *ibid.* However, an interview with Michel Delahaye (*Cahiers du Cinéma* [in English], No. 5 [1966]) Riefenstahl claimed that the film was cheaply done and that she had only two cameras. She also claimed that the film was "purely historical" and an example of *film vérité*.

18. Alan Bullock, *Hitler: A Study in Tyranny* (New York, Harper, 1952), p. 420.

19. Committee on Fair Play in Sports, *Preserve the Olympic Ideal: A Statement of the Case Against American Participation in the Olympic Games in Berlin* (New York, 20 Vesey Street [1935]), pp. 31–32.

20. William L. Shirer, *The Rise and Fall of the Third Reich* (New York, Simon and Schuster, 1960), p. 234.

21. August 1, 1933, quoted in *ibid.*, p. 51.

22. Committee on Fair Play . . ., pp. 7ff. The information was taken from German newspapers and *The New York Times*.

23. Bruno Malitz, *Die Leibesübungen in der Nationalsozialistischen Idee* (Munich, F. Eher, 1933), p. 3.

24. Committee on Fair Play . . . , p. 14.

25. Malitz, p. 21.

26. *Ibid.*, p. 42.

27. Committee on Fair Play . . . , p. 28.

28. *Ibid.*, p. 56.

29. See the list of Jewish Olympic victors in Bernard Postal, Jesse Silver, and Roy Silver, *Encyclopedia of Jews in Sports* (New York, Bloch, 1965), pp. 391–395.

30. Natan later made a reputation as a literary critic and scholar. He retained his interest in sports. For a refreshingly bitter appraisal of the impact of international sports on peace, see his essay in the book he edited, *Sport and Society: A Symposium* (London, Bowes and Bowes, 1958).

31. But he never again achieved international renown. Postal, p. 451.
32. *The New York Times*, April 24, 1933.
33. Postal, p. 201.
34. *The New York Times*, November 24, 1933.

CHAPTER 3

1. See Colin Cross, *The Fascists in Britain* (London, Barrie and Rockcliff, 1962).
2. London, Trades Union Congress General Council, 1936, 31 pp.
3. See "Baker," *Olympiade à Berlin?* (Paris, Editions universelles, 1936), 24 pp.
4. *Ibid.*, p. 3.
5. Postal, p. 398.
6. Committee on Fair Play . . . , frontispiece.
7. Postal, p. 398.
8. *Ibid.*, p. 399.
9. See *The New York Times*, October 21, 1935.
10. *The New York Times*, October 22, 1935.
11. *The New York Times*, October 23, 1935.
12. Postal, p. 400.
13. *The New York Times*, October 24, 1935.
14. *The New York Times*, November 27, 1935.
15. Committee on Fair Play . . . , p. 22.
16. Postal, p. 201.
17. November 8, 1935, p. 41.
18. Committee on Fair Play . . . , p. 39.
19. *Ibid.*, p. 40.
20. *Ibid.*, p. 40.
21. *Ibid.*, p. 42.
22. *Ibid.*, p. 44.
23. Postal, p. 400.
24. Two pamphlets explaining the case *for* participation are *Fair Play for American Athletes* (A publication of the American Olympic Committee [1936?] 18pp.) and Gustavus T. Kirby, *Some Why's and Wherefore's of the Olympic Games of 1936* (13 pp.).
25. *The New York Times*, December 9, 1935.
26. Letter from S. Brodetsky dated November 12, 1935. *Bulletin officiel du Comité international olympique*, 10ième année, No. 30 (December 1935), p. 6.
27. Postal, p. 402.
28. He also edited the British official report on the 1936 Olympics—a report which is remarkable for its utter lack of political discussion.
29. This interesting sideshow has been almost forgotten. No American magazine reported on these Games, though *The New York Times* gave the preparation and the events courteous attention.

30. "Report of the Chairman of the Finance Committee," in Frederick W. Rubien (ed.), *Report of the American Olympic Committee: Games of the XIth Olympiad* (New York, American Olympic Committee, 1936), p. 73. Henceforth, *American Olympic Committee 1936.*

31. *Memoirs 1925–1950* (Boston, Little, Brown, 1967), p. 77.

32. Comité Olympique français, *La Participation française aux jeux de la XIième Olympiade* (Paris, 1936), p. 26.

33. The reader can consult the notes on Diem's scholarly work in Chapter 9.

34. Organisationskomitee für die XI. Olympiade Berlin 1936. *Official Report* (Berlin, W. Limpert, 1937), I, p. 57. Henceforth, *German Official Report 1936.* This is a straightforward translation (a French edition was also issued) of the German *Amtlicher Bericht* published in 1936 by Limpert.

35. *Olympic Games 1936: Official Organ of the XI. Olympic Games,* No. 2 (July 1935), p. 16.

36. *German Official Report 1936,* I, p. 61.

37. *American Olympic Committee 1936,* p. 207.

38. British Olympic Association. *The Official Report of the XIth Olympiad Berlin 1936* (London, British Olympic Association, 1937), p. 31.

39. *German Official Report 1936,* I, pp. 240–242.

40. *American Olympic Committee 1936,* p. 7.

41. *Ibid.,* p. 72.

42. *The New York Times,* August 21, 23, 1936.

43. André G. Poplimont, "Berlin 1936," *Bulletin du Comité international olympique,* No. 56 (October 15, 1956), pp. 19–20.

CHAPTER 4

1. Organisationskomitee für die Olympischen Winterspiele 1936 Garmisch-Partenkirchen, *Amtlicher Bericht* (Berlin, Reichssportverlag, 1936), p. 103.

2. There were thorough preparations including special tracks and towers for an official filming of the winter Olympics of 1936, but I have been unable to determine if this film was ever completed or shown.

3. See the *New York World-Telegram,* February 17 and 19, 1936.

4. William L. Shirer, *Berlin Diary: The Journal of a Foreign Correspondent 1934–1941* (New York, Knopf, 1941), p. 47.

5. Alice Damrosch Wolfe in Frederick W. Rubien (ed.), *American Olympic Committee 1936,* p. 346.

6. *The New York Times,* February 16, 1936.

7. Organisationskomitee für die Olympischen Winterspiele 1936, p. 244.

8. See Heinrich Müller, "Die IV. Olympischen Winterspiele im Lichte ausländischer Presseberichte," *Die neueren Sprachen,* XLIV (1936), 369–376.

9. Alice Damrosch Wolfe, p. 345.

10. Walter Goerlitz, *The German General Staff 1657–1945* (New York, Praeger, 1952), p. 306.

11. Gordon A. Craig, *The Politics of the Prussian Army 1640–1945* (New York, Oxford, 1955), p. 487.

12. From the memoirs of Paul Schmidt, quoted in Alan Bullock, *Hitler: A Study in Tyranny* (New York, Harper, 1952), p. 302.

13. Kim, *Saturday Review*, CLI (March 14, 1936), 328–329.

14. Craig, p. 487.

15. Max Doremus (ed.), *Hitler: Reden und Proklamationen 1932–1945*, Band I, Zweiter Halbband (Munich, Süddeutscher Verlag, 1963), p. 597.

16. In his "revisionist" *Origins of the Second World War* (London, Hamish Hamilton, 1961) A. J. P. Taylor claims that because Germany was no longer defenseless, she encouraged her potential attackers. The Rhineland crisis laid the psychological basis for Allied rearmament and "this was a double turning point. It opened the door for Germany's success. It also opened the door for her ultimate defeat" (p. 101).

17. Without citing the vast literature, I believe the respectable consensus then (and now) was that the blow was not a foul. In any case, Jacobs fouled when he set his foot in the ring.

18. Jonathan Mitchell, "Joe Louis Never Smiles," *The New Republic*, LXXXIV, No. 1088 (October 9, 1935), p. 239.

19. Lester Bromberg, *Boxing's Unforgettable Fights* (New York, Ronald, 1962), p. 219.

20. *The New York Times*, June 19, 1936.

21. Max Schmeling, "This Way I Beat Joe Louis" (As told to Paul Gallico), *The Saturday Evening Post*, CCIX, No. 10 (September 5, 1936), p. 10.

22. *Ibid.*, p. 32.

23. *The New York Times*, June 1, 1936.

24. *Ibid.*

25. *The New York Times*, December 18, 1936.

CHAPTER 5

1. See *Sport der Hellenen: Austellung der Griechischen Bildwerke* (Berlin, Verlag für Kunstwissenschaft, 1936).

2. *Welt am Sonntag* (Berlin), January 12, 1969.

3. *German Official Report 1936*, p. 111.

4. *Ibid.*, p. 113.

5. *Ibid.* p. 113.

6. *Ibid.*, p. 116.

7. Quoted in *ibid.*, p. 517–518.

8. *Ibid.*, p. 513.

9. *German Official Report 1936* quoted, p. 520.

10. *Ibid.*, p. 527.

11. The first sports event to be televised in the United States was a double-header baseball game on May 17, 1939, between Columbia University and Princeton at Baker Field in New York.
12. "Olympic Berlin," *The Spectator*, No. 5641 (August 7, 1936), p. 229.
13. *The New York Times*, July 6, 1936.
14. Quoted in *The New York Times*, July 18, 1936.
15. *German Official Report 1936*, p. 446.
16. *Ibid.*, pp. 447–448.
17. *The New York Times*, July 30, 1936.
18. *The New York Times*, letter, July 25, 1936.
19. In a characteristic effort at glossing over the rough moments, the American official report states that "the greeting to the American team was noisily enthusiastic both on entering and leaving the stadium." *Report of the American Olympic Committee 1936*, p. 93. All other reports would verify the description in my text.
20. The XIth Olympic Games, Berlin, 1936, *Official Report . . .* , p. 446.
21. And ungrammatical. *"Ich verkünde die Spiele von Berlin zur Feier der elften Olympiade neuer Zeitrechnung als eröffnet."* In an attempt at pompousness Hitler's speech was awkward in German. His use of "verkünde" (proclaim or prophesy) was clumsy and incorrect.
22. Erich Ebermayer and Hans Roos, *Gefährtin des Teufels* (Hamburg, Hoffmann und Campe, 1952), pp. 210–211 quoted in Ernest K. Bramsted, *Goebbels and National Socialist Propaganda 1925–1945* (Lansing, Michigan, Michigan State University Press, 1965), p. 152.
23. Bella Fromm, *Blood and Banquets: A Berlin Social Diary* (New York, Harper, 1947), p. 226.

CHAPTER 6

1. *The New York Times*, August 5, 1936.
2. R. L. Quercetani, *A World History of Track and Field Athletics 1864–1964* (London, Oxford, 1964), p. 188.
3. "Are Girl Athletes Really Girls?" *Life*, LXI, No. 15 (October 7, 1966), p. 66.
4. *The New York Times*, August 9, 1936.
5. H. G. Salsinger quoted in *American Olympic Committee 1936*, p. 175.
6. Quoted in *The New York Times*, August 17, 1936.
7. *Ibid.*, August 8, 1936.
8. *Ibid.*, August 13, 1936.
9. The point tabulations were always called "unofficial" and the American Olympic Committee's report on the 1936 Games noted, "The International Olympic Committee is opposed to all point scoring systems." See *American Olympic Committee 1936*, p. 22.
10. *Ibid.*
11. See the discussion in Donald E. Fuoss, "An Analysis of Incidents in the Olympic Games from 1924 to 1948 . . . ," pp. 194–196.

12. *The New York Times*, August 4, 1936.
13. Canadian Olympic Committee, *Canada at the Eleventh Olympiad 1936 in Germany* (Danville, Ontario, 1936), p. 63.
14. *American Olympic Committee 1936*, p. 22.
15. August 17, 1936.

CHAPTER 7

1. Quoted in Quentin Reynolds, "Galloping Gal," *Colliers*, XCVIII (July 25, 1936), p. 22.
2. This phrase is part of the letterhead still used by Miss Stephens. In her letter to me (which also contains a picture of young Helen about to break a finish tape and a list of her eight records) Miss Stephens wrote, "I don't believe you should have too much difficulty supporting your justification for including me as one of the stars of the 1936 Olympics."
3. I use the better-known form. For a complimentary article on Son (or Sohn) as a Korean patriot see Hal Drake, "The Conquerors Won Thanks to the Conquered," *Sports Illustrated*, XXVIII, No. 20 (May 20, 1968), 95–96.
4. *Ibid.*, p. 96.
5. There are other versions of the nexus between Harper and Son. The official British report claimed Harper and Son were actually competing all the while and Son later claimed he needed no advice; that he was always in control (see Drake, *loc. cit.*, p. 95). Still several observers on the spot have recorded that the two conversed and this can be seen in Leni Riefenstahl's film.
6. *Ibid.*, p. 96.
7. See some of the stories in Edwin Bancroft Henderson, *Negro in Sports* (Washington, D.C., Associated, 1939).
8. That there are epic proportions in some of these stories has been realized only in Howard Sackler's *The Great White Hope*, the stunningly effective (and successful) Broadway play.
9. Paul Gallico, *Farewell to Sport* (New York, Knopf, 1938), p. 300.
10. See Paul Gallico's discussion of the case of Willis Ward of the University of Michigan *ibid.*, pp. 304–305. Gallico's inability to combat racial injustice in sport made him "curl with shame," yet he too may have feared the Negro boxer: "He is generally a magnificent physical specimen, powerfully wiry, hard, and not nearly so sensible to pain as his white brother. He has a hard, thick skull . . . ," *ibid.*, p. 306.
11. R. L. Quercetani, *A World History of Track and Field Athletics, 1864–1964* (London, Oxford, 1964), p. 18.
12. Lawrence N. Snyder, "My Boy Jesse," *Saturday Evening Post*, CCIX, No. 19 (November 7, 1936), p. 15.
13. *Ibid.*
14. *Ibid.*

15. R. A. Hewins, "Owens' Olympiad," *Observer*, August 9. 1936.

16. *Ibid.*

17. Quoted in Donald E. Fuoss, "An Analysis of Incidents in the Olympic Games from 1924 to 1948 . . . ," p. 186. This version is Jesse Owens' alone and is characteristic of other later inventions demonstrating the world's love of their author. Even Larry Snyder, though stating that Jesse was cheered as loudly as any Aryan, believed that either Hitler was waving to a countryman or that the tale is a fabrication (*loc. cit.*, p. 97).

18. The Chancellor was actually merely a guest—no more. He had, however, succeeded in placing himself in a position of exceptional prominence which led later to the establishment of stricter protocols by the International Olympic Committee against the political use of the ceremonies of the Olympics by politicians.

19. See the discussion in Fuoss, *op. cit.*, 181–188.

20. Jesse's coach claimed his star was tired of running and was not eager to go to Cologne. But the A.O.C. held him to his contract—for the German officials promised 15 per cent of the gate with Jesse; 10 per cent without. Snyder, *loc. cit.*, p. 97.

21. "Even today some experts maintain that he could have done better in this or that event if he had shown a greater singleness of purpose." Quercetani, *op. cit.*, p. 22.

22. Quercetani (*op. cit.*, p. 22) gives no source for this tale. If his source is Jesse Owens, I would place it in the category of Jesse Owens' apocrypha.

23. Snyder, *loc. cit.*, p. 97.

24. *The New York Times*, August 16, 1936.

25. Norman Katkov, "Jesse Owens Revisited," *The World of Sport*, ed. by Al Silverman (New York, Holt, Rinehart and Winston, 1962), p. 289.

26. I have taken the lists of competitors from Charles H. Williams, "Negro Athletes in the Eleventh Olympiad," *The Southern Workman*, LXVI (1937), 45–59.

27. *Ibid.*, pp. 58–59.

28. Hewins, *loc. cit.*

29. Gallico, *op cit.*, p. 309.

CHAPTER 8

1. *Mein Kampf* (Munich, NSDAP, 1940), p. 454.

2. *Ibid.*, p. 456.

3. *Ibid.*, pp. 396–397.

4. *Ibid.*, p. 458.

5. Otto Dietrich, *Zwölf Jahre mit Hitler* (Munich, Isar, 1955), p. 176, quoted in Hajo Bernett (ed.), *Nationalsozialistische Leibeserziehung* (Stuttgart, Karl Hofmann, 1966), p. 18.

6. Baldur von Schirach, *Ich glaubte an Hitler* (Hamburg, Mosaik, 1967), p. 217–218.
7. Bernett, *op. cit.*, p. 204, n. 4.
8. Information obtained in the course of an interview in January 1969 with Frau Dr. Liselott Diem.
9. *Ibid.*
10. One can examine his "Drei Völker—Drei Freunde: Deutschland, Japan, Bulgarien" *Reichssportblatt* (March 8, 1941).
11. *Bibliographie Carl Diem* (Cologne, Carl-Diem Institut, n.d., ca. 1966).
12. Information obtained in an interview with Mme. Zanchi, a close associate of Coubertin, in Lausanne in June 1968.
13. *Bibliographie Carl Diem.*
14. All in Berlin: Terramare Institut, 1942.
15. Diem died in 1962 in Cologne where he had established a new (and much smaller) center for German physical education. His scholarly productivity revived in the 1950's. Diem left unpublished memoirs of his years under the Nazis. A biography of the man is needed and I offer the topic as a necessary and fascinating one.
16. Page 11 of the American Olympic Committee's *Handbook*. The handbook was reprinted in *American Olympic Committee 1936*, pp. 51–55.
17. See the discussion in Chapter 3. The quote is from Robert Shaplen, "Amateur," *The New Yorker*, XXXVI (July 23, 1960), p. 32.
18. Quoted in Jack Scott, "The White Olympics," *Ramparts*, May 1968, p. 54.
19. My primary source for the lady's insensibility is a mimeographed press release of the American Olympic Committee. It is signed by Avery Brundage and Fred Rubien, Secretary of the American Olympic Committee.
20. "I Like Champagne," *Time*, XXVIII, No. 5 (August 3, 1936), p. 21.
21. *Newsweek*, VIII, No. 5 (August 1, 1936), p. 20.
22. *Time, loc. cit.*
23. *The New York Times*, October 22, 1936.
24. *The New York Times*, July 21, 1944.

CHAPTER 9

1. Robert Gardner in his "Can the Will Triumph?" *Film Comment*, III, No. 1 (Winter 1965), p. 30, says that a German film critic, Lotte Eisner, claimed that Leni was half-Jewish.
2. David Gunston, "Leni Riefenstahl," *Film Quarterly*, XIV, No. 1 (Autumn 1960), p. 5. As one has a right to suspect in the case of movie stars, she may be older. Successive issues of *Who's Who in Germany* have advanced her birth date. The latest gives her birth as 1912.
3. *Ibid.*, p. 2.

4. Leipzig, Hesse and Becker, 1933, 133 pp.

5. Riefenstahl has been adamant on this point.

6. Ernst "Putzi" Hanfstängl, *Hitler: The Missing Years* (London, Eyre and Spottiswood, 1956), p. 194.

7. *Ibid.*

8. Gunston, p. 14.

9. It won a gold medal at the Paris Exposition of 1937.

10. See Riefenstahl's *Hinter den Kulissen des Reichsparteitagfilms* (Munich, Zentralverlag der NSDAP, 1935), 104 pp.

11. Gardner, p. 30.

12. Quoted in Michel Delahaye, "Leni and the Wolf," *Cahiers du Cinéma* (in English), No. 5 (1966), p. 52.

13. Gordon Hitchens, "An Interview with a Legend," *Film Comment*, III, No. 1 (Winter 1965), p. 7.

14. *German Official Report 1936*, p. 331. The official author of this part of the report is Dr. Carl Diem. The "tone" and confidence in this section lead me to the inescapable conclusion that the author was, in fact, Leni Riefenstahl, edited slightly by Diem.

15. Letter quoted, *ibid.*

16. See *German Official Report 1936*, p. 333. We cannot take seriously her later claim, "We didn't have gigantic resources for the good reason that we didn't have gigantic sums of money." Delahaye, p. 53.

17. Delahaye, p. 53.

18. *Ibid.*

19. *German Official Report 1936*, p. 334.

20. Delahaye, p. 53.

21. The secondary literature customarily says there were many versions made with generous footage of the winners of each of the destined national versions. I have not yet seen conclusive evidence of altered footage in the versions I have seen. What did happen was that the Americans censored out a great deal of the footage of Hitler and of the nudes in the opening part of the film. Also, I believe there were only a German, a French, an Italian, and an English version.

22. No one has been able to unconvince me that one soft-focused view of a nude female, a tall blonde with an aquiline nose, is not Leni Riefenstahl herself.

23. Gérard d'Houville, "Les Dieux du stade," *Revue des deux mondes*, 8 période, XLVI (15 August 1938), p. 935.

24. Henry McLemore. The quotes are from a clipping copyrighted 1938, but otherwise undated, from the *Los Angeles Evening News*, part of a file on Leni Riefenstahl at the Museum of Modern Art, New York.

25. Pierre Bost, "Les Dieux du stade," *Les Annales politiques et littéraires*, 56 année, No. 2607 (25 July 1938), p. 104.

26. Riefenstahl claims it even made a substantial profit. See the interview with Delahaye, *loc. cit.*, p. 53.

27. Review by James Manilla done in November 1938 and reprinted in *Film Comment*, III, No. 1 (Winter 1965), p. 23.

28. *New York Herald-Tribune*, May 18, 1945.

29. "Nazi Pin-up Girl," *Saturday Evening Post*, CCXVIII, No. 39 (March 30, 1946), pp. 11, 36, 39, 41.

30. Alfred Polgar, "Two Ladies of the Regime," *Commentary*, IX, No. 6 (June, 1950), p. 553.

31. Letter by Leni Riefenstahl in *Film Comment*, III, No. 1 (Winter 1965), p. 126.

CHAPTER 10

1. My historically interpolated conclusions, of course, leave out the accomplishments of the democratic Scandinavians who, if medal-winners-in-proportion-to-population was the criterion, would be the indisputable victors with Finland or conceivably Estonia clearly winning the palm. But this confounding notion was not taken into account by the Germans or the Americans or anyone else—except, possibly, the Scandinavians themselves. For further discussion, see Charles D. Snyder, "Real Winners of the 1936 Olympic Games," *Scientific Monthly*, XLIII (October 1936), 372–374. Snyder draws racist conclusions. For example, he noted that the Negro winners "were trained by white men in the white man's institutions." Snyder used his article to oppose racial mixing and to celebrate "the great northern races" except for the Danes who, he claims, performed badly because they were so "mixed."

2. Quoted in *The New York Times*, August 4, 1936.

3. *Deutsche Volkswirtschaft* quoted in *The New York Times*, August 4, 1936.

4. *La Participation française aux jeux de la XIième Olympiade* (Paris, Comité français olympique, 1937), p. 5.

5. The whole proclamation was printed in the *Völkischer Beobachter*, August 3, 1936, and republished many times afterward.

6. Ludwig Drees, *Olympia: Gods, Artists and Athletes* (New York, Frederick A. Praeger, 1968), p. 167.

7. The first volume of the meticulously documented and illustrated official reports appeared in 1938. Subsequent volumes appeared irregularly and had various editors and publishers. Volume VII was published in 1958 by Walter de Gruyter in Berlin. All the reports can be traced through the general titles *Ausgrabungen in Olympia* or *Bericht über die Ausgrabungen in Olympia*.

8. "I Like Champagne," *Time*, XXVIII, No. 5 (August 3, 1936), p. 21.

9. All serious writers on sport, including Diem and Coubertin, have asked the questions, "What is sport?" and "Why sport?" The literature is vast and most of it is pathetically naïve. Two of the most rigorous and provoking works are Roger Caillois, *Man, Play and Games* (Glencoe, Ill., Free Press, 1961) and Johan Huizinga, *Homo Ludens* (Boston, Beacon, 1949).

10. For more on this one can consult the manual for coaches by Bruce C. Ogilvie and Thomas A. Tutko, *Problem Athletes and How to Handle*

Them (London, Pelham, 1966). I have passed over the drug problem which became very serious in the 1960's. The drugs, of course, work on the body. But we must be aware of the corruptions of spirit which lead to the use of drugs and their attendant risk of bodily wreckage. The causes of these conscienceless abominations are the ideologues' distorted (dare we say, "mad") lust for victory and new records.

11. Jack Scott in his *Athletics for Athletes* (Oakland, California, Other Ways, 1969) makes the point that the most authoritarian methods of training Olympic-class athletes are those used by Soviets and Americans.

12. *The New York Times*, January 13, 1938.

13. Hitler, "Schlussrede auf dem Reichsparteitag 1937," quoted in Hajo Bernett, *Nationalsozialistische Leibeserziehung* (Stuttgart, Karl Hofmann, 1966), p. 212.

14. Hans Grass, *Politische Leibeserziehung* quoted in Bernett, p. 214.

15. Albert Speer, *Inside the Third Reich* (New York, Macmillan, 1970), p. 70.

Index

A.A.U. *See* Amateur Athletic Union

Abba, Captain Silvano, 172

Abrahams, Harold M., 80

Airplanes at 1936 Games, 155

Albritton, David, 166, 228, 231

Amateur Athletic Union: meeting in November 1933, 71; supported Brundage for years, 72; resolution of November 1933, 73; meeting in December 1933, 78–80; Eleanor Holm Jarrett case, 243; mentioned, 42, 73, 229

Amateurism in sports: Brundage personifies many rigidities, 72; yachting races at Kiel in 1936, 186; Eleanor Holm Jarrett case, 243–249; Americans compared with Soviets, 287. *See also* Professionalism in sports

American Federation of Labor, 77

American National Society of Mural Painters, 78

American Olympic Association, 72

American Olympic Committee, 73, 83

American point tabulation of 1936 Games, 206

Amsterdam Games 1928, 38, 63

Amsterdam News, 81

Amyot, Francis, 185

Angriff, Der: quoted on Louis-Schmeling fight, 120–121; instructs Germans to be charming, 140; on "Black auxiliaries," 202; on German victories, 281–282; mentioned, 46

Anti-Comintern Pact, 282

Anti-Semitism in Germany: 1933–1936, 57–64; part of *Gleichschaltung*, 57; signs in Garmisch-Partenkirchen, 59; American reactions to, 70–80 *passim;* Fuerstner case, 92–93; Hitler agrees to relent for 1936 Games, 93–94, 237; Jews forbidden to fly swastika, 142; eased for 1936 Games, 143; Jews serve as bureaucrats for Carl Diem, 239; Americans boycott film *Olympia*, 270–271; no new measures in 1937, 282

Antwerp Games 1920, 36–37

"Aquacades," 248

Arai, Shigeo, 175

Arndt, Gisela, 177

Arnstein, "Nicky," 248

Art competitions of 1936 Games, German point tabulations, 208

Askola, Arvo, 163

Astylus of Croton, 5

Athens Games (mid-nineteenth century), 15–16